THE PERSONAL IS POLITICAL

Praise for *The Personal Is Political*

'Indian democracy is in deep trouble at this time, but its flame has been kept alive by a multitude of vibrant collectives working on the ground. Aruna Roy and her colleagues in the Mazdoor Kisan Shakti Sangathan have played a leading role in this effort to defend and expand democratic space. They have not only contributed to many historic changes, such as India's Right to Information Act, but also sharpened the methods of public action. The foundation of their approach lies in valuing the knowledge, wisdom and power of working people. In this enlightening book, Aruna Roy reflects on this life of deep engagement, weaving the personal and political. A great inspiration.'

—**Amartya Sen**, economist and philosopher, and **Jean Drèze**, welfare economist and activist

'This is the most unusual yet compelling of memoirs: a chiaroscuro of thought and emotion, seen through the refracting prism of memory. Aruna Roy has had an extraordinary life of social activism and struggle, often very effective, always deeply committed and courageous, and constantly able to find strength, joy and learning in collectives and camaraderie. Her determined fight over decades for social justice and rights-based strategies is legendary. But in this thoughtful exploration, she shows that she has also been aware of contradictions, of shades of meaning and reality, conscious of her privileges even as she seeks to reduce them, and is able to recognize the need for compromise in specific situations and coalitions to strive for the most important goals. At one point Roy notes that "political action is also born from intense personal sharing". This remarkable book, interspersing personal experience with complex Indian social reality and political economy developments, exemplifies this. It is a feminist tract, a deeply humanist tract—and a very engaging read.'

—**Jayati Ghosh**, development economist

'Aruna Roy's remarkable life overlaps almost completely with the life of independent India. Her memoirs, therefore, read also as a necessary narrative of growing up in democratic India, of its dreams and also its fractured freedoms. Aruna writes as a feminist, a humanist, a socialist. Her accounts are unfailingly riveting, of being raised in a progressive middle-class Tamil household; her marriage to a charismatic Brahmo Samaji and national squash champion who is drawn to an unexpected offbeat vocation of changing rural India; her brief years in the elite Indian Administrative Service, her resignation and her voyage of discovery of rural India; her rage at the inequities of gender, caste and class; her wonder at the wisdom of the unlettered; and her struggles for gender equity, for labour rights, for the right to work and, for what she will most be remembered, the right to information. In these pages, wisdom, political insights, grace, pique, humour and outrage all alternate to weave together a compelling, illuminating and engaging account of an extraordinary life of meaning. There is hope, there is audacity, there is struggle, and there is bearing witness to the persistence of stubborn historical injustices combined with the new ones that free India brought in its wake.'

—**Harsh Mander**, author, researcher and social activist

'This book encompasses the hope, the despair that all of us "midnight's children" have experienced. Aruna tells her story, weaving many threads into a pattern that fascinates and stuns the reader. With the occasional flavour of Rajasthani language, she intersperses in her narrative stories of women and men who became her lifelong humsafars. Seamlessly she narrates histories of movements and tehriks that give dignity and power to the marginalized who live in the villages of Rajasthan. Beginning with one state, we witness in the book how these movements spread across the country, ultimately becoming the government's policies and programmes. A child of principled and privileged parents, given the best education, honed in culture, she steps into a career highly coveted by all. With the same resolution and grace, she steps off that road and moves into a rural setting to lead a life of frugality and starkness, where she gathers her wealth by transforming the lives of people across the country. The words of Allama Iqbal best describe Aruna Roy:

Nigah buland sukhan dilnawaz jaan pur soz
Yehi hai rakht e safar mir e karvaan ke liye!

Lofty vision, dulcet speech, feeling heart
This is the only kit of the caravan's leader!'

—Syeda Hameed, women's rights activist, educationist and writer

'A diagram of social movement in India, written by one of the most well-known civil society leaders. The book offers the perspective and intelligence guarded in the mind of a great activist. Aruna Roy is a godmother to many urban-educated youths inclined towards justice in India. This book is, indeed, a marvellous appearance in the deck of social movements and its categorical history and pursuits. It is written with such care that the reader will identify with the author and will relate to her as a friend. Roy validates the emotions, fears and bodily expressions of activists and women. Trained by Dalit women in rural parts, Aruna resurrects the important contribution of Dalit women in her life and in bringing civility to India. This book is sure to serve as a guide to many activists and organizers. Alternating between memoir, experiential theory and commentary, Roy has successfully written a reflective tract.'

—**Suraj Yengde**, author, scholar and Dalit rights activist

'For decades now, Aruna Roy has been the touchstone on how to engage in socio-political activism, especially for those of us from social privilege. This book is one too—a critical reflection on a life lived with utmost honesty, and rich with the willingness to listen and learn.'

—**T.M. Krishna**, musician, author and activist

'Aruna Roy, a giant in the social justice movement, has generously translated fifty years of tireless work in rural India into a brilliant and riveting feminist manifesta for social change. Not only has she given her life to fighting poverty, discrimination, inequality and corruption, she has done it with the embodied and radical understanding that the personal is political and the heart is equal to the head.'

—**V (formerly Eve Ensler)**, American playwright, author, performer and feminist activist

'You need to read this book. It works at the intersection of so many processes: gender, labour, feminism, activism, social movements, politics, policymaking, culture, communal violence and more. You'd think that's too big a stretch in one book. But the author manages it gracefully and analytically. This is a book that could probably only have been written by Aruna Roy. The simplicity and honesty of its expression actually walks us through what are truly complex questions. It's more than a fine memoir, it captures an era in our history.

Aruna Roy's stories and anecdotes of her interaction with everyday people are captivating (including an early one where a village woman in Rajasthan asked her to get lost, saying she had no time for the likes of the former IAS officer turned earnest activist). It's hard to find a major political-religious-social event she has missed out on—from the sati of Deorala to people's power at Shaheen Bagh. Always linking every single milestone to those questions: What is democracy—and what is happening to it in India? And how important freedom of expression and the space for dissent are to both. And, as she says of her book, it is meant to foster dialogue, "For, much that is written in these chapters, cannot have a conclusion as they are conversations in progress."'

—**P. Sainath**, author

'Unlike most people, Aruna Roy does not keep her personal and public life in separate silos. To live by the same ideals that one speaks of is not an easy endeavour. Aruna Roy has lived such a life. A major part of the book is about her interactions with people. There are many who speak but very few who act. This book is a testimonial to the fact that change comes only with action and reinforces the proverb, "Actions are the best words spoken".'

—**Perumal Murugan**, writer, scholar and literary chronicler

'Aruna Roy in her writer's incarnation continues to be the activist, the thinker, the inspiring co-traveller. The book analytically unfolds our collective journeys of decades ago, of the personal being political. These journeys were very powerful and kept our hopes alive. Even today they remain undated stories for the contemporary reader as if playing out now. A must-read for all those working with a perspective of strengthening processes and institutions for socioeconomic justice for poor women.'

—**Kavita Srivastava**, human rights activist

'This book is deeply significant. It is an account of a pivotal moment for civil society in India and an untold part of the history of India. When Aruna Roy and the Mazdoor Kisan Shakti Sangathan (MKSS) began their work, issue-based and funded NGOs proliferated. The MKSS was fundamentally different; being non-funded and not aligned with a political party allowed them the space to analyse every government and occupy an independent space of critique and dissent. This book shows us how that distinct movement and politics was built, brick by brick. Aruna Roy and the MKSS have been vital and significant for the National Federation of Indian Women and me. Our common vision and purpose brought us together. One of the greatest arts that Aruna has is to carry joint movements and struggles. She makes sure that every organization is included equally in national issues and conventions, is given space and made to feel empowered and dignified. In the book we find this intersectionality and involvement in many connected struggles reflected. Today, the MKSS has also played a leading role in a new phase of Indian politics, which is the bringing together of civil society organizations, people's movements and democratic, secular, political parties. The feminist character of the book is reflected in Aruna's writing about the personal struggles that women have faced at different times in work in social movements. Several chapters document her evolving understanding of feminist politics, her life in rural India and the building of friendship and solidarity across class and caste. It is a personal and intimate account of an extraordinary life and the shaping of our history.'

—**Annie Raja**, Indian politician and general secretary of the National Federation of Indian Women

THE PERSONAL IS POLITICAL

AN ACTIVIST'S MEMOIR

ARUNA ROY

FOREWORD BY
GOPALKRISHNA GANDHI

HarperCollins *Publishers* India

First published in India by
HarperCollins *Publishers* 2024
4th Floor, Tower A, Building No. 10, DLF Cyber City,
DLF Phase II, Gurugram, Haryana—122002
www.harpercollins.co.in

22

P-ISBN: 978-93-5699-859-9
E-ISBN: 978-93-5699-652-6

Typeset in 11.5/16.3 Dante MT Std at
Manipal Technologies Limited, Manipal

Printed and bound at
Nutech Print Services, India

FSC
www.fsc.org
MIX
Paper | Supporting responsible forestry
FSC® C195953

This book is printed on FSC® certified paper
which ensures responsible forest management.

Many of us dream of a better world, of sharing privilege and for an equal right to live with dignity. This is a narrative of some collective stories which began with independence and the solitary journeys within our minds that continue to worry us. No matter how much life changes, the fulfilling creativity of the personal meeting the political transcends generations, and the story continues.

The detailed notes pertaining to this book are available on the HarperCollins website. Scan this QR code to access the same.

Contents

Foreword

A, OR ALPHA, the letter with which the Greek alphabet starts, is nothing more than just one of the twenty-four characters in that language or the twenty-six in the Latin. But being the inaugural character in the sequence that follows, it has a certain stature attached to it.

As do the vowels अ in Devanagari or அ in Tamil.

There is an atrial personality to the sound and sense of that letter or vowel, a very particular strength. And when a person's name begins with that 'A', something of the power of that opening sound flows into their name and image. Does that mean that the rest of the letters in an alphabet, from beta to omega, or from A to Z in the Latin, have a strength-deficit, a power-loss? Only a cretin or a deliberate and dubious distorter of reality would say that. But I do believe that Thiruvalluvar was not naïve or ignorant to begin his 1,330 couplets in the *Tirukkural* by privileging A with a role and a responsibility:

அகரமுதலஎழுத்தெல்லாம்ஆதி
பகவன்முதற்றேஉலகு

As the letter A is the first of all letters,
So the eternal God is first in the world

And as it happens I have found that A plays a role in 'maintaining' more than the flow of speech; it infuses the texture of a name beginning with it and—here I may be being totally callow—invests it with something of the privileges of primogeniture. Adam Smith would have been as sharp an economist had he been called, say, Giles Smith, Abraham Lincoln as great a statesman if he had been called Mortimer Abraham and Albert Einstein would, without doubt, have given the world his theory of relativity even if he had been Daniel Einstein. And in the pits of perversity and slums of sadism, Adolf would have been all that Hitler was, even if his first name had started with any other letter from B to *Z*.

Somehow first names beginning with A go well with their lasting fames or infamies.

Five women in modern India's history whose names began with A and whose personalities were of the first order come to mind:

Annie Besant (1847–1933)

Anasuya Sarabhai (1885–1972)

Amrit Kaur (1887–1964)

Aijaz Rasul (1909–2001)

Aruna Asaf Ali (1909–1996)

The first, third and fifth are well known, the second and fourth not that much. But they deserve to be.

Annie Besant is celebrated for her campaigns for democracy in India. But she also was in her younger and more fiery days, as Annie Wood, an activist to be reckoned with, having been in the thick of 'Bloody Sunday', the 1887 demonstration in London, England, where marchers protesting unemployment and demanding the release of MP William O'Brien clashed with the Metropolitan Police. She also was a 'flame' in the London matchgirls' strike of 1888 by the women and teenage girls working at the Bryant & May match factory in Bow, London, protesting fourteen-hour workdays, shockingly low wages, unjust fines and health complications caused by working with white phosphorus.

Anasuya Sarabhai, a sister of the mill-owner friend of M.K. Gandhi, came under Fabian influence while studying at the London School of Economics, participated in the suffragette movement there and, on returning to India, pioneered the then very new and revolutionary concept of a women's labour movement in India. Founding the Ahmedabad Textile Labour Association (Majoor Mahajan Sangh), the country's oldest union of textile workers, in 1920 and Kanyagruha in 1927 to educate girls of the mills, she was a prime factor in the just settlement of the strike in 1914 called by the mill-workers in her brother's factory, under Gandhi's leadership. While his fast is definitely what led to the strike's termination, Anasuya's steadfast solidarity with the strikers was another undeniable factor.

Amrit Kaur, born to the Protestant wing of the Sikh princely family of Kapurthala in the Punjab, took to a life of simplicity (not to be confused with slatternliness) under the influence of Gandhi and, joining different phases of the Indian freedom struggle, suffered imprisonment by the British. Gender issues were an abiding interest of hers and co-founding the All India Women's Conference in 1927, she was later appointed its secretary in 1930 and president in 1933. Unflinchingly courageous and equally consistently a believer in non-violence, she went, in 1937, on a mission of goodwill to Bannu, in the present-day Khyber Pakhtunkhwa region of Pakistan, to strengthen communal trust and harmony, and was charged and arrested for sedition.

Aijaz Rasul, like Amrit Kaur, came from an aristocratic family in the Punjab, but from Malerkotla's Muslim half. Of strong views of her own on equity, she was an advocate for land reforms and for the abolition, no less, of zamindari. She was also a determined advocate of Hindu–Muslim unity, and in the 1937 elections successfully contested from a non-reserved seat and was elected to the U.P. legislative assembly. Begum Aijaz Rasul was also elected to India's Constituent Assembly where, as a member of the Minority Rights Drafting Subcommittee, she created consensus among the Muslim leadership to voluntarily give up the demand for reserved seats for religious minorities—a view which most of them came to appreciate. Radical, revolutionary even, Aijaz Rasul remained to the end a believer in negotiation as the first and best instrument for change.

Aruna is so well-known as Aruna Asaf Ali, the grey-haired leftist firebrand who feared nothing and sought no office (except for having been mayor of Delhi once), and, though married to a celebrity, was so much her own person throughout that one forgets that she was, as Aruna Ganguly, once a very young nationalist who, at the time of the salt satyagraha of 1939, was jailed for, guess what, vagrancy! And when, after Gandhi's iconic agreement with Viceroy Lord Irwin, all political prisoners were released, Aruna was not. Why? For she had been booked as a vagrant! The word 'vagrant' suited her, for it means 'one without a fixed abode, a roamer, a wanderer'. Being restless and ever on the move, including, during the Quit India Movement of 1942, in the underground, Aruna Asaf Ali—with the A in her name being present three times over—became a legend. And, like all those who are legends, she has a fluttering image of her legendary being: Aruna, hoisting the Indian national flag at the Gowalia Tank maidan, Bombay, during the Quit India Movement in 1942.

Aruna Roy, named, as she tells me, after the fifth, has in her something of the personality of all five and they, hers. She has Annie Besant's passion for justice, Anasuya Sarabhai's steadfastness in solidarity with the underprivileged, Amrit Kaur's determination in struggle, Aijaz Rasul's singular clarity of purpose and Aruna Asaf Ali's elegant flair for cocking a snook at the arrogance of power. She is an alpha in all these qualities. And her very own composure in the midst of the commotion around her, her ability to face challenges without flinching at the risks involved, her readiness to suffer the maximum penalties for the cause she believes in are values that all five would have cherished.

But there is more. Aruna has something else in her biochemistry that is totally hers. I am not suggesting that the great five did not have that 'something else'; they did, but in Aruna's case it has become a special attribute because of the dynamics of her socio-political setting. I refer to Aruna being Aruna, and not Aruna the Democrat, Aruna the Unionist, Aruna the Nationalist, Aruna the Leftist. Or, in more contemporary terms, Aruna the Feminist, Aruna the Activist, Aruna the Dissenter. She is all of these but is still not. There is an A in Aruna being Aruna that defies co-option, eludes homogenization. Be she with the left and she will yet be to the left of the most leftward. She is of the left but can never be termed a 'leftie'. Be she with the democrats (indeed, she has inspired the School for Democracy in Rajasthan) but can never attract the jibe 'libocrat'. Be she the toast of all dissent but she cannot be the 'AutoNayer'.

Aruna does not have to prove either her patriotism to the right or her independence to the left.

Never one to wear her learning on the borders of her stunningly spartan handwoven saris, Aruna does not hide her love of art or books. Never one to struggle, as an English-speaker of class, for the right words in Hindi or Tamil, Aruna will speak a patois with the gender casings mixed up in her Hindi and Tam-Brahm colloquialisms sprinkled liberally over her Tamil. She is a stranger to racial prejudice, but she will not try like some do, ineffectively, to deracinate her origins. She will court prosecution but not popularity.

She speaks, when called for, the language of the crossroads but reads Shakespeare, Blake and Yeats. Reading this book you will find it peopled by men like Mohanji of the Mazdoor Kisan Shakti Sangathan, whom she calls 'our unlettered bard', and fascinating individuals from the deserts of Rajasthan like Naurti, Billan, Mangi and Haseena, Bhuli and Kesar, as also Brecht, Eduardo Galeano, Ibsen, Victor Hugo, Francis Bacon, Huxley and Orwell. She sings songs of protest with fire, not music, in them, but is a connoisseur of Carnatic music. She will rage, because rage rages in her, but she will not miss a chance if she can to see high-end dance.

This book is about the human conscience examining itself—an unusual exercise. We know of that word being used to elevate the user's status, or used to deflate another person or institution. But Aruna Roy, being what she is, uses the chance to recollect her life's major passages by asking herself whether her conscience has been up to self-deception, has taken to moral policing others or has been its own critic and corrector. Can conscience judge itself? Can water wash itself?

Aruna shows it can.

Searingly honest about her own quest for personal and public honesty, this book is more than a memoir, more even than a story of the writer's times. It is a seismograph recording moral pulsations on scales Richter would miss for they are so small or for they are so large as to cross Richter 10.

I marvel at both Aruna's self-confidence and her self-restraint in writing as she does about her lived experience.

To have known Aruna Roy and her extraordinary husband, Bunker Roy, to have been her house guest in her official home in Pondicherry and later in her own dwelling in Devdungri and the home where Bunker and she spend time together, Tilonia, has been a privilege. To have heard her speak in Kolkata, Chennai, Delhi and also in villages in Rajasthan and Bengal and heard her talk to groups outside India as well is to have seen the very best by way of modern India examining itself—an instruction. But to have read this book, which contains the essence of her life story, is to have understood what I have not seen better described—The Discomfort of Conscience.

A truer phrase I have not come across. Trevor Huddleston (1913–1998), who was an Anglican Bishop and anti-apartheid crusader, wrote a memoir called *Naught for Your Comfort*, the phrase drawn from G.K. Chesterton. In the alphabet of that genre of books, Aruna's is the alpha that its author is.

Bengaluru **Gopalkrishna Gandhi**
7 September 2023

1
A Prelude

IT WAS SOMETIME early in 1975 when I resigned from the Indian Administrative Service (IAS) and left Delhi for Tilonia, a village in Rajasthan, to join a not-for-profit non-governmental organization (NGO), Social Work and Research Centre (SWRC for short and better known as the Barefoot College), to work with the rural poor.[1] As an IAS officer, I had trained in Tamil Nadu and visited several villages in the state as well as in the union territories (UTs) of Pondicherry (now Puducherry) and Delhi (then a UT and now a state). What could be so different in Tilonia? Impatient to begin, I requested a village colleague to take me to someone with whom I could begin a conversation. He led me to a small courtyard that had two rooms at right angles, and a hut for a kitchen where animals were also tethered. A woman emerged from the kitchen with some pots and pans in her hands. My colleague left, indicating that no woman would speak freely if he (a male) was present.

The woman was striking. She was tall, and had a sharp look and, as I soon discovered, a sharper tongue. Suspicion was writ large on her face. We were the same colour but that is where all similarities ended. She said in Rajasthani, which though close to Hindi is another language, 'Why have you come?' I replied in my most cheerful voice,

'I have just come to your village and thought we could talk.' She looked me up and down (I was shorter) and, having sized me up, said, 'Get lost! I neither want literacy nor a job. I have my hands full and no time to waste on the likes of you!'

I was taken aback. What had happened between my experiences in south India and Delhi, and now? Then it dawned on me that I had made my way to Tilonia leaving behind the trappings of power. I had assumed that as a former IAS officer I would be able to talk with ease to both local men and women. I was wrong. It had been the name of the Revenue Department that had, in all its glory, preceded me in the earlier experiences, proclaiming my privilege, 'status' and power. Without that symbol of authority I would have struggled there too.

Smarting with chagrin and irritation, rebuffed and perplexed, I sat wondering how I would even begin to work with the people here. I knew that somewhere I had approached the issue wrong. It was a cultural gaffe or an intrusion by a strange species upsetting the area of comfort of a solidly created and impenetrable pattern of manners. Later, when two women came to the Barefoot College campus where I lived, I was somewhat wiser. I learnt that they belonged to a Dalit community and were daily wage workers. The statutory minimum wage was Rs 3 at that time. It was beyond my imagination that such a small amount could cover their daily necessities.

The two women, Bhuli and Kesar, were my first teachers. I tentatively asked if I could visit them and they welcomed me. Theirs was the first home I stepped into. The houses had no windows, only a small hole in the wall, because they believed windows were dangerous, making it easier for thieves to enter. The kitchen stove was a chulha, and I had my first taste of bajra roti and chilli-garlic chutney, which I washed down with buttermilk. My conversation with them that evening marked the beginning of my education about the India which was to be my home. At every turn my assumptions were questioned and opinions challenged. The women were warm and forthcoming. To some extent they saw me as the person who had hired them to work, but also as a woman. I am embarrassed to think of the questions they asked me to make sure I was, in fact, a woman and married. Where, they asked, were the traditional indicators on my person that proclaimed my marital status? I could have been a Martian! As I left their home I met some others, who were shocked that a woman of privilege from the city would dine in a Dalit home. They assumed I was a Christian come to convert them.

The woman who refused to communicate with me belonged to a community listed under Other Backward Classes (OBC). They all seemed alike in dress and ornaments—beautiful big silver or white metal bangles, anklets and a stiff necklace. I was daunted by the cumulative weight of their accessories. What perhaps shocked me the most when I met them was the huge challenge to fight privilege, looking at the hiatus between them and me. This was a time of great internal upheaval and relearning. All my scholastic learning and my training in the IAS went out through the hole in the wall. I could not roll a roti or grind chilli-garlic paste; I addressed my husband by his given name; I did not cover my face—my upbringing was faulty! I had no books to guide me and no one to tell me how one made friends across cultures.

Soon I learnt that affection and persistence were the way to open doors to dialogue and learning. But I had to come to terms with facing chasms between people who claimed the same country, had the same skin colour, but had an ocean dividing them in privilege and world view. I found justification had to be made to a patriarchal system that set store by material gain and benefits, but saw little value in making conversation or friends. Many questions arose. The hurdles and difficulties of crossing cultural boundaries had to be navigated within one's mind.

My journey from urban middle class to rural marginalized India is interwoven with the warp and weft of other people's lives. It has never been solitary. There has been the joy of living, working and learning with people. The so-called 'vulnerable, oppressed, marginalized and deprived' never lost their affection, humour, common sense, wisdom and sense of fun even in the direst of circumstances. The ugly picture circulated of stark poverty, representing deprivation at its worst, joyless and bleak, was rubbished in living with each other. In its place we found colour, beauty, joy, laughter and tremendous grit to struggle every day. As Sunil Gupta, a friend and now an internationally known photographer, said to me in the 1980s on the dispute between colour and black-and-white photography: 'The others see us as black and white; we see ourselves in colour.' Obviously, we always remain multidimensional to ourselves, no matter how starkly we may be projected in polarities. It is this multidimensional perception that forms the basis of understanding and change.

One of my first cultural shocks in my transition from urban to rural India was the non-existence of any concept of privacy, except traditional modesty of course. (According to Rajasthani rural etiquette, you could expose your bosom, but not your face. You could not look at men and had to be very modest with the in-laws.) Doors were never shut, visitors walked in and opened trunks to peer in to see the contents. Every item that was different, be it furniture or anything else, was the topic of discussion at the well where women gathered. Who came and went was in full view of the ever curious. Woven into the political, personal life became a public theatre. Even expressions of emotion became a part of the public persona, unless one bottled them up for the night when everyone was asleep.

One of the important motivations that pushed me to live with people was the worry and guilt about inequality and privilege. However, poverty of the extreme kind that one encounters in a town or city slum was not to be seen in a village. Here it bred another kind of endemic hunger and need that ran through a lifetime. Throw in caste exploitation and the picture was complete. These factors were internalized often to an illogical degree, creating fault lines in the 'idyllic', apparently peaceful rural scenario that were just waiting to erupt. The authoritarian feudal system did not take to questioning easily. Everyone compromised to keep the peace, either with consent or with fear.

I realize that life, if we have to choose a metaphor, is like a river. It flows, overflows and moves constantly. The personal has to exist in this space. The mind, being private and hidden, is allowed the freedom to accept inadequacies, the unconventional, without fear of social disapproval. The categories we continually evolve to define our work and our lives are like an ever-changing choice of different sieves through which we pass our experiences, thoughts, emotions, ideas, hopes, failures and achievements. The choice of sieve, a fine mesh or a larger one, defines the nature of analysis and the way we present our experiences, thoughts.

In the world outside we are told rationality is, or should be, the dominant frame within which the 'I' (the inner voice; the mind) must reinvent itself from time to time. In this 'rational' world, emotions must frequently struggle to occupy primary space and, at moments, grab the space they need to assert their right to be. The women I have met in village India have not created these fragmenting walls—

emotion and thought are a continuum, and I have often envied them. In living with them these last fifty years I have readjusted to see myself holistically.

In many ways, our childhood prepared my siblings and me to shape our lives without conforming to conventional definitions. Ours was a small home that housed the immense mental space of the universe, elastic and capable of the craziest assumptions and expansions. The outside world was a mosaic of the strict rules of tradition and conventionality. Each community was tight and exact in its conservative propriety. Yet tolerant of others. There was no public need to identify oneself in any one specific category at all times. This gave me, for instance, the liberty to be within the larger fold of cultural Hinduism, in my love for classical music and dance. It equally allowed me to appreciate the church choir, an azaan or kirtans. Friends went to the local government school and also to private schools, Christian and non-Christian. Festivals came and went, and all of us siblings could be seen at every celebration. My mother tried to bring the children together to edit a small paper, celebrate a doll's wedding without traditional ceremonies, etc.

It was the era before moral policing and self-righteousness had taken over public space. Gandhi's battle for tolerance, which he paid for with his life, had left its protective shadow. Ambedkar and Ramaswami Naicker were in living memory. You could not dismiss or wage war for your opinions or perspectives; you argued or withdrew.

Othering

On 14 May 2015 in Dangawas, a village in Nagaur district of Rajasthan, five Dalits were brutally killed by powerful upper-caste farmers when they legitimately claimed their right to harvest their crop. The police station stood a mere 2 kilometres from where the incident took place. It was manned by OBC and upper-caste men, who took two hours to respond to the call.[2] It took several weeks and several street protests in Jaipur for a case to be registered against the upper-caste farmers. Three years later, in 2018, justice was still awaited.[3] Demands for justice are tempered by the complexity of human reactions, conditioned by prejudice, ignorance and the deliberate denial of factual conditions. Justice in a case of violence often descends immediately into intersectional loyalties and social inequality—caste, religion, gender—leading to delays and compromise.

Justice is often set aside by identity politics and overlaid by power equations. One of the constant ways to attack the 'other' has been stereotyping and its internalization. The internalizing of stereotypes has led to violence and irrationality. It is often an unconscious process. Dissent and critique are born out of questioning these prejudices and their influence on public action—in present times these prejudices and their influence seem to be in their worst manifestation.

The perception of feminine beauty has strong overtones of 'othering'. A strongly articulated critique of this predicament came from the initial feminists, who talked of liberation from dominant perceptions of beauty that forced women to squeeze themselves into roles and body shapes to please the viewer's aesthetic, often a male one. For instance, most Indian models are light skinned and have Caucasian figures. Some people have asked, with political innuendo and sarcasm, where the darker-skinned, hour-glass-shaped female body, more common in India, is to be found in this representation. And where do women from the north-eastern states find space? The dominant ideas of beauty come from a market that controls what we think and buy. Feminism has become all the richer for including these perceptions and variables as part of its political discourse. There are many stereotypes—race, ethnicity, sexuality, caste, religion, rich, poor, educated, uneducated, etc.—that influence the debate on freedom of choice and equality. In a village, gender, religion and caste untouchability raise their ugly heads many times a day when people are forced into positions of subordination.

Deprivation and injustice must be universally damned. There are many journeys and many travellers; Indians committed to doing something about what they believe is injustice fight millions of daily battles. The emotional fuelling of public action comes from anger, need, compassion, angst and grief arising out of the despicable treatment of human beings, as much as a denial of rights. Structural violence, which attempts to break the will of the powerless, provokes a continual search for ways to resolve issues.

'What is your version of the truth?'

In 1988, some people sat to gherao the local authority in protest against the non-payment of minimum wages.[4] The protest took place inside a square that housed the offices of the sub-divisional magistrate (SDM), the tehsildar and the subordinate court. A few days later, when a friend visited the district office on some work, the district collector complained the protestors had blocked the road to prevent Sita Devi, wife of late Prime Minister V.P. Singh, from getting past them to Deogarh, her parental town.

The highway on which she travelled was 1 kilometre away from the SDM's office, where the gherao had taken place!

Distortion of truth is one of the many categories of lies by which political protest is often maligned.

In the decade 2005–14, the rights-based legislations made promises of looking at privilege and access to power rationally in a progressive understanding of democratic participation.[5] The legislative response (the rights-based laws) grew out of an acceptance of observed truths and through building policy with people. Ironically, the same government that made these rights-based legislations invoked the bogey of extremism and initiated 'Operation Green Hunt' to counter the protest of Adivasis. In contemporary India, Hindutva nationalism has clubbed all protest and dissent under the threat of anti-nationalism and sedition, stoking mass public sentiment to deny justice and compassion. The system says it is concerned about corruption and endemic hunger, but fails to listen to the people. Their opinions are brushed aside and the planners do not pay attention to what the people can or cannot do, what they want and do not want to do. Power pushes pre-conceived non-participatory solutions, forcing people to accept what is impractical. Naturally, they reject it. The best example is of the toilet and the obsession with open defecation that has a laudable end, but refuses to see the impossibility of the means and is blind to reality. The quarrel over fact has often been misrepresented by bureaucratic privilege as 'what is your version of the truth?' Truth stands alone in its inviolability. Facts can have versions. The deliberate distortion of truth becomes possible only when there is a war between versions—my version and that of the 'other'.

Well-known Indian historian D.D. Kosambi once argued that the documented histories that we take so seriously are written from the perspective of the privileged.[6] The people's history, on the contrary, has been kept alive for centuries through a rich oral tradition, in the form of poetry, songs and stories.

People and the Oral History Tradition

Cultural conditioning often plays a huge role in human responses. During my forty years of struggle and learning in Rajasthan, the region's culture has had an immense influence on my politics. The parables, folk stories, folklore, historical narratives of local deities, the myths have all helped me understand a community very different from the one I grew up in. I have learnt to understand cultural history from a plethora of forms. From women's songs sung when they work—tilling the soil and bringing the water up from the well—to when people wed and when they die. The sonorous music of the Marwari khayals, the repetitive refrains of the phads, the songs of Bulleh Shah and Latif, the music of the Langas and Manganiyars, the Kabirpanthis, the funny anecdotes and the sombre tragedies, the richness of the interweaving between fact, fiction and wisdom are part of a continuing tradition.

Telling a tale effectively and engaging the attention of the listener is a craft, an art, which weaves together the magic of words and the consummate dexterity of a communicator. These stories are universally remembered not necessarily for their morality or the strength of their perceptive insights, but because they are good stories, their language is easily understood and they relate to lives people still lead. Two communities in the state—the Bhatts and the Charans—are masters of this craft and carry forward Rajasthan's rich oral history traditions.[7] The Bhatts go from village to village narrating personal histories of valour, while the Charans narrate the personal stories of kings and the powerful. We once met a sub-inspector (SI) of police, who charmed us with his narration of a criminal investigation. He collected a crowd of admiring listeners. We discovered he was a Charan first, then an SI! He could not resist turning a criminal report into a story.

In my experience, Rajasthanis are oral historians and, in general, reluctant readers. I am surrounded by Rajasthani friends, acquaintances and others who are fascinated by the spoken word but find little joy in reading. The written word is a mystery they can do without. Even in contemporary times reading is a habit fostered and protected in very small exclusive communities in Rajasthan. Books are largely a part of the décor or just a means of establishing class. The reason: exclusion, more than seventy years ago, from schools and scholastic pursuits—a chasm yet to be bridged. However, the great folk-story writer Vijaydan Detha (Bijji), writing in twentieth-century Rajasthan, captured the popular imagination like none other. Bijji wrote as if he were speaking—he recreated Rajasthani folklore. He evoked its universal and topical relevance, reaching across time and space. His books, which are akin to the fables of Aesop and Kabir, have been translated into multiple languages, so great is their appeal.

I loved listening to Bijji read his stories aloud, traditional in their setting and very modern in psychological content and implicit analysis. The stories often question inequality and social conditioning, like the famous retelling of 'Dohri Joon' (the English translation is called 'Double Life'[8]), where two women are tricked into getting married because of a pledge by their parents. What follows is unorthodox and contemporary. Bijji's powerful retelling of folk narratives brings to mind the Mazdoor Kisan Shakti Sangathan's (MKSS) much-loved narrator Galkuma's[9] fables of animals to lampoon the unjust government, and the interwoven narratives in an Eduardo Galeano[10] speech on politics. Their works communicate so easily. I have grown up reading and cannot imagine a world without books: short-story collections, novels, non-fiction. While friends, and conversations, have to be organized, books sit waiting on the shelf, ready to suit my mood and time. Choosing to write has something to do with that, and much to do with the fact that narratives have reclaimed the value of many worlds lost to us.

Audio-visual media is steadily leading an entire generation away from the wonder of the written word. Nevertheless, storytelling in the form of podcasts underscores the age-old understanding that knowledge can come from listening as much as reading. There is something compelling in a human voice and we hope the oral history tradition will survive. Politically distorted oral narratives also find space in printed form and repetitive narration in contemporary India. Sadly, the once-continuing informal modes to build narratives and counter-narratives are fast losing space to social media. The stories about struggles—individual and collective—have been taken over by manufactured stories to manipulate people's emotions and prejudice to negate and destroy. We are now in a world where propaganda is masquerading as history. So much so that in contemporary India many are willing to believe that Godse is a nationalist martyr, and Gandhi the opposite. How do we begin to regain the space to tell our stories and talk of equality, justice and compassion, of loving people and cultural differences? Can we begin to dream again?

When propaganda claims historical veracity, one way of countering it is by recording life experiences that speak for themselves. Ordinary people manage to live amidst multiple and sometimes cross-connecting pressures and issues. Life as it is lived and perceived becomes the history of individuals. Thus, the people's history continues to live and thrive in charcha (informal conversations) in the chaupal, in the teashop and at the adda.[11] Poetry, songs and tales of protest of today draw deeply from the rich foundations of our oral historical traditions. Their rhythm, metre and passionate conviction serve to express outrage, agony and the aspirations of today.

Our unlettered bard Mohanji, of the MKSS, once sang:

Pehle wallah chor bhaiyan bandukaon marta o
Abbe wallah chor to kalmaon mare re, raj choronko.

(Thieves of old, brothers, used guns to kill / Thieves today use the pen to kill; it is these thieves who rule.)

We hope he will continue to awaken people to the power of hidden secrets in files (once as paper and now as data in computers).

Songs of protest and their lyrics evoke the texture of political action. They rekindle collectively shared moments of commitment. Especially during campaigns, such songs give birth to new energies that lift flagging spirits. Campaigns thrive on creative energy and promote yet more. Poetry, kathas (stories, including personal stories of activism) and the humble 'parcha' (an inexpensive pamphlet printed and circulated widely and quickly) remain a witness to such moments. The parcha, though written in a hurry, stokes collective and personal memory for generations to come as it brings home the immediacy of the moment even though that moment is long gone. It does not, however, find respectability or space in the theoretical universe or in recorded history.

Narratives, based on facts as perceived by the disempowered, form much of the oral folk tradition. Every narrative has its internal logic, but what if the sum of many such narratives speaks a truth born not out of indoctrination but of experienced realities? Today what remains of many protests is a dry newspaper report, while many fascinating stories born of such struggles go unrecorded for posterity. Sadly it is the written word that has appropriated and dominated history even though the oral tradition relies on memory and continuity and is vibrantly textured historical recall. Personal stories of activism are absorbing and stay longer in one's memories;

they are often only part of an oral tradition. Folklore born of struggle dies as memories fade. Women's voices, the complexity of emotions—where success can also be loss, and defeat, a moment of realization—are also unrecorded and lost to posterity. This makes most written histories dull, a set of dates and dry events that fail to kindle the imagination. Such dry detailing of events leaves the reader, especially the next generation, indifferent to moments of change and courage.

In the political context the written word helps to explain the logic of a personal choice, making it more universal. For the unlettered, the written word is a mystery and a challenge; its absence opens them up to exploitation and domination. I recall sitting in a literacy class with Naurti, Billan, Mangi and Haseena in 1982, as I had with many mature women before. They looked at me with something akin to dislike. They were oppressed by the chalk and the board and the squiggles. They had developed thoughts that they could not put down in writing. Their chagrin was totally understandable. Mangi, the intellectual, wanted to read to lessen her dependence on the literate. Naurti, to make sure her wage was correct. Billan, just to be with everybody. Haseena was there to please me. What price to pay for functional literacy?

Forty-odd years in rural India and meeting people all over the world—political writers like Eduardo Galeano, for example—have strengthened the admiration I have for my friends in the village who have a story for every political thought. Narratives stay embedded in our consciousness and come up unexpectedly to answer very knotty political dilemmas. The storyteller has the huge advantage of digressing, embellishing and moving back and forth between thought and feeling, and the past, present and future. The critique of meandering linearity in a book is often countered by the storyteller's magic of engaging the reader.

2

'The Personal Is Political'

IT IS NATURAL to want to express oneself. There is of course the universal desire to share, communicate and enjoy the comfort of belonging to a community. Many stories and histories belong to the collective, even though the story, when narrated, is a unique personal experience. Chanting slogans together empowers and connects individuals to a collective, but the emotions behind different voices are highly individual. The collective unified chant empowers individual thought. From this nourishing dialectic between the person and the collective emerges the seminal feminist slogan: 'The Personal Is Political'.

Good slogans rarely have a single author. They come from a collective experience sifting through years of struggle. Slogans emerge with a finely crafted string of words that communicates perfectly. 'The Personal Is Political' is one such collective slogan that will surely live forever. Gloria Steinem said that to ascribe authorship for this slogan to a single individual would be like attempting to claim or ascribe authorship to the First World War! This slogan has the power and life of a statement of truth that evokes both the political history of women and the meeting point between theory and practice.

The slogan gives a theoretical niche for the two beings I shelter within my body—the first, a capable, confident social activist sure of herself; and the second, a questioning woman who asks as many questions of herself as of others. The first welcomes confrontation if necessary to fight injustice and inequality, and the second one believes that there is room for compassionate dialogue. For the outside world, I am stereotypical and categorized. For myself, I am complex and beyond cataloguing.

Many feminists have entered mainstream politics. No political movement, however, has sought to give space to both the personal and the political, and to the more holistic and realistic learning they engender. Despite its universal appeal, 'The Personal Is Political' is not merely a feminist slogan in origin but, as contemporary events have established, it has democratic logic behind it. The last two decades have been a gradual learning of how intimately connected our personal lives are with political events, processes and the character of our institutions.

The politics of the state encroaches on, among many, two personal domains: the right to religion and right to marry a partner of choice. Such as a law that actually interferes with the personal choice of a marriage partner, like the 'Uttar Pradesh Prohibition of Unlawful Conversion of Religion Ordinance, 2020', which contests inter-community marriages. Though debated and with a sizeable number of Indian women protesting, the law, now popularly labelled the 'love jihad law',[1] still stands—a witness to growing patriarchy and religious fanaticism.

In the 2020s, the Indian republic's journey entered our homes and even our personal dreams and choices, compelling us to confront the cocoons of comfort and the consequent paradigms of deliberate ignorance we have built for ourselves. The slogan has been vindicated and comes home to us—at a terrible cost. We have had to witness large-scale violence against women and the hollowing out of the constitutional guarantee to equality. There is too the polarity of contemporary political rhetoric, forcing binaries and denying complexity, a world of black and white, ignoring the grey. I remember Kuldip Nayar addressing a public gathering in 2004 in Delhi, where he argued that life is lived in the area of grey, and resolutions will only come when we step out of these false dichotomies of black and white.

The word 'political' became an important part of the feminist vocabulary in the 1960s. We grew slowly to understand that politics is not merely that which constitutes our external realities—electoral politics, parties, the vote and the now rampant system of payoffs and corruption—but is everywhere. It is present in each personal choice and nuance. It is there in varied experiences, in hunger and the kind of food we eat, the clothes we choose to wear, in the kinds of inequality we choose to tolerate or oppose. The political is also at times the thread that connects the various parts of the personal narratives.

What seems, what is

People see me and say
That's a strong face
Determined to walk on
The fist raised.
The courage, we must
Show with
Our fingers curled into a ball.

But I know the paradoxes
That uncurl that fist,
Making the sun dip or shine.
The abyss gapes
Its jaws luring me
Into its menacing darkness.

Reason comes through
The bird in flight, the child
Crying of hunger,
Pushing me out to what must
Must be done.

The rhythm of daily chores
Again
Look at the new, harmonious
Reality sharp in focus
Through the photographic lens
Of a Leica,
Nudges me to comprehending hunger.

I look at my life
I feel my dreams
They change, they fade,
New ones come and
The cycle begins.[2]

Conflict between Home and Work

As women, we are often asked how we manage between the demands of family and struggle. Family (the personal) and activism (the political) are perceived as two contesting obligations. Let us take the example of the dharna (sit-down strikes, protests) where circumstances do not allow protagonists to move from where we are. Children, home are put on the back-burner; a feeling of guilt follows. Outrage is not baggage that an activist can leave at the dharna site; we carry the seeds of discontent home. Women have a more highly developed sense of duty and are more sensitive about family needs, about themselves and to each other. They often have to leave protests to tend to children and those who are critically ill in the family. These are difficult choices. It does require a shifting prism of perception and a juggling of pressing demands on time.

Ideologies, ethics, discriminatory politics, principles, emotions define the permissible limits of what a social group may decide as proper. The angst of forgotten children, the spouse who may feel marginalized, ignored social obligations—all keep us forever juggling time. The guilt of prioritizing one over the other stays with us as a footnote to trouble our conscience. Conflicting obligations and choices between personal commitments and public action tend to occupy contentious space. To some extent, smudging the boundaries between work and home has helped.

To my mind, anyone who acts on principles and stated public concerns is an activist, female or male. 'Activism' is but a label we give that set of actions. It can be about anything. It undoubtedly originates in a commitment to ethical ideas and ideology. It also emerges from a background of life experiences that have led actors to choose this method of self-expression. The political (aka choosing to take public action) is also at times the thread that connects the various parts of one's personal narrative.

All of us have several identities. My primary identity, if there is one, can only be gender. Like millions of women in my generation,

I treasure the empowerment of the feminine consciousness in the twentieth and now in the twenty-first century. I have had many lessons from women before me, to cite a few examples: my grandmother Lalita, who pushed the boundaries of social freedom using privilege to break the stranglehold of custom like many others of her generation in India; Virginia Woolf; the women in Tilonia—Naurti, whom I met at a literacy class in 1982, and from whom I learnt of the politics of poverty; and Bhuriya, the rugged old woman who gave us the courage to fight economic and feudal oppression head on in the initial struggles of the MKSS.

Understanding is both an emotive and intellectual comprehension of reality. These women moved me emotionally; it is only later that I groped for categories to express the complexities. We, as women, have struggled to place emotion on par with thought. The language of communication has a male and female vocabulary. Virginia Woolf says in *A Room of One's Own*: 'Women have served all these centuries as looking glasses possessing the magic and delicious power of reflecting the figure of man at twice its natural size.'[3]

Woe to those women who chose to confront not only ideas but ways of expressing them! When one talks of setting women's bodies free, the feminine mind too needs acceptance. The artificial divide and hierarchy between imagination and logic must dissolve to an extent. One should be able to see the logic in imagination, and imagination in logic. Dr S. Anandalakshmy titled her collection of essays *Thinking with the Heart*.[4] Women's expressions combine emotion and logic. The relationship of a woman to language is as intriguing as her relationship with her body. It is a similar fear of expression. The words women use, their style and the concepts that emerge from them can often topple the male citadel—not merely by use of language, but by thought itself. Vocabulary traps emotions and pins the mind to work within a frame, and deviants are punished.

Community approval of both thought and language matter in the public domain. That is why perhaps Shakespeare, who broke all rules, wrote a language that had the power of emotion and unorthodoxy as well as the clarity of rationality. But the world we live in has become adept at producing seductive arguments for comfort and consumerism. It has weakened both our ability to demand rational answers, and the collective resolve to resist self-destruction. At the same time the dilemma—between individual aspiration and the greater common good—etches out the drama of today's political scenario.

We continually evolve categories or classifications as tools to order one's mind. They exist only to facilitate. But the rigidity of the category often takes over at the cost of reason. Thinking about the intersectionality of identities challenges the basic binaries. Many women have a tendency to think laterally. A woman is a person with many identities—a Dalit, from a minority, poor—all intersecting in a skewed socio-economic-political scenario. How much of her oppression comes from where? Questions like this are essential to address in a search for access to equality.

Equality, as a principle, draws its legal and constitutional validity from a personal human condition of discrimination. When the divide between the personal and political blurs, the compassion of seeing another's point of view takes shape and becomes the basis for understanding. It would help understand how Naurti's struggle for minimum wages, or Bhanwari Devi's fight against rape in the 1980s, or recently in the 2020s, Bilkis Dadi's crusade against discrimination and a threatening citizenship law, in Shaheen Bagh, transformed perceptions.

To plunge into action requires courage. Pondering over choices endlessly can lead to inaction, a Hamletian dilemma. The shaping of a question for public examination too requires courage. And the fashioning of the question itself, ingenuity and honesty. The process has also to be collective for better public action. The two personas, the personal and the political, act as monitors to correct self-justification and self-righteousness.

Some of us have the misfortune of being conscious witnesses to our own public actions, which is a blessing and a curse. Very often, as I stand to address people, I am both the speaker and the one who listens. This witness offers a constant critique. In one dharna, while addressing already furious women, I had a moment when I knew that a word uttered without moderation could incite the protest to become unruly. This consciousness averted what could have led to uncontrolled violence. Our internal conflicts—of which there are always many—and their predicaments are shaped by and resolved in relationships in action and with other people. Women have always instinctively broken the boundaries between the personal and the political; witness how quick we are to seek listeners and share our sorrows and joys even in public places.

Activists are seen as exaggerating statements of concern and our frank articulation forces the fence sitters to address uncomfortable questions. The activist's biggest challenge is to keep hoping. How do we define and keep alive the possibility of a utopia in our minds despite cynics telling us it is a complete waste of time? The answer lies perhaps in recognizing that each one of us can make a difference. The trouble is that these actions do not often measure up to our dreams of a grand design. We fail to understand that these processes need to be kept alive for the possibility of regaining normative constitutional values. Obsessed with the grand design, we often fail to see the small beginnings or recognize the material existence of a dream next door.

What keeps public action going in the darkest of times is hope, faith in human compassion and kindness as a value that will survive the worst. It is perhaps this positive faith, kindled and kept alive, that makes possible the hope for resurgence and revival of a world most of us cherish as the definitive framework for public action. It energizes our resistance against what seem indomitable odds. As Bertolt Brecht wrote:

> In the dark times
> Will there also be singing?
> Yes, there will also be singing.
> About the dark times.[5]

Someone asked Eduardo Galeano about utopia and he said, 'Utopia is on the horizon. I move two steps closer; it moves two steps further away. I walk another ten steps and the horizon runs ten steps further away. As much as I may walk, I'll never reach it. So what's the point of utopia? The point is this: to keep walking.'[6]

Courage lies in walking towards what may always recede.

3

Our Politics, Our Bodies, Our Lives

A Footnote to the Discourse

I have watched the faces
    Of many of my kind
Shaped different, of different colour
    Hair parted in front
    Or knotted behind.

Faces alit with laughter
    Eyes watchful and wary
Mouths prim and strained, sometimes
    Parting, the beginning of a smile.

In all of you my friends
    I see a bit of myself—
My body's burden,
    The pain and the delight;
The desire to break into dance.

I see too in the stiff
    Legs and hands
And those bowed with
    The continuous strain—
The oppression on us.

But I know the spirit
    Which makes us share
The other's pain and pleasure;
    To empathize with the churnings
We have known,
    Have felt in our gut
And in our marrow bone.

I celebrate with you my friends
    women who toil,
The joy, the beauty
    The compassion of our kind.[1]

IT IS A truth universally acknowledged that girls and women who fight for equality, decency and dignity are usually called aggressive. To be damned they must simply be strong, expressive women and able to win their argument, or just different from the stereotypical woman of the conservative male imagination. The ones who assert their rights understand that being called aggressive may even be an acknowledgement of shifting power. From the moment the female identity is established in the womb to the moment death takes us, an 'inferior species' is subtly managed and manipulated.

Feminist theory and writings by Mary Wollstonecraft, Virginia Woolf, Germaine Greer, Jill Tweedie, Vina Mazumdar and Devaki

Jain have all provided me a framework to lodge many of the questions that troubled me as a young middle-class woman. That was the beginning. Later, in rural India and in the many years with Naurti, Bhuriya and many other rural working-class women, inequality was first and foremost a question of hunger and work. They kept reminding me that gender inequality worsened the situation, but the basic inequality was of class and caste.[2] The most obvious was the idiom and the language of communication itself. The women talked through experiences—stories from which facts emerged and evolved into theoretical understanding. Very often the stories went on a ramble with anecdotes and subplots. This was a different logic and method that needed to be understood. The act of listening had to be relearnt and learning reorganized.

Women meet people holistically; they absorb a whole range of sensory perceptions—from nuanced expression to the colours and details of dress. We are often accused of dressing up to please the male, but we equally dress up for each other (as can be seen in the giving and receiving of compliments and approval within women's groups). But what stands out as a sensitive value is that we are alerted to observe emotion, we note the stresses and strains of facial expressions and gestures, and we empathize. We are also quick to respond, sympathetically and with concern. Love is not confrontational and competitive. Women understand this. It affords great reassurances, and is missing almost entirely from the male world. A quick hug or a smile of understanding makes dealing with the day easier.

I was born into an unequal gender. I was, by circumstances of birth and privilege, protected from confronting issues of gender inequality till I entered a co-educational institution. The complexities of gender inequality dawned on me in my teens, when I heard my very intelligent mother complain that she wanted a profession. Though a very accomplished person, she had been left sitting at home, mothering her children. She sowed the seeds of feminist equality in her daughters to choose a profession, and showed by negative example that as women we needed to be assertive in claiming those rights. My father was supportive, but did not push her to break the boundaries of social and familial conditioning.

Most of her generation, and even today, women are demoralized when they internalize social values! Demanding freedom to choose is not easy. It is a struggle with each step and every day. Progress is still dominated by traditional conditioning and women continue to be affected by centuries of prejudice. The issues my great-grandmother, grandmother and mother dealt with made my battles much easier. When we step out of the frame of traditional roles, etiquette and convention, we are free to build our own ethical constructs.

My great-grandmother Neelamma sent her daughter Lalita (my grandmother) to school, till she finished her Senior Cambridge in 1918; she set standards for schooling for girls in the family. She also sold her land to send her brother to Oxford to study. He returned the favour by promising to organize Lalita's wedding. Fresh from a continent openly discussing equality and the political upheavals in Russia, he was radical enough to look for life partners for his niece and himself from another sub-caste of the community that he was born into. It was revolutionary in the extremely rigid and conservative south India of that era to do so. My grandmother Lalita Krishnaswami was the first social worker in my maternal family. She worked with leprosy patients and with women and children in slums from the 1920s to the 1950s. She was even an honorary magistrate. Her concern for the poor and her disregard for caste and religious divides shaped and changed values permanently in the family.

The identifiers of these divides were many, as I learnt by observing Ellamma, who had brought up my cousins, and from the poor woman next door to my grandparents' home in suburban Chennai in the 1950s. Women—domestic, agricultural or construction workers—not only spoke and dressed differently but also appeared to belong to a completely different political landscape. The brawls that took place among them frightened me but they never pushed me away; curiosity and inquiry remained. I often wondered what mystery lay within their 'beautiful' thatched huts. Poverty was not frightening.

Merging the Personal with the Political

The personal and political merged for me in the mud-and-stone hut in Devdungri in Rajsamand district of Rajasthan that became my home and office from 1987. It was here that I learnt that according to rural protocol newcomers had to address the men, the power elite, before talking to the women. I also realized that I did not have as clear an understanding of gender politics in rural India as that of caste and class politics.

It was curious how the men would never look me in the eye. If I addressed a question to a man, he would invariably reply to any male colleague of mine standing nearby. This irritated me. Later, however, I came to be accepted and even appreciated by the macho society I had entered. But for strange reasons—that I could drive a jeep, both on the national highway and in the more difficult alleys in the village; that I could stand up to and fight the men in the village; that I could say 'no' in categorical terms; and finally (and this acceptance was very grudgingly given), that I could understand their power structure and fight it.

The many Dalit and poor women were construction workers, and exposed to urban ways as they often travelled to Jammu (in the then state of Jammu and Kashmir), Kanpur (in Uttar Pradesh) and to towns and cities in Madhya Pradesh. They understood the challenges of exclusion and oppression in rural patriarchal society and were quicker to respond to calls for women's solidarity. The first strong battles against inequality I was part of were fought by women workers who hailed from the OBC and Dalit communities. The enumeration of people who submit Right to Information (RTI) applications may tell us that there are fewer women applicants than men; but the struggle to get the RTI Bill passed in Parliament was waged by rural women. We could even argue that the RTI has a more 'feminist' understanding of change, i.e., change without violence to transform the relationship between power and the powerless.[3]

Our Bodies, Our Selves

As women, we are defined by our bodies. Conditioning over the years has made our bodies a contentious space. The feminist debate has helped us dissolve some of these contradictions or artificial polarities. Eventually we have partially disengaged ourselves from the image of the stereotypical woman.

The dichotomy between the body and the self is just one of many dichotomies that women face.[4] The global debate it triggered in the 1960s made women look at conflict and fragmentation. Strong emotions were frowned upon by patriarchal and traditional morality and guilt followed. Logic did not provide answers (after all we are all tutored by Aristotelian logic). The body becomes a battle ground for conflicting value systems. The damned body is yet the focus of commercial attention. Markets continue to shape consumer dreams that are built on the ideal Caucasian figure. These dreams end in nightmares, persecution and violence against women, and sometimes even in death.

To talk of women as one category is perhaps naive. In this continual dispute, where women struggle at home, at the workplace, in the family and outside against multiple kinds of inequality, there are powerful and constant divides as well as overlapping oppressions. Indian women have to contend constantly with other identities taking over, caste and religion specifically.

My introduction to transgender people was through my mother, who typically explained the scientific or biological predicament of people born either sexually different, born 'male' or 'female' but who did not identify with their societally prescribed gender. The adult understanding came when my sister Manya did her thesis for her master's in social work on the transgender community and the dismal and inhuman conditions in which they lived and survived. Her stories made their plight a matter of concern. Sensitivities were further heightened when I heard the personal story of a trans woman. I was appalled, containing my tears at a public meeting, even though I was acquainted with her condition. She said, 'You continually talk of sexuality, but we too want love, romance, a home. We want a family. Every gathering looks at mere political equality; what about our sensibilities?' Even legal remedies were so callously conceived and humiliating. Transgender people fall into a predicament where, beginning with toilets and questionnaires, they are denied identity and existence. Some of those battles have now been won, but they continue to face social ostracism, often visible even in progressive circles.

Anyone working with oppressed communities, including women, identified 'intersectionality' long before American civil rights advocate Kimberlé Crenshaw coined the term.[5] No understanding of Indian feminism is possible without understanding the intersectionality of caste, religion, class and other identities. For instance, just looking at oppression as a gender issue would be limiting, as it would bypass poverty, caste and religious prejudice among women. Upper-class women talk of gender equality, but do not focus on other oppressions that women may face. In rural India, often the question first asked is: 'What is your caste?'

Women's discourse is also personal, and brings in the specifics of our conditions—we do relate to larger ideologies and positions, but we tend to start with the personal to go to the political. Women bond over all differences when their physical bodies are abused. But there are several issues that still divide us—inequality, caste, religion and class; the gender difference then becomes a subsidiary issue.

Power of office does not make much difference to the way women are treated. During my IAS training at Lal Bahadur Shastri National Academy of Administration (LBSNAA), Mussoorie, my expectations of a free, equal and friendly atmosphere among fellow officers were only partially realized. In the first few days I met a misogynist, confronted patriarchy and had to deal with the crude boyish-group sexual behaviour modified by a veneer of politeness from many fellow officers. There were of course many exceptions, men who were friendly and equal in their friendship with women, who behaved with propriety and a camaraderie that has remained for fifty years in bonds of friendship. Political inequality and gender differences were raised and discussed outside classrooms.

The curricula then did not include women's studies, which it now does. The most shocking of all was the anachronistic *Probationer's Handbook*, circulated to probationers and printed many decades earlier by the British colonial government. It was a book on manners, designed and delivered to a subordinate population by its imperial masters. It hilariously and pompously stated that if a gentleman crossed a lady on the left, he should take off his solar topi with his right hand and bow, which did not make sense even in 1968. I kept my copy, as testimony to colonialism and sexist conditions in the civil service, till it was borrowed and never returned. The IAS Academy is still a protected environment and though the male officers have to be educated in gender equality, there is recourse to legal processes at hand. It is always unpleasant, but the structure has now adjusted to the growing awareness about women's rights.

The Myth of the 'Uneducated' Rural Woman

I had moved to rural India to address poverty. Once there, I saw that women were economically and socially at the bottom of the pile. These women saw their political and personal–political as a continuum. The trajectory of democratic cultural politics, the personal to the political, the social to the cultural and psychological, was amply evident in their lives. The women did not segregate discussions into themes and topics; a wage protest and sexual assault would be discussed at the same time. The personal organically slipped into the political. This capacity to break artificial boundaries makes us women take on larger political issues as a natural corollary.

My women's politics was defined by my worker friends who struggled for food, work and shelter and questioned inequality across boundaries. I learnt women's politics from Naurti, a Dalit wage worker, who has been my friend and mentor for fifty years. These women set my agenda for political action—struggle against feudal sati, violence and rape, struggle with the system for wages and work.

The middle-class urban entrant to rural development came with a formula of action under certain heads: literacy, toilets and traditional malpractices. Self-styled reformers, who were very often genuine protestors against privilege, nonetheless came with all the additional baggage of superiority and arrogance. The initial interactions on literacy for women led to important understanding and earlier perceptions were constantly revised. For instance, learning a skill needs time; literacy is no different from, say, tailoring. An adult needs to see literacy as the acquisition of a skill, as a tool for establishing oneself.

Literacy classes ran at night, failing to acknowledge a woman's physical incapacity to study after a hard twelve-hour workday, or to appreciate her intelligence. After coming to terms with the arrogance of the 'let's teach them' attitude, the process was reversed. An experiment with literacy began with a woman's real predicament at the centre of its concerns. We reckoned that women needed both time and space to deal with learning the skill. The programme for literacy at the Barefoot College, Tilonia, was designed by its women workers. Using an existing training capsule called Training Rural Youth for Self-Employment (TRYSEM) it was decided to dedicate eight hours a day for six months to a literacy training programme. Four women leaders, across caste and religion—Naurti, Mangi, Billan and Haseena—volunteered to attend the course, with a daily honorarium to compensate for loss of wages.

The early '80s were days of intense learning for the four who came to learn a skill, and the dozen or so of us who came to be educated. The mornings were board, chalk and writing. Painful for these mature women who sometimes flung the chalk and asked instead for a shovel and the task of digging, where they were adults, skilled and competent. In the afternoons the positions were reversed. The women taught us the politics of gender in the village, its nuances, their understanding of power and oppression, their joys and how they sought expressions for liberation from oppression. We sang, laughed and enjoyed each other's company. Women from other states working in Tilonia—Omana and Vidhya—who were part of this training began great programmes for women in Wayanad, Kerala, and Koraput, Odisha, respectively. Their initial orientation and 'gurus' were these extraordinary women from rural Rajasthan. At the end of those six months there was cross-cultural learning and the birth of collective women's action, which lasted for decades.

The Government of Rajasthan decided to build on this experience, as well as work in villages in Silora block, where Tilonia is located—women's collectives in the village had begun to form effective groups. The argument that leaders cannot be created but can be identified and empowered with skills, and gaps in information attended to, gained ground. Anil Bordia, an enlightened civil servant working as development commissioner, inspired by this and other processes of empowering women, initiated the Women's Development Programme (WDP). The mainstream discourse on feminism in India was burgeoning and WDP managed to bring in the essence of some of its arguments. The seeds of this expansion demanded a dialectic between action and reflection, as well as the ability to steer between the rigidity of a government programme and the flexibility inherent in an NGO experiment. It sought to bring the varied experiences with women's activism together, within the structure and authority of government. The Rajasthan civil service, no different from other male-dominated spaces, was firmly entrenched between patriarchy and feudalism. But the WDP was a significant breakthrough. Women invited to plan the programme and design training were given space to bring in contemporary views on women's issues as well as modes of exchanging knowledge and skills.

To quote from a 'Pracheta Training'[6] report written with Dr Sharada Jain and the Institute of Development Studies (IDS), Jaipur:

> We talked without having mothers, fathers, officers, husbands around—with a sense of space. These voices around describe us in various ways, forcing us to see ourselves falling in strange brackets—almost shaping and moulding us ...[7]

This experience taught the 'trainers' as much as it taught the 'trainees' to open minds conditioned by prejudice, balance participation with self-appointed authority, to keep a separate identity as trainer and yet participate equally and fully.

There were sceptics, but as the training progressed many gradually lost their scepticism and a friendly and creative critique took its place. We lived together, challenging untouchability and prejudices of caste hierarchy. We shared stories of gender and the fear of violence, but in every other way—familial, social, economic and political—we were different. We had to be constantly vigilant so that our hackles did not rise while listening to issues that arose from a traditional and unequal belief in caste and religious prejudice. Women shared thoughts, feelings and predicaments. The sharing of these stories bonded us, as they have millions of women around the world. We became collectively exhilarated and responded holistically to reach out to each other. Reason and analysis followed these sessions to locate our political battles. To quote Dr S. Anandalakshmy, we were 'thinking with our hearts'.[8] What we learnt in the early 1980s is now accepted in theory and practice: political action is also born from intense personal sharing.

It was an attempt to link action with reflection, practice with theory.

The Mahila Mela 1985

> *'Mele me kain hoosi? Hivdari bataan.'*
>
> (What will happen at the mela? We will discuss matters of the heart.)

The year 1985 celebrated the first decade of the international women's struggle for equality, with a meeting in Nairobi. The Norwegian Agency for Development Cooperation (NORAD) was willing to sponsor me. These international celebrations are designed for leaders who can speak English or an internationally accepted language of communication and only the privileged among women managed to satisfy these requirements. Many of us wanted to celebrate the decade with our fellow activists in struggle, the less privileged women with whom we had grown to understand empowerment. The negotiations with NORAD were successful and an equivalent of my fare plus a little more was enough to organize a 'Women's Mela' with 1,000 women in the campus of the Barefoot College in Tilonia. It turned out to be a phenomenal experience for the women gathered there.

It was a challenge to transform the collective exhilaration of a small gathering at the training of Prachetas into mass excitement of sharing. The shift from isolation to togetherness was what made women's participatory trainings so special—the sharing of laughter, sorrow and joy. Could the process, so successful with just twenty-five of us, be effective in a large assembly? The Mahila Mela actually and miraculously experienced the power of the collective upsurge of emotions in 1985. Many who came from earlier trainings brought their memories with them. Words cannot do justice to the magic of those moments, when literally many personal dreams and sharing transformed into the collective political strength of the march against rape in the neighbouring town of Kishangarh, which concluded the mela.

A great deal of preparation went into the organization of the Mahila Mela. It was planned participatively. We discussed the processes, the schedule and the agendas with many groups. Of the 1,000 women who came together, 100 were from middle-class backgrounds, and the remaining 900 came from the rural working class. They came from Kerala, erstwhile united Andhra Pradesh, Tamil Nadu, Odisha, Madhya Pradesh, Himachal Pradesh, Uttarakhand, Haryana and a huge number from Rajasthan. Eleven villages hosted the rural women for three days before they came to the mela. In those three days they made friends and played innovative games like who cut grass faster, dug quicker. They exchanged information about marriage customs and were intrigued to know about polyandry in Uttarakhand and bride price in Rajasthan. Their clothes and jewellery, so different and varied, were examined, admired and talked about. They sang their songs and danced in different styles.

When they came to the mela three days later they brought along newly made women friends from the host villages. The unexpected happened, and friendships blossomed without a common language or custom. They came to the mela singing and holding hands. A collective gathering was a challenge without a common language. Mangi (my Dalit friend who is also my mentor) suggested that we use the traditional method of the 'prabhat pheri', a joint early morning walk through a village, with each group singing their songs and inviting other women to come. It was a success and amazingly energizing. The procession was led by the traditional Rajasthani bankia (a musical instrument similar to a trumpet) and dhol, a big drum. We came back for breakfast dancing.

The four-day mela had space for many activities: drawing, sculpting with clay, learning to cycle, focussed discussions on health, assault on women and wages, etc. Every evening the women opted to play 'men's games', such as tug-of-war with 300 women on each side. In a non-competitive atmosphere, even kismet was on our side. Each side won once and in the third and final attempt, the rope broke, leaving both sides winners, dancing to the drums, the drummers drumming with different beats tirelessly. The Mahila Mela is still remembered by its participants for its layered understanding and extraordinary experiences at the political, social and psychological level. Bonding left us with a greater understanding of public mobilization and how one could actually transform these singular moments of insight and joy into a very large collective expression. It has become a Tilonia tradition since and is now celebrated on International Women's Day.

The mela also addressed the complexity of the deep anxiety that the aftermath of rape produces. Such a discussion in a public space was almost unheard of. In fact, until the mid-1980s public discussion about rape was taboo in rural Rajasthan as much as anywhere else in India. I recall meeting many frightened women in the early 1970s who had been raped—out of wedlock, widows raped by brothers-in-law, sometimes by the father-in-law—and were terrified by the possibility of becoming pregnant. They were traumatized, threatened with ostracization by family and society, and there was no counselling.

A large number of rapes are of Dalit, poor or underprivileged women. Rape is not an assertion of mere lust. It is always an expression of power, often by upper-caste men on lower-caste women, revenge and punishment by the powerful on the powerless. A demand for justice or equality, even asking questions, is seen as a threat and can trigger anger and revenge. In communal riots or confrontations women are raped, and such rapes are often unfortunately condoned by many women who belong to the community of the rapist. In war too, through the centuries, women and their bodies have been part of the spoils of the plundering victor.

In 1985 a man from Indoli (in Ajmer district) brought his eleven-year-old daughter, a survivor of rape, to us at the Mahila Mela for justice. She was innocent and unable to understand her predicament. The offender was a neighbour, a boy in his late teens who belonged to the OBC community. Her condition drew hundreds of women into a debate on sexual violence. The discussion ended with a public rally in the town of Kishangarh, the first big rally of its kind in this part of Rajasthan. Of the 1,000 women attending the mela, the local Rajasthani women covered their faces to conform to propriety, but carried placards. It was a silent procession as many of the women were worried about the reactions from their families for being part of a public rally. Before shocked onlookers, a petrified SDM timidly stepped out to receive the petition. The women symbolically tied their black armbands on a thorny babul tree outside the court as a reminder to the SDM and others to render justice to the innocent rape survivor.

The Mahila Mela also validated my choice of wanting to stay primarily connected to the working class and to make sure that the intersectional concerns of social and gender equality found equal space. It was interesting that the definition of women's rights to sexual equality were nuanced differently by the women depending upon class and privilege. The working-class women were much more preoccupied with fertility and control over reproduction. They were forced to produce the male heir. Infant mortality rates were very high and children were an investment for one's old age and had to survive preventable diseases and dangers such as snake bites or accidents. Infertility was a stigma. Even if men were infertile, the women were blamed and social norms made them outcastes. They were often treated worse than the lowest in the caste hierarchy. Once a woman was labelled infertile, a second wife soon appeared, violating all legalities.

Women may see themselves as one community from time to time but in the junction of intersectionality, caste may often be the dominant identity. The few large holistic mobilizations of women in Rajasthan that invariably addressed the violence against women's bodies stand apart as significant statements that these borders can be crossed sometimes.

Roop Kanwar: The Last Sati in India

In 1987, a young Rajput woman of eighteen self-immolated in Deorala, Sikar district. Her name was Roop Kanwar and it was alleged that she 'chose' to be burnt alive on the funeral pyre with her dead husband. This sent shock waves across India. It was all the more incomprehensible as some members of the family were serving personnel in the Indian Air Force and they too supported her sati. Rajasthan's women came together to protest. The sati showed how upper-caste men were still belligerent promoters of patriarchy and casteism. The district collector had delayed taking action. Bureaucratic helplessness was primarily responsible for allowing this tragedy to unfold, by not enforcing the law. Women in Rajasthan came together for the first time regardless of other divisions, but unfortunately some Rajput women joined a counter rally led by Rajput men in support of the sati.

Before we went to protest in Jaipur, close to 500 women discussed sati into the night. All the women believed in the power of 'sat', i.e., truth and faith. They believed that if the woman was 'pure' she could ignite the wood on the funeral pyre with the power of her faith and mind. All agreed that Roop Kanwar's burning was not 'sat', as her brother-in-law had lit the funeral pyre. The small urban group present that evening challenged the women about 'sat', saying it was a belief that was not based on fact. The rural women produced fake photos of the sati. The argument was locked in an impasse. Finally after hours of simmering discontent, an older woman stood up and said to me, 'Beta, you believe that man landed on the moon?' I said, 'Yes.' 'Did you see him there?' she asked. I answered that I had seen it on TV. 'You saw a moving photo and believed it; we see photos and believe in them. Let's leave this argument for now. Let's agree that Roop Kanwar was burnt to death, and proceed tomorrow for the rally.' Her admonition could not be faulted at the level of a logical argument.

This protest on sati saw the emergence of important women leaders like Naurti, a Dalit, who subsequently became an icon for Rajasthani women. Eventually, however, Sati temples were constructed on the site and continue to bring in huge revenues. A Special Court acquitted all the eleven accused in the Roop Kanwar case, thereby dealing a blow to the women's organizations that had fought hard to put more stringent laws against sati in place.[9]

Bhanwari Devi: Rape and Public Protest

A huge collective of Rajasthani women came together once again. This time to protest against the rape of Bhanwari Devi (1992).

Bhanwari worked with the WDP as a sathin (a woman leader from a village). She was expected to help implement government programmes for women in a panchayat. The district administration had issued orders to stop child marriage. She carried out the directive and restricted a Gujjar family from performing a child marriage in her village. The irate family planned revenge, and five men gang-raped the forty-five-year-old Bhanwari in front of her husband, who was gagged and tied. The rape drew outrage from almost all of Rajasthan and many parts of the country. The mobilization of Rajasthani women who came to support Bhanwari laid the foundations of a loose formation in the state known as Mahila Atyachar Virodhi Jan Andolan (MAVJA).[10] The MKSS stood with other organizations and was at the frontline of protestors who broke the barricade to gain access to the secretariat to present their demands. The state government refused to engage in a dialogue, and failed to respond quickly. The case in court was even more unfortunate: the district and sessions courts found her rapists innocent and acquitted them. Their assertions that no upper-caste man would rape a lower-caste woman, that a middle-aged woman had no sex appeal to attract men and that no man could passively watch his wife being raped were shocking.

The rape discourse, which began with the Mathura rape case, the custodial rape of a minor Adivasi girl,[11] took time to build, but when it did it drew a cross-section of women into the demand for a special law to protect them.

Women in subordinate positions in the workplace were often asked for sexual favours in return for their rights—whether it was salary, promotion or leave; whether blue-collar workers, including daily wage labourers, or white-collar workers. If they did not 'cooperate', they could end up losing their jobs. Women began to politically assert their rights and demand legal redress for sexual harassment in the workplace. The Vishaka Judgment (1997) logically followed the issues raised in the many meetings with women, including the government-run WDP.[12]

Rajasthan has contributed to jurisprudence on rape, though by all conventional indicators it should not have; female literacy was low and political awareness still lower. But the presence and contribution of NGOs working with women prepared the grounds even for a progressive women's programme—the WDP—which drew on the experience of Barefoot College, Astha and Sewa Mandir. A new generation of women grew up with this history, facilitating an understanding of the right to fight rape, and rejecting its stigma. The Nirbhaya case, which followed much later, prominent among many others, is a case in point.[13] These processes established that determined and focused public action can culminate in the drafting of new laws and the amending of older ones. These campaigns were strengthened by demands for public consultations in framing policy in a constitutional democracy.

The initial voices against rape in most of these cases (barring the Nirbhaya case) were raised by women who did not belong to elite groups or the middle class. They were essentially women from the poorer sections of society, particularly Dalit and backward communities. Violence against women workers by their landlords or employers, a fairly regular phenomenon, violence within the family, violence against women in rural social groupings on charges such as 'witchcraft', are also important points in discussions on violence against women. Witchcraft has resurfaced and the violence against middle-aged women has been appalling.

Articulation on rape by the middle class is comparatively more recent. The 'Me Too' movement, naming and shaming men who have sexually harassed women, has a wider base with younger women coming from a cross-section of urban classes and communities. Though rape is no longer a stigma and the rape survivor an object of hatred, the trauma of a rape survivor has had very little institutional support and even women's groups are ill-equipped to help the person adjust to daily life. The death penalty has not worked effectively as a deterrent, and rapes are on the increase. Men need to be addressed as much as women. We have dealt somewhat with the politics of rape, but the personal is yet to find peace and a cessation of anguish.

Women and Reservation

Electoral politics are still male-dominated. Women have become more visible, but are unable to carry the genuine debates on equality into Parliament and the state assemblies. They still lack agency when it comes to setting the agenda and taking over the reins of governance and state power.

In local self-government elections for the position of sarpanch (head of the village panchayat/council) in Rajasthan, 50 per cent of the seats are reserved for women. It has made a difference and a few extraordinary women Dalit sarpanches have made a mark. But on the whole the women are represented by their menfolk, as the sarpanch is an administrative head of office and the job requires both training and competence in matters of governance. Three very good women friends, Naurti from Harmara, Rukmini from Vijaypura and Kamla from Tilonia, all Dalits, made good sarpanches. They made the programmes work for the poor, especially the Mahatma Gandhi National Rural Employment Guarantee Act (MGNREGA), removed encroachments and were also able to take difficult decisions like restoring burial grounds to Muslims. For the first time, by using the office of the sarpanch for development and practical delivery of constitutional rights, women experienced the possibilities of using power for justice. The transparency provisions and anti-corruption structures were also put in place. These women had structured institutional back-up with the MKSS and were astute in forming their own networks with women in Rajasthan. The campaigns in which they had participated earlier, for transparency and the right to work and food, formed the base of their political education. A footnote to the careers of these three women should include their defiance of patriarchy, of hierarchy and of caste as a political structure of suppression.

It has always been a struggle to get spaces for articulation on critical issues. The problems and complexities of patriarchy never entered the public debate on equality. Subtle issues of language and cultural superiority continued to oppress women. In an interesting moment I was asked, 'Are you a left-feminist or a feminist?' Feminism minus the 'left' was probably interpreted as largely elitist, leaving the questions of poverty and other aspects of privilege out of the discussion. There were concerns with sexuality. There have been dissident voices, especially from Dalit women, who have argued that such formations are not inclusive.

Women too are conditioned culturally and politically by intersectionalities—class, caste and religion. Women's organizations have also been formed on political ideologies, special groups of women with inequalities arising from caste and religious identity. The National Federation of Indian Women (NFIW), All India Democratic Women's Association (AIDWA) and the National Federation of Dalit Women (NFDW) are a few examples. These national networks became part of movements struggling against inequality and governance, such as the National Campaign for People's Right to

Information (NCPRI), Peoples' Action for Employment Guarantee (PAEG) and Right to Food campaigns, to bring in the rights-based legislations (the RTI, MGNREGA and the Right to Food). Women in the NFIW have been able to look holistically at women's issues.

Feminism and Social Mores

My educated and literate parents took upon themselves the task of talking scientifically about procreation and socially about sexual morality. In any education that includes an understanding of literature and visual art, there is space to talk of propriety, the body and its perception. India abounds in sexual visibility in its ancient temples, for instance, Konark and Khajuraho. Reading Hermann Hesse's *Siddhartha*, or even hearing stories, were part of life.[14]

Women have internalized the male notion of female sexuality and with it a sense of shame, for the bodies that bulge too much or not enough. The political still gets discussed, the personal is largely private. There was always the fear that prudishness, propriety and delicacy will be invaded if the personal became public. The middle-class Indian woman was monitored by a moral code, set in a rigid set of approvals and disapprovals. In the absence of sensible discussion, we often have sensationalism, obscenity and vulgarity taking over the discourse.

Soon after the women's trainings in WDP, meeting sathins and prachetas, I came across the book *Our Bodies, Ourselves*, which marks a turning point in middle-class women's understanding of their sexuality.[15] It accidentally surfaced in a meeting on fixing wages and looking at work and employment. I was tentative about showing the book to them. But as it turned out, the women could have educated many of the urban and even Western women on sexuality! It was often the topic of their conversations. For once, I wished I had a ghunghat behind which I could hide my extraordinary discomfiture. I was embarrassed, but they took it casually. In the discussions that followed, I realized that discussing sexuality was natural among them; it was the middle-class woman who was scared to do so. In the intense trainings with women, sexuality was discussed freely along with fertility and birth control.

Naurti, Mangi, Billan and I travelled the feminist path together. When my middle-class shyness of my body was matched by Naurti's own, we were both confronted by Billan, who, with her beauty and brashness, talked about anything that came into her head and questioned us relentlessly. Working-class women's politics was taught to me by these 'professors' who knew and articulated the thought in an idiom much more compelling and communicative than mine could have been. They stated their own limitations and made me see and accept some of mine. I understood women's politics and its contribution to mainstream political thought through various discussions with them. We were inhibited by different factors. They were constrained within a village community and a caste from which they did not want to/could not break away.

The women in my life have been mentors and the greatest of friends. Conversations with older women, like my mother, Hema, the designer Shona Ray, and educationists S. Anandalakshmy and Sharada Jain, continue to inform me. Women friends from college and university, my siblings, and scores of friends across ages and backgrounds continue to bond in rather special ways.

Jill Tweedie was my first educator in the theory of feminism. We spent ten intense days together in a village in Rajasthan. She wrote to me asking if I could help her interview a typical Indian woman. I answered her that I could, but how did she see an average Indian woman? A woman from the working class? A working woman from the middle-class? Which caste? Literate or illiterate? Many choices followed. She was baffled by the intersections. She left the choice to me, and came to an unknown and bewildering culture and difficult living conditions. Despite looking for a single representative woman she had to settle for one of the many variables of an underprivileged 'typical Indian woman' to understand Chothi, a poor Dalit woman. We became friends, and she walked me through my first lessons in feminist theory. She had a great sense of politics and humour. Her book *Letters from a Fainthearted Feminist* is a treasure.[16] Two sisters write to each other critiquing the other's extremism and compromise. We learn about modern sensibility and the nuanced differences between and among progressive women. After the discussions with Jill on sexuality, Rajasthani working-class rural women seemed more liberated than their urban counterparts.

She talked of the men in her life and the journey to find a partner who accepted equality in practice. She introduced me to feminist words and concepts of the 1960s—the three slogans 'Personal Is Political', 'My Life Is a Revolution' and 'Intimate Enemy' (defining intimate male relations). The last, an acceptance of the presence of men in special relationships and the struggle for equality embedded in each of them. She introduced me to the concept of gender. There have been many men who have been supportive of women's rights and struggles. Equality does not mean a denial of the right to differ. But the difference cannot be premised on inequality. It is the equal right to act on one's convictions without imputing motives to a disparate point of view or imposing a claim. We have the right to differ, given a shared acceptance of values.

These discussions helped put my life of breaking with tradition within the framework of feminism.

The progression and regression of women's position in society is varied. But we cannot doubt that we have managed to claim much that we could not before in terms of legal rights to land and property, to fight dowry and to claim equality in marriage. Yet, as long as we stay trapped socially in identities like caste, religion and class, these gains will remain more legalistic than actual. The state plays a primary role in guaranteeing women their rights. There have to be choices permitted on basic fundamental rights and in a system where equality and secularism as a state value is implacable. That is why the law on 'love jihad' is regressive, unequal, anti-women and anti-humanity. The right to choose, the right to love and marry across communities, the right to equality—these are all part of the feminist struggle.

Being a woman is not easy in a patriarchal universe. Many like me have had no desire to be a man. I have always rejoiced in the complexity of a woman's vision, the ability to multitask and think laterally, to live fully, to surrender to one's feelings occasionally, to cherish love and compassion as a value and so much else. The inability to define absolute equality does not disvalue it as some pundits argue. Equality and freedom will remain values. The politics of women's equality in numbers and visibility is achievable. The other forms of real equality will remain in perspective and will be better understood over a passage of time.

However, in the world, and more specifically in India, we have structured cultural and social divides. A woman's decision is determined by a plethora of other variables. These and the human conditions of dependence, familiarity, familial loyalties may make a woman choose differently. In any case of violence that arises from a structural identification other than gender, women stand divided and this weakens public action.

There are the classic cases where women in broken marriages have illogically rallied around to protect the husband; the desire for reconciliation at any cost is more pronounced than the desire for justice. In the hundreds of interfaces with rural women there has been the constant refrain that 'women are the worst enemies of women', quoting the classic mother-in-law–daughter-in-law syndrome of incompatibility. It is theoretically and structurally perceived that mothers-in-law are as much victims of patriarchy as daughters-in-law. But daily attrition, anger, abuse and the welling of hate seems to be irreparable. It is ultimately a sharing of power within the small confines of domestic decision-making that makes the situation impossible! Switch the scenario to a working woman with a homebound mother-in-law and the dynamic changes to some extent. But the clash of temperament and priorities is ever present. Men who occupy the high moral ground should just look at their own predicament. They choose permanent remedies, even killing over property, land, money or women. Some of the great wars were fought for these possessions. Killing thousands and justified by political reasoning.

The constant refrain of equality is the most significant contribution of women's movements at all levels to democratic politics. At one stroke it brings 50 per cent of the world together, exponentially raising the confidence of women. Even the smallest protest is backed by these numbers. Feminism has been able to contest competition by defining a huge collective, by similarity. This collective assertion even led women to a collective nomination: '1,000 Women for the Nobel Peace Prize in 2005'.[17]

One of the most important theories of feminism is its position against war. The use of non-violent methods of protest, such as civil disobedience, are feminist in concept and in practice. However, feminism's singular failure is its inability to initiate a national/international discourse on peace. Arguments about equality and power and its distribution are issues central to the feminist debate. An entire philosophy based on equality is inevitably involved with definitions of power and leadership. Leadership in the first quarter of the twenty-first century stands precariously balanced on the edge of totalitarian states and dictatorial governments. It is perhaps the flip side of all the dreams of collective leadership nurtured by the feminist movement. Essential values of feminism are inverted and a distorted view of power and leadership has taken hold of the world's imagination. Various media, social and otherwise, have betrayed readers and viewers in bypassing real and substantive debate about politics and leadership. On the contrary they have further singled out men driven by the hunger for power and iconized them. The definition and use of unequal power is the base of the structure of corporate media and corporate politics. This unholy alliance has been contested in the democratic space of activism and alternate media politics.

Women's groups have been successful in raising consciousness about sexual abuse to transform it into a national concern, and employ legal instruments, when it did not threaten other identities. The country, which was aflame after the Nirbhaya incident, did not show the same spirit when women were raped and attacked in Kashmir or in other parts of the country. Many right-wing women's formations placed 'nationalism' and identity politics above justice and gender. It was no surprise that women split across religion, caste and region. Collective leadership and shared power have been the victims in this potpourri of mixed and contradictory feelings and reactions. The biggest victor has been patriarchy and the greatest failure—the return of the macho dictator.

The failure of the collective spirit is reflected in the fact that individual rights are dominant in struggles. Access to rights must be seen as collective for real empowerment. The feminist world view for peace, against war and redefining leadership, stands waiting in the wings.

We believe with Maya Angelou that: 'Each time a woman stands up for herself, without knowing it possibly, without claiming it, she stands up for all women.'[18]

4

Our 'Development' ... at Their Cost

'Unless our hands go hand-in-hand with our heads, we will be able to do nothing whatsoever.'

—Mohandas Karamchand Gandhi

I WAS TUTORED BY an intelligent mother, who was gifted with skills in mathematics and a love for physics but was trapped in domesticity. I learnt the value of relating to the larger universe by watching her daily angst and witnessing her inability to fight the odds stacked against her. As I grew up I realized it was not my father who prevented her, but rather the principles and obligations she wove into her web of defeat. I was determined to resist that mould because of my own childhood recognition of inequality.

The consciousness about work and its value is perhaps universal. It is not merely that it translates into money. It is one of the first steps one takes into the world outside the home. It is the freedom to choose one's space. Work establishes a relationship with the external world and connects us to it with logic and a routine. However, we define it in various ways. For instance, the wealthy consumerist world defines (and will continue to define) the state of 'worklessness' as a worthy cause to aspire to, while women in the middle and upper classes feel caged in the limitations of the 'home'. From the time of Ibsen and his powerful capturing of the 'trap' of domestic bliss in his play *A Doll's House*, we have all fought this spurious paradise sold to us persistently by a consumer-driven society and the patriarchal world.[1]

I admire my rural women friends, who made the transition from home to work so gracefully, with an ease and harmony defying the fragmentation of people who separate work from daily life. I recall a hot sunny day. The heat was relentless. I saw two women in thick skirts of hand-woven cotton, thin backless blouses ('kanchli') tied with string, muslin veils ('odhni') over their heads, digging and carrying earth. I felt a combination of awe and guilt. I may have had no electricity, no fans and no cooling in my home, but unlike the two women I did not have to suffer in the blazing sun. I stood in the shade of the margosa (neem) tree outside the stone-and-lime building that was my home-cum-office. I was always curious about the elegance of their lives, even tinged with envy of the romance of living a simple life. Being able to feel the earth, to be in contact with the smell of life. I saw them working, bearing their physical burden, sometimes with song. I realized later that this emotion can only rise in a woman who sees from a point of privilege and comfort. As a Dalit friend said disdainfully, 'I will trade your life with mine. You can have the earth, I will have your comforts.'

For me, the issue of work has always had a context that has led to growth and an ability to understand myself through an external connect. But it has also been the relationship of honesty between the external world and me. As my friend Chunni Singh (a founder member of the MKSS) says, '*Karni aur kathni mein pharak nahin honi chahiye.*' (Walk your talk; there should be no difference between word and deed.) A principle or an idea succeeds or fails only in action. I recall my first meeting with Chunni Singh: he looked like a possessed human being, fierce in his look, beard unkempt, his hair wild—but compassionate in his understanding of poverty. We met on a long protest march, a 'yatra', seeking government intervention against drought. The acquaintance blossomed into a friendship and he became a comrade in all struggles. His wide understanding of democratic politics was housed in a formal schooling of two years. He had to leave home at the age of four to wash utensils in dhabas. His knowledge and experience of life and work was immense.

My notion of work, as employment or engagement with the world outside domesticity, was shaped by the gender-based division of work and labour that is apparent in all classes and castes, which even exists in some liberal households that aspire to be more egalitarian.

My siblings and I saw our parents as equally well-informed people engaged with the polity. They fought over the *Statesman* crossword and the spoils were even. We heard them discussing the national budget and the politics of Nehruvian welfare. They often had opposing points of view. My mother was always more moderate in her critique. My father took extreme positions. We found that neither of them gave in often. These arguments and counterarguments were actually lessons to us in contemporary affairs. A word or a phrase, even if prejudiced, worked its way to some familiarity and understanding of an idea later. What worried me was why Appa, my father, had social sanction and the right to go away for eight hours, leaving my mother walled within her home, vocalizing her dislike of domesticity.

When I was around eleven, she advised me to never succumb to pressure to marry and be caught in the cycle of the home and its chores. She urged us all to look for opportunities for self-expression, mainly outside the home. I so internalized her persuasive and emotive arguments that when I imagined a future, it was a life with work outside home. Yet, Amma taught me to cook when I was thirteen, not because I was a girl, but because she felt it was a life skill. She, as the intelligent, academically inclined daughter of a middle-class family, studied and learnt the veena, won the all-rounder prize with her skill in sports, but found herself uneducated on the simple skills of living.

With this background I planned my future at twenty-one. The first option was to see where I could get employment. My father's financial situation was such that I could not indefinitely be a dependent. Once I passed my MA in English literature, I was offered a teaching job in three Delhi colleges. I chose to go back to my alma mater, Indraprastha. I love literature and it should have been an exciting prospect, but teaching a largely unenthusiastic class proved daunting. Most young women gathered the degree as part of the marital dowry. I discovered that teaching, as opposed to learning, could be tedious and I did not have enough experience to create interesting learning conditions.

The hierarchical shift from student to 'lecturer' was within the confines of the known, yet it felt strange to enter the staff room as a right. It was also a formidable challenge to confront the curious gaze of friends who were now my students, assessing my competence. Teaching was tough. I did not see myself as a teacher for any length of time, but I could not imagine not being meaningfully occupied. If nothing else worked out, I would continue to teach. The social class stratification in college made me think that at least I would be of use to the less privileged. I don't really know how the classes went, I just hope that my enthusiasm for literature prevailed and persuaded some of the students to see its imaginative possibilities. I think my main learning from teaching was how important it is to have students interested in learning.

While teaching at Indraprastha College I was, among other things, studying for the civil services exam (conducted by the Union Public Service Commission), so I was really busy. The civil services exam, or the IAS, as it is referred to in India, is a national challenge to young seekers of employment. We filled the form in droves. The assessment was not frightening, but just one more in a series of exams. My decision to prepare for the UPSC stemmed in part from wanting to do well in a non-arbitrary process, where I would get a job without having to ask anyone for a favour. As a woman, being a civil servant also seemed to offer independence and equality. However, many inherent biases of the IAS would be revealed to me in the years to come. Qualifying for the civil services also pitched me into a world of 'special' beings. Even if an individual was unaware of its significance, all of society stood at the elbow to steer one into self-esteem and arrogance.

My parents, who had no special love for authority, were worried that my becoming an IAS officer might cause me to develop an unwelcome sense of self-importance. My younger siblings were aghast that I had joined 'the establishment'; they were lovers of the Beatles and the anti-establishment philosophy of those days. All this was sufficient to deflate any ego that may have expected to grow and I was apologetic on having acquired my 'status'.

The Civil Service: In Uncivil Times

Days as a probationer at LBSNAA were chaotic. I was twenty-two and happy that any and all exams were now behind me. While the future was distant, the present meant dealing with the fear of horse-riding. No less frightening were the 'formal evenings', very colonial and unimaginative. Patriarchy was as much present there as anywhere else. It was not easy being a woman officer. I was not invited to join the 'old boys' network and remained in part an outsider to the rank and file of officers. Curiously corruption was a non-issue, though the arbitrary use of power as nepotism and control over authority was seen and acknowledged. Little was said about it though.

I discovered that many men gossiped and were obsessively neurotic about those women and men officers who became friends. In fact, the men who made friends with women officers (numbering at just a tenth of the total batch) bore the brunt of comments among other things. It was very reminiscent of undergraduate life in Delhi University.

Absorption of information was not based on any real experience and remained largely academic. Few of us had ever visited a village, seen real poverty, known hunger or for that matter been inside a government office or police station. The 1968 batch lobbied for and got the course design changed. Probationers were sent to camp with NGOs and other organizations to experience the harder lives people lived so they could understand the reality of the ordinary citizen. The civil service was still under the hangover of colonial India.

The 'protectionist colonial approach' took some time to go, but since then a new corporate culture has taken its place—the current scenario post-liberalization does not make sense. Probationers now go abroad not to look at poverty but to elite institutions to learn about business management, investment and finance. The interactions between pro-welfare people and probationers have been replaced with representatives of business and multinational concerns. Acquiring, keeping and using power to get choice postings, transfers, etc., was the gist of general conversations and was the 'normal'. Questions of poverty or the Constitution remained issues discussed in smaller groups among friends and did not steer the general discourse outside the classes.

Instructors initiated classroom discussions on administration and the intricacies of the judicial system, which were unfamiliar to the probationers in an immediate sense. The class on office procedure remained abstract as few had been in an office environment and dealt with dak (official papers/paperwork). The *Tottenham System of Office Procedure and Management*, for instance, made sense to me only when I became a sub-collector in Pondicherry (now Puducherry) and was handling an office. Classes on law and other academic subjects made sense, but in the absence of the physical knowledge of a court or village administration, the mechanics of its functioning, they remained abstract. Political governance was not discussed and the status quo was taken as given. For the majority, Naxalbari may not have happened for all the impact it had on their discussions! This uprising had taken place just a year earlier and had given birth to a movement and ideology that would dominate one part of the national discourse for decades. That one year of training made many of us friends and these relationships were to mature in later years to lay the grounds for policy and public intervention. When governance expanded its boundaries and included civil society in its deliberations, the year in training was often recalled.

The IAS woman probationer's life was often a lonely one. She inhabited a society coiled in its own contradictions—it barely tolerated women as equals and revered the civil service. It was a dilemma that did not get resolved in the late 1960s; women were still seen as unwelcome encroachers of male privilege. The day after

I arrived to join duty in Tiruchirappalli, the collector told me that he would find it difficult to take me with him on field trips as his wife would object. To my astonished response that I was an officer under training who needed to learn and field visits were mandatory, he issued orders that I was to work in the office. I stormed off to the chief secretary and complained that I had come for training in the varied jobs that fell to the lot of the IAS, not to be trained as a clerk. I think he was part amused and part sympathetic and transferred me to North Arcot, where the collector would strictly see me as an 'IAS officer under training'.

The move worked well and thereafter I learnt a great deal under two excellent collectors, who took the task of working with probationers quite seriously. Learning about commitment to service and understanding the professional nature of the job, including filling a daily diary and submitting it to the collector, brought rigour to our training. Despite this, I was left with many unanswered structural questions.

Then came my first posting as sub-collector, Pondicherry. The initial six months were difficult and continued to expose the fault lines in training (though it was the best that one could have had in those times). I lived on the first floor of the Labour Department in Place de Pondicherry, within hearing distance of the sea. The domestic worker who took care of my house spoke in French and Tamil. The first chief minister of Pondicherry, Monsieur Goubert (1963–64), spoke Tamil and French, and considered English a barbarian language. The 'karnam' or 'patwari' spoke pidgin French, just as his counterpart in other states and union territories spoke pidgin English. From then onwards the trajectory took me to Delhi, and on to various jobs. They were years of understanding law and order. For the first time I felt the real-life tension between believing in protest and dissent, and being part of a mechanism of power that by its very nature opposed it.

This period was also my first exposure to political privilege, nepotism and corruption. Life zigzagged between facing an assembly of protesting people (satyagrahis) defying illegal orders, and the ambivalent system, and learning to deal with democratic processes. The service continued with the colonial attitude, advising its officers to keep distance from people, to sustain its image of neutrality. The fact that I mixed with office staff was not seen as conducive to 'proper' behaviour; one senior officer, in fact, said it was curious that despite many years in the service I still looked like 'a waif'!

The seven years I spent in the system were important years of learning about governance and were to stand in good stead in poverty-related public action, which demanded engagement with the system. There were moments of tension for a troubled and guilt-ridden young woman of privilege, wondering every day about the ethics of her actions. I was suspicious of every official who put up a file, seniors who could not be overruled and politicians who, though more timid than they are today, were still a force to reckon with.

At a time when an SDM drew Rs 400–900 a month, innocent citizens were paying anywhere between Rs 70 and Rs 100 as a bribe to get a free entitlement. Official jeeps ran personal errands, and when a law-and-order situation broke out, as it so often did in Delhi, the jeep pool reported that there were no vehicles available. In a series of events the thumb rule was often not delivery but personal comfort, if not gain. Important discussions and discourse were not about the poor, whom in some remote way we had pledged to serve.

There were excellent officers who shone by their integrity and probity. This escape from the irresolvable tension between the desire for democratic transformation and the status quo resulted in my understanding that the possibility of change was continually shrinking. The primary function of the IAS was to maintain the status quo as dictated by the party in power. As contemporary governance in 2014–23 has amply proved, this primary function remains the same even now. This also answers the question I am asked most often: 'Why did you resign from the IAS?'

Resigning from the IAS

There is a subtle divide between those working for the people, i.e., for constitutional guarantees, and those working for power. In today's context, the Constitution is being systematically pushed aside, its values degraded. In Rajasthan, serving civil servants witnessed the lynching of Afrazul Khan and Pehlu Khan[2] and remained largely silent. What is the mandate of a civil servant? Whom do they work for?

My years in the system (1968–75) taught me to face a hitherto unknown reality behind the glamour of 'power' and the mechanisms, such as the interface with corruption and its insidious ways, used to subvert it. Most people who were in government—the elite and subordinate services—had joined up for stability of income and excellent working or non-working conditions. There were very few cases of retrenchment because of non-delivery or poor performance.

By the time I joined, a substantial part of the system had accepted that there were two incomes, one legitimate and the other illegitimate. Questions were asked: '*Upar ka kitna, niche se kitna hai?*' (What is your salary and how much do you earn under the table?) Even the matrimonial prospects of officers in all services fell victim to this mentality. Lavish marriage ceremonies were the fashion. Male IAS officers were offered dowry, which defied the 'Dowry Act'. Neither the system nor the officer's conscience stirred in discomfort.

A marriage alliance with a government servant meant stability and access to power, and overall it increasingly became right to bend the law and claim impunity from accountability.

I came home every day wondering whether I should not have heeded the advice of a tehsildar or section officer, because of their susceptibility to graft. Or which senior officer was delaying a decision or making it under pressure from the power elite. Ultimately there are points in which legality alone does not help. Despite having grown up in Delhi, I was seeing a side of its polity that I had never seen before. It also became gradually apparent as I visited rural Delhi and saw the resettlement colonies and heard and discharged people booked under the vagrancy sections of the Criminal Procedure Code (CrPC) that the civil services failed to provide many opportunities to remove inequality and injustice. This was for a number of reasons. While the business of running the government provided challenges to the serious, it provided opportunities with impunity, to those who sought to misuse power. The levels of abuse by public servants of facilities increased daily, but the systems of accountability were inadequate to bring in the rule of law. Any questioning from within was seen as interference or insubordination.

Yet, almost every aspirant parent wanted their child to qualify for the IAS. Appearing for the IAS, as one young person said in the mid-1970s, was the national pastime! Some are incredibly idealistic and say that they want to do service for the poor, or for the country. But when one is inside the system most people's character and personality change; very few retain their idealism. Why does this happen? The answer lies in the analysis of what power does to an individual.

The bureaucracy has always shone in the minds of the aspirant middle-class and the elite for its status in society and for its 'power' and access to security. Power is so placed in the mechanics of governance that it has got divorced from moral and constitutional authority and mandate. In this divorce the people of India have been sacrificed at the altar of careers and comforts. The power vested in the civil servant, as S.R. Sankaran, Harsh Mander and many others have stated, should have been used to put constitutional rights and promises into practice. The power to do good was somehow pushed to the back-burner (and there it remains) thanks to a slew of skewed orders from a deeply corrupt political establishment. These orders were (and are) carried out by officers lured by the promise of plum postings and foreign assignments. Repeatedly, over the years, good officers have been penalized for respecting the rule of law.

The civil services are at a very critical juncture today. Individuals from the private sector have been recruited laterally to the office of the Prime Minister (PMO). As a critic of the performance of the bureaucratic mindset, I would still argue that we need a permanent civil service. We need continuity, to keep a check on the whimsicalities of changing political governments and for accountability. We need a structure that guarantees steadiness and causal logic. One that ensures that work begun is not pushed back or dismissed irrationally, and cautions civil servants about violation of laws and rules. It is incumbent upon those of us within the structure to not only maintain its integrity but also make sure it works for constitutional values and principles.

When I was posted in Delhi, I never knew when I had taken a wrong decision because of being misled by the 'discretion' of 'experienced' subordinates. Yet one had to work with them, or not at all. When I was leaving the service, my senior officers tried to persuade me with a posting of my choice, or at the very least by granting me long leave. I resigned and felt free and liberated when

I did so. The civil service is a constant in public life—a structure that will remain no matter what ideological political frame we may subscribe to. Those years in the civil service prepared me to understand its critical role in ensuring that there was no slipping away from the rule of law, and to watch out for the lure to be corrupt and arbitrary in the use of power.

My search for a system for delivery of justice to the common citizen reads like a list of predicaments and obstacles that prevented that from happening. I left the civil service in 1975, frustrated by the status quo's failure to deal with good, honest people fighting a daily battle, and its injustice. Transparency was a forbidden word and the Official Secrets Act and Conduct Rules weighed heavily against public discussion of misdemeanours and increasing lack of probity. While the honest were penalized for sharing information through proper channels, illegal leakages were the order of the day—the paradox of the civil service. There seemed no way to chart a path of action to collectively fight this misuse of power.

The IAS has, potentially, a singular and a powerful role to play—of intervener, protector and defender of constitutional rights. It still retains its unique position and some of its promise. This explains why activism and, for that matter, all of us who engage with the system are in search of the good babu and officer. Committed IAS officers, few as they are, can and do make a significant difference to the response of the government.

Governance is part of the daily business of public life in one form or another. Having left the service without bitterness, I have since tried to follow logical patterns to see how the marginalized could get their rights to a share of benefits. My shift from the civil service to an NGO, Barefoot College SWRC, was the result of constant comparisons between work within government and an ethical workspace without transfers. It was the outcome of my desire to be a part of a logical causality in addressing a problem—from the beginning, to the middle and a possible end.

From 'Paperwork' to People

The gap between 'life' and 'work' shrank when I started working directly with people, post the IAS. In the civil service, people continued to be an abstraction, faces and real lives remaining untouched. In this life, on the contrary, distinct faces brought the human condition to life. There was a persistent daily interaction with people and a community. Personal lives became the context for welfare and equality.

The first ideas of 'doing good' take us back to simple service: feed the hungry, clothe the ill-clad and so on. Gandhi defined public action in three categories: sewa (service), nirman (create)and sangharsh (struggle). The first is service to people. What follows is constructive work—working with development infrastructure and processes. But even service and constructive work must recognize the value of struggle to go beyond its own limitations. Public struggle is often based on rights and constitutional ethics. The resistance of the status quo to struggle is often defined by the fear of diminishing impunity and power.

Shifting to a village, simplicity and continual commitment

Bunker Roy, whom I married, was a classmate in Delhi University and had spent a summer, while in college, in Palamu in Bihar (now in Jharkhand) during the 1966 famine. The impact on him was so profound that he decided to abandon his search for a 'job' and work with the poor to change their lives. In the years that our professional concerns ran parallel, I saw great virtue in the framework of what was then called 'voluntary work'.

Despite the apprehension of many friends that it would ring the end of professional independence, and narrow me down to a wife-in-attendance, I packed my bag, dismantled my middle-class home and left for rural Rajasthan, travelling by train from Delhi without reservation, sitting in a crowded compartment. The village I lived in, Tilonia, in Kishangarh tehsil of Ajmer district, had no access to piped water, electricity or other amenities that were so taken for granted elsewhere. An abandoned 'pucca' TB sanatorium and its deserted campus became home. The fears of my shrinking into a 'female' were not unwarranted. When I had visited Tilonia's Barefoot College SWRC in its initial years (1972–74, when I was still in the IAS), Tejaram, the cook, assumed that, as a woman, I would take over the community kitchen and would give himself a holiday whenever I visited. I would end up cooking in rather primitive conditions in a mess that catered to two dozen people.

Patriarchal resistance continued to come not only from the community but also from fellow workers who were happy to see me cook, but resented the suggestions I made about management, which, after all, had become my specialization courtesy the IAS! Needless to say, the change from Delhi to Tilonia, barely 360 kilometres away from New Delhi, was dramatic.

It was not merely the physical location or the community of suspicious villagers one had to befriend, but the fact that I had to explain the context about almost everything! It was a transition from being an employee to a voluntary worker. It used to be called voluntary work because conscious choice preceded involvement. Remuneration was also only subsistence from an urban point of view. Living conditions were basic. Water had to be rationed and services we expect as normal were not available. You entered a different world in every way, yet Delhi was only 360 kilometres away. The system of working within the Barefoot College SWRC was very different.

Apart from the simplicity of lifestyle and the informality of the relationships, one faced birth, death, illness without a filter. They had to be dealt with; you could not shut yourself away. The concept of privacy did not exist. One's world view had to be re-adjusted and new tools of interaction and exchange had to be constructed and internalized.

The limitations of a rigid, traditional caste-based community had to be challenged, fighting injustice. The OBCs who called themselves the 'upper caste' were unchallenged in their privilege and power. If this position was implicitly or explicitly threatened, there was violence. The Constitution, and even Dr Ambedkar's name, was a very distant reality. Age-old pejorative terms were used to describe the scheduled castes, and the term 'Dalit' unheard of. They had to get off bicycles and could not sit on charpoys or chairs when the OBCs and savarnas made an appearance.

Within the campus of Barefoot College SWRC, there were few rules and everyone lived almost as equals. The professionals from elite institutions perforce learnt every day to acknowledge that unlearning was an important part of putting theory into practice. It was exciting to see geophysicists, social workers from Tata Institute of Social Sciences (TISS) and young people with professional degrees working shoulder to shoulder with rural people. The illusion of an idyllic rural village was, however, challenged by the somewhat vicious and street-smart manipulation of the naïve outsider by locals. It was stark and soon led to the abandonment of any romantic notion of the 'innocent villager'. The villagers were as fallible to the foibles in the human condition as their peers in towns. Equally there was sympathy, kindness and common sense. The last is an exceptional quality lost in the battle for 'book learning'. It was common sense that discovered fire, made the wheel and the plough, and tamed the wild horse in a world where there were no intellectual property rights and no patents. This world, which contributed towards food security and services of various sorts, allowed the intellect space to grow.

The problems of adjustment were daunting. I was also unhappy that the IAS background pushed me into administrative work, auditing and accounts of this nascent organization. Work had to conform to certain standards, but processes could not be hierarchical. It was a challenge to evolve a system that could blend financial and work accountability within a humane frame. Slowly but inevitably the management pattern in Barefoot College SWRC shifted to participatory management practices. Collective decision-making and participatory management require collective acceptance of norms and consequent processes. All these took time and patience to evolve, with many debates and discussions.

By 1980 what emerged at Barefoot College SWRC was a strong participatory structure with stated values and collective acceptance. This included acknowledging the role of democratically designated power to individuals to monitor the working of the system as per norms. This structure underscored transparency and information to all workers, as a basis for making informed choices and sound decisions.

My role as the coordinator and motivator was shaped in major part by the critical need for internal democracy and accountability. The immersion in this process and steering it to a conclusion was a great stage in my learning and went into building the MKSS and its campaigns. The need for an RTI law was built brick by brick, incident by incident. If the IAS showed what should not be, Barefoot College SWRC gave me a platform to evolve what should be.

Negotiating rural hierarchies

In any meeting with villagers as an IAS officer, I had met only the elite. Even without the hierarchy of the civil service in Tilonia, I came across traditional power structures that had well-constructed barriers to prevent the poor from meeting people. In the village too there were many kinds of hurdles in reaching the last person.

Many things intimidate the really marginalized from accessing or meeting outsiders. Their very presence proclaims a sense of equality with the richer, privileged-caste residents, who invariably want to take over the entire conversation and resent the poor being there. The powerful prevent any genuine interaction with the poor. They produce the token 'poor person' but who is tutored to say what will not reveal real oppression. For the most part the poor are part of a system of dependence and almost bondage. They are often under oath to corroborate the statement of the power elite. The penalty for deviation is ruthless. This explains why the marginalized seem to speak in blatant contrast to their condition and contrary to self-interest.

The poor live in very small houses and as families grow there is hardly any space left for the newcomers. One of the first projects I undertook was to mobilize the Berwa, a Dalit community, to apply for housing plots and talked to the collector for a small but comprehensive housing project. He agreed. After talking to the caste leader, about 100 families agreed to deposit Rs 100 each in favour of their stake in the new housing scheme. An architect of repute came down from Delhi and designed the colony. The money was deposited and patta (claim deeds) to existing plots were issued. Suddenly, overnight, the Berwa community withdrew their money and declared they were not interested in the scheme.

The reason behind this abrupt reversal was the pressure put by the forward class on the Dalits to quit the deal. The Berwa community was threatened that if they went ahead with the scheme, their dues (any payments/debts) would be extracted any which way. The land that should have gone to the colony was encroached upon by the dominant community within the year.

The demand from the marginalized is distinctly different from that of the privileged. The well-off want infrastructure; the marginalized want access to livelihood, work, wages and basic necessities. The outsider's ignorance of power dynamics, language, geography and culture prevents them from effectively reaching the poorest and most marginalized. However, none of this is insurmountable, provided there is a commitment of time and a willingness to learn and understand. It took me a year to penetrate the layers of social privilege to reach the genuine cases and win their confidence. Language skills had to be acquired, timing of meetings revised to late afternoon and evenings, spaces for conversations understood and claimed with intelligence and sensitivity. The TISS group educated me on patience and to be unobtrusive in meeting people, and to give time to absorb ideas and plans. The natural intelligence and prejudice of individuals had to be given space to be expressed, and confidence had to be built to share our ideas. Equality was a necessary value in practice. New ideas emerged out of the exchange, impacting knowledge, skill and capacity. Along with the burgeoning of new ideas, there was the necessary but mundane—keeping records of these meetings so that analyses necessary for planning could be based on genuine feedback. The pace was slow, but change, when it came, was effective.

I owe these nine years of patient learning in Tilonia a great deal. It laid the foundations of understanding work in its any manifestations and the accompanying complexities. It was in a sense my alma mater for understanding the details of practical social action.

5

Work as Politics of Inequality and Justice in Practice

Creating Alternatives

I UNDERSTOOD THE POLITICS and emotional toll of migration when I met Mangi, a Dalit woman, who belonged to the Berwa community, a sub-caste of the community of leather workers who have answered a nationwide call to never touch raw or processed leather. She worked as a 'beldar' and accompanied her husband, a mistri (mason), as they repeatedly migrated to various parts of India seeking work. I finally understood the lived context of the word 'migration'. Mangi had lost six children because of lack of access to medical care at the time of delivery. At the time I met her she was anxious to keep the baby she was carrying. She was getting on in years and it was crucial to have children, both from a social and economic point of view, not to mention her maternal needs. In successfully delivering her baby in the Tilonia[1] dispensary, with Dr Arti Sawhny and medical social worker Manya Jayaram attending on her, Barefoot College both gained the trust of the community and made a case for safe delivery. It also established that the work women did was hazardous. Women had to work to survive but needed diversity and options to cut down hazardous migration, which affected their health.

Work in rural India was caste-based, and had traditional skills of livelihood. Mechanization had displaced artisans and farming roles, creating joblessness and displacing and downgrading the value of many skills. All these emphasized the absolute need for alternate sources for employment for the rural poor. Mangi was an artisan; her craft was her skill. However, she was part of an economic order where rural artisans / crafts persons were exploited and ignored. The negative impact, of all of the facts listed above, is doubled if you are a woman. Mangi's situation afforded a view into the many aspects of the disempowerment of women and revealed her determined attempts to make herself equal, against great odds.

The Regers, another sub-caste of leather workers, worked using traditional methods—where the entire skin of an animal was sewn and then filled with water and a special bark. The dripping of this mixture through the skin tanned it and this process was called bag-tanning. The actual skinning of the animal was not done by the Reger but by a community that is a notch lower in the caste hierarchy—the Valmikis. The pits where the Regers carried out bag-tanning were located in their own homes and they lived with the odour, which was far less offensive than that of a tannery.[2]

The Regers were the first group of artisans whom I met as a cohesive group in Harmara. The first among them to meet me was Sua, despite being warned that he would be taken away to Saudi Arabia or converted to Christianity. It was brave of him and he became a friend and a worthy adversary of great skill. But his reaching out started a long and fruitful relationship. Long after he died and circumstances changed, we—the community and I—remain friends. I spent hours with members of the Reger community and learnt about their social life and their history as written by them. They claim a common ancestry with the Rajputs. (In Rajasthan the aspiration for upward mobility is to identify with the Rajputs, the dominant community.) According to folklore, they were condemned to earn a living by tanning leather after losing a battle.

In the 1970s I would often walk the 4 kilometres between Tilonia and Harmara and spend the day with the Regers. I ate with them and drank water in their homes, defying caste taboos. My entry to Brahmin and Rajput houses was barred. So much so that a Brahmin woman was insistent that I only drink from my cupped hand as she poured water from a pitcher held eight inches above. I was disallowed entry and touch, the two sacrosanct tenets of caste behaviour. Curiously though when a specialist from the Central Leather Research Institute (CLRI), who was a Brahmin, came to test the bag-tanning process, he tested the water by sipping it! Science (and powerful outsiders) were permitted to break some barriers.

The leather worker community was on the lookout for new markets, and many of its members had already migrated to Mumbai and Kanpur's leather-making units. The diesel pump, the tractor and the company Bata had seduced the local buyers. There was no demand for leather buckets for irrigation or the 'jooties' made from bag-tanned leather. The community was also looking at craftwork, as an option to continue with their livelihood.

I found that the weaver community was also facing similar problems. Pit looms were fast disappearing, as they could only weave cloth 24 inches in width. Some had, however, shifted to handlooms. The handloom made a dramatic, positive change possible, by not only increasing the width of the cloth, and income, but also helping to fight caste taboos as the loom shifted out of the home to sheds anywhere. This permitted other castes and communities to take up weaving. However, to adopt mechanization and appropriate technological innovations the community needed money to invest and turned to local moneylenders (read, the handful of affluent business communities in the village). These moneylenders used every opportunity to give small loans with a substantial collateral and/or huge compound interest. Sadly, the weavers were bonded to them through the huge compound interest that could, in fact, never be repaid. Moneylending was a flourishing local white-collar crime. So, despite the progress that came to the weavers and other craftspersons with mechanization and appropriate technological innovations, their economic condition never really improved.

Indebtedness was part of the system of the market, the purchase of raw materials, the structures to design and sell. In the mid 1970s, well-known designer Shona Ray, after her fundamental contribution to the building of crafts,[3] decided to help with the idea of bringing these craftspersons to Delhi to sell their wares. The idea of the Tilonia Bazaar was born. Along with sculptor Mrinalini Mukherjee, she played an important role in expanding the horizons for possibilities of working with craftspersons. The first bazaar held in 1975 brought the blessings of Kamaladevi Chattopadhyay, Pupul Jayakar, L.C. Jain—leading lights of the handicraft world.

Shona Ray also came down to Harmara to meet Sua and then went to meet printers in Kishangarh and Roopangarh, where she shared skills of layouts for basic design using traditional colours and patterns. We had already identified local handicrafts and found women who made small items for the household. One such item—a mobile with stuffed cloth birds—was redesigned by some of us, with a small copper bell that every goat had round its neck, which became the famous 'Tilonia bell tota', which has sold millions. My contribution to creativity, small as it was, made my administrative work more tolerable.

Mrs Sridharani and the Triveni Kala Sangam in Delhi were persuaded to rent out the premises, and the Tilonia Bazaar was off on its long and eventful journey. The prevailing urban market had bypassed these craftspersons, and the average urban buyer was unaware of India's abundant and long history with crafts. The concept of the bazaar goes back to India's ancient past and continues till today. What better frame for an entry of a bazaar than an unusual space in an urban elite spot, like Triveni. The bazaar was a resounding success and later Dastakar followed with a grander design.

But the journey had only just begun. The hundreds who came to find work at the Tilonia Bazaar could not be absorbed, the per capita investment was too high and the risks could not be underwritten. Business was ruthless, but a voluntary organization lives with a perpetual duality—the struggle (for better lives for the poorest craftspersons) and guilt (because marketability pushed those whose products were not marketable out of the running). Impossible as it was to sever from the intent to enable income-generation for the poor, the attempt to market their products meant we had to find newer ways of displaying handicrafts to potential buyers. After the initial euphoria and success, it was apparent that large numbers of unemployed were still out of the net. The hiatus between the world of the craftsperson and the buyer only grew larger and arguments to create collectives did not succeed. After further intensive work with bag-tanning, leather, design and receiving financial support through banks and donations, we were able to establish a co-operative. Here we spent months to bridge the gap between the skills of the craftspersons and market demands. Many new and now familiar items were fashioned.

Sadly in the end the co-operative established for the purpose fell victim to structural corruption and the work became individual-based. Sua and his friends came together in a loose formation called Harmara Leather Workers. However, they were not happy with this either. How could any production unit work with corruption in the department and the individualism of buyers, they asked. The buyers harassed them for bargains, asked for impossible discounts, and were utterly unconcerned about how these discounts were rendering profitless the items they bought; the livelihood of these craftspersons and their economic health were still taking a hit.

By the time one understood the crafts embedded in caste and market, the political in the craft became more than visible. I realized that the only way the market and hierarchical class-ridden values could be contested was through mobilization in large numbers.

'Dispensable People' versus 'Exploited People'

Poverty and work are inextricably linked. Poverty should shock every Indian. Urban poverty should shock everyone even more, because it leaves no room for illusion—the contrast with its environs is so sharp. Poverty challenges us to look at our lives, questions our levels of consumption, condemns our indifference and prods us to revisit the complicity hidden in our silence.

The poor work. They build our homes but live under the flyovers, in railway stations, under plastic sheets, in cement pipes; they clean our toilets but have none they can use. They clean our mess, wasteful plastic and rubbish we strew, and we call them 'rag pickers'. They grow our food, they craft to make our homes look chic, but we grumble at their subsidies and are angry when they die by suicide. They toil, but when they reach a dead end and return from the labour market without work, we call them lazy and good for nothing. The complete illogic of the popular discourse that labels them 'a burden' remains unchallenged.

I chose to live with people in rural India, where poverty still has the veneer of dignity. Many leave the familiarity of their homes and migrate in the hope of getting work in some unknown metropolis. They go from dignity and kinship to an alien, indifferent and callous environment in the city. Millions of poor people do not beg. In the first decade of my life with the poor, their single constant demand was for work. They, like all of us, want to live with dignity. Their capital is their labour, a devalued currency in the modern global environment.

The film *Slumdog Millionaire* (2008) may have been a hit, books on slums may have become bestsellers and a couple of children may have escaped poverty and misery, but the inequality and the injustice of poverty remain, goading us to ask relevant and critical questions and push the wheel of change, which is mired in the inability to perceive and act. In a celebrated fable, a child's voice once stated starkly that the emperor was naked, dispelling the myopia that he was clothed in grand clothes. The children in these pictures and books blow the myth that 'India shines', raising questions that are pertinent and critical, questions that we need to address urgently.

In 2013–14 the Pension Parishad was in protest, and assembled at Parliament Street in Delhi. There were hundreds of elderly from the unorganized sector who wanted an increase in the measly Rs 200 monthly pension approved by the Government of India. The mockery of a pension valued at Rs 200 a month does not need detailing. Some states have, however, raised it to a somewhat dignified amount.

A frail and haggard old rickshaw puller from Muzzafarpur in Bihar came to us and took out from a secret pocket in his vest the array of government-beneficiary cards that are issued to people. He said, 'I have them all, and now I am in the capital, can I go home with a reassurance of a larger pension? My wife is paralysed and my son is mentally ill. I peddle a cycle-rickshaw for a living, and it is becoming difficult.' I asked him what he would do with the increased pension of Rs 2,000 per month that we were then demanding. He said he would take his wife to hospital in an auto-rickshaw and have enough food to eat. In the call at the dharna for donations from the middle-class attendees, some pensioners took out from a layered bag, a small pouch and laboriously counted out Rs 5. It was equivalent to Rs 5 lakh for an industrialist who damned the existence of the poor for 'draining the economy'.

A decade after our Pension Parishad march, the central government continues to give a pension of Rs 200 a month, such is the callousness of an elected government. It is hurtful to see the indifference of structural response to rectifying human misery and injustice, and addressing the predicament of the unemployed and hungry. After having spent their healthy years in relentless toil, they are victims in old age to endemic poverty, ill health and early death. Respect for fellow beings has to translate into policy and laws that assure them of work and protection from such malignant aftereffects. Are they not citizens and a part of this country? The new policies of market liberalization have brought in new relationships between the worker and the employer, where the worker is actually seen as dispensable, not only for production but even as a human being.

Work safety, healthcare, health insurance?

Stone quarrying, mining and the setting up of cement and other such factories have all increased to develop India's 'Smart Cities' and to build ostentatious government and private structures. Those suffering from endemic poverty and faced with unemployment and hunger often have no option but to go to work as labourers in these factories, mine stone, chisel gods and goddesses for temples and make fancy stoneware for the rich. Owners of quarries and factories routinely bypass minimum safety precautions and the impact on the health of lakhs of workers is nothing short of criminal.

The most shocking outcome of bypassing these precautions is silicosis—a disease caused by the inhalation of fine dust that contains particles of silica, a mineral found in sand, stone, concrete, glass and rocks. The inhaled silica particles attack the lungs, causing them to deteriorate quickly; the disease occurs mostly among people in the construction and mining industries.[4] Silicosis patients go to work daily knowing full well that their lives are being cut short; they carry on working just so that their families can survive. When they die prematurely their children are forced, by poverty, to take up the same jobs and choose the same fate.

Mechanization has dealt two further body blows. First, it has sped up the work process in the stone-cutting, mining and construction industries, but the workers who operate these machines are now exposed to much higher levels of fine dust when they use the machines. They inhale much more particulate silica daily than they did using hand-operated tools such as the chisel. Secondly, mechanization has replaced workers with machines, increasing joblessness and poverty. Poverty-ridden workers are now not merely talked about as those who drain 'economic growth' but are also seen as dispensable. Not long ago we met an Italian Gandhian economist who predicted that the world would progress towards not an eradication of poverty but an eradication of the poor themselves. We listened to him, but could not bring ourselves to believe in his terrible prophesy.

Coming back to silicosis, in Rajasthan alone about thirteen districts are affected by the disease. In 2016, it was estimated that about 1,00,000 people had been tested for silicosis in just one district of Rajasthan—Karauli; this shows the extent of its suspected spread in the state. The compensation allotted for workers with silicosis has changed from time to time. It began with Rs 1 lakh to those living with silicosis and Rs 3 lakh to their families when they died; in 2021 it was changed to Rs 3 lakh for the affected workers and Rs 2 lakh for their families. Far beyond being simply exploited, those working in mines and stone and marble factories are treated as one would treat disposable teacups.

The testing procedures for silicosis are slow and at times arbitrary, extending the emotional and physical pain of the patient and the economic hardship of their family. In 2018, at a public hearing for silicosis patients from nine districts in Jaipur, many reported the difficulties they faced in getting a silicosis confirmation certificate from the Pneumoconiosis Board; and even if the certificate was released, they shared that the government took its time over sending them the compensation money.[5]

It is a cruel reality that normalizes the exchange of a person's labour for their quality and length of life. Where are their constitutional and societal guarantees? How many of us know that the stone we use in our homes and in kitchens comes from this process? Development cannot be at the cost of blood money. The

MKSS joined this struggle, and later worked with the Rajasthan government on a silicosis policy to address this ongoing tragedy.

In the neoliberal rush for economic growth, we have always short-changed the rights of the labourer and worker. However, before 2014 there was the space for dissent and protest and many rights for workers had been won through collective mobilization and struggle.[6] Laws were passed dubiously in Parliament through a voice vote, along with restraints on protest, mobilization and freedom of the most vulnerable, for claiming their rights.[7] We can hardly call such governance democratic. The incentive to increase production cannot come at the cost of the workforce. The denial of basic conditions—ventilation, lighting, toilets, sitting facilities, first-aid boxes, protective equipment, canteens, crèches, weekly holidays, rest breaks, drinking water—reminds us of the days when slavery was the accepted practice. Even early Bollywood films portrayed the inhumanity of those conditions that free India managed to reduce but not eradicate and now wants to ignore.

Unemployment has remained a primary concern for people in India since Independence, especially for those who work in the unorganized sector. The critique of the worthlessness of labour is so internalized that the response was often: '*Mein kayina karoon, bas dhool aur gaarnakoon.*' (I do nothing, I just dig and scatter mud.) That is how many women described their back-breaking, underpaid work as daily wage workers on public works, farms and construction sites. Unpaid work, or grossly underpaid work, has lost its value even in social terms. This echoes what women say about unpaid and unacknowledged work at home as well. Even if he tills less than a bigha of land, the man is still 'the farmer'; but the woman's work and labour, key to a family's well-being, is called 'surplus' and made cheap.

Unemployment and endemic underemployment in rural India lead to migration to urban areas. There are three kinds of migration. The first is migration for work, which seeks any paid work; with increasing literacy, skilled workers especially go to towns and cities hoping to upscale their earning with blue-collar jobs that are hard to come by at home. The second is migrating to move away from the constricting caste oppression in the village. The third is migration of farm labour in huge numbers across states, from poor to rich agrarian economies.

The substantive numbers of semi-skilled and skilled workers, not to mention the unskilled domestic and other workers, have led to a phenomenal increase in urban populations, which has put pressure for an Urban Employment Guarantee Act. It nevertheless adds insult to injury when such people are called a 'drain' on the economy, especially when they fill such a basic economic need in urban economies and connect to our well-being.

Defining 'Drudgery'

In a study on 'drudgery', published in 1984, designed by the Department of Science and Technology (DST), Government of India, the very definition of the term was questioned by the respondents. The study as proposed by the DST was accepted by the Barefoot College SWRC, but women respondents contacted during the study found the hypothesis and definition of drudgery unacceptable. The study had unwittingly been fashioned to satisfy an assumption that was faulty.

Even in its frailest form we cannot fail to notice that work itself is contentious and very complex. At the bottom of the pyramid is the wage worker with no say in the making of policy, no role in the planning and fixing of emoluments. It is impossible in contemporary India to make out a case for equal wages for all work. Nor is it easy to evaluate the wage with regard to how much (or how little) each particular skill contributes to the survival of the human race. Understanding work demands contextualization and understanding conceptual flaws. It requires the systematic unpacking of many concepts. This leads to an appreciation of the intersectional relationship of any kind of work, with multiple variables. An important aspect of these processes is the perception of the gap between the technical/research point of view and the subject being studied. Often the subjects are human beings, complex in and of themselves, situated in a state of powerlessness; the transaction between the researcher and respondent is unequal. Add to this the fact that the hypothesis that the study hopes to prove or confirm is formed far away in a 'laboratory' situation, where the respondent is a faceless end object, even though the success of the research depends on the acceptance of the hypothesis by the respondents. Any such study, unwittingly fashioned to satisfy an assumption that is faulty, becomes little more than a formality to reassert an already foregone and formulated conclusion.

In the case of the 1984-85 study on 'drudgery',[8] the research team had concluded (before the study was completed) that the use of the smokeless chulha and solar cookers must be promoted among rural women as the solution to 'drudgery'. All the women friends I had made during my eight-year stay in Rajasthan told me this would not work. Neither the solar cooker nor the smokeless chulha met the requirements for making rotis from bajra (millet) and makka (maize), which was the staple diet. Both kinds of rotis required a direct flame of a much larger circumference than the smokeless chulha permitted. The solar cooker could cook rice and dal, neither of which was part of their diet. To use the smokeless chulha and the solar cooker they would have to change their diet *and* spend on buying rice and dal. These foods were neither easily available nor affordable. Local women deemed the solar cooker and the smokeless chulha redundant, even before these could enter their kitchen. It was obvious that the research team had got both the definition and solution of drudgery wrong.

The first demand we made as preliminary to conducting the study was that 'drudgery' be defined by the women themselves. It took a great deal of persistence and contestation to finally get the DST to agree to a participatory methodology in conducting the study. If it had not been for support from the feminist economist Devaki Jain, then advisor to the DST, this would not have been possible. We wanted the questionnaire (and its yes/no answer format) to be replaced with a focus group discussion (FGD) in eleven village clusters or groups, where women would gather to 'define drudgery'. These FGDs were recorded on a battery-operated tape recorder and later transcribed. Thanks to the FGDs, instead of a simple 'yes' or 'no' to questions raised, the complexity of choices also became apparent.

The rigour of the revised pattern of the study lay in its attempt to work scientifically from a given condition to possibilities within that predicament. From previous experience with health and with toilets, one knew that leading questions gave you predetermined, politically correct answers, which did not tally with reality and possibilities. One had to accept the hiatus between our academic hypotheses and the reality of living conditions to evolve sound policy. It was important, therefore, to look at and understand women's predicament at work. The veracity of the statements in the FGDs spoke for themselves. The study then categorized and analysed the responses to the questions.

The women eventually defined drudgery as 'hunger, arduous physical work and unemployment'. Under 'arduous physical work' they had listed 'collecting fuel' at the top of the list, followed by 'construction labour', 'work related to frequently climbing-descending ladders', 'weeding' and 'digging'. 'Cooking', which the research team had included under drudgery, was considered relaxing.

The DST's solution—pushing a pre-determined output (solar cookers and the smokeless chulha)—was not linked to addressing the real drudgery of hunger and poverty. It also became apparent that the work that women did needed to be reclaimed and valued economically.

This entire experience resonated with a similar discussion with famous orthopaedist Dr P.K. Sethi. The focus of the discussion with Dr Sethi was on the mismatch between the intent and reality. He cited an example from his own experience. As a young, idealistic doctor, he had travelled far and wide to deliver callipers to patients whose legs were afflicted with polio or other problems. But during follow-up visits he often found the callipers hanging on a nail and the patient still a victim of lack of mobility. He was irritated with the non-use until one day, instead of asking what was wrong with the beneficiaries, he asked himself a different question: What is wrong with the planning? In that question lay the answer. The patients were poor and wore Indian clothes, and their footwear, if they had any, were slippers. The calliper had a solid shoe. Also, it was impossible to sit cross-legged with the calliper or climb a tree with it on. The beneficiary had a shoe on one foot and nothing or a slipper on the other. A picture that spoke for itself. Dr Sethi then designed the now famous Jaipur Foot. He had the integrity and honesty to accept that his hypothesis was faulty, and sought rational and correct solutions. The famous Jaipur Foot is a bare foot, light and easy to wear and take off, and has benefitted lakhs of Indians. Policymakers need to understand that people's responses cannot be dismissed as unintelligent or regressive.

The reality was that the user did not want the calliper, the chulha, the solar cooker or the toilet (a flush toilet in an area where water is scarce is a luxury the poor can do without). If the cause of resistance among beneficiaries is logical, one must concede and rework the hypothesis.

When working with people, it is important to listen to them and involve them in the decision-making process. Participatory policymaking in a democracy is a sound principle, value and process. To place people in the centre of the discussion and to consult them as equals is the way to real development. Those preoccupied with efficiency and implementation should understand that planning done without reference to the conditions of people begins with a false premise.

Understanding Skilled and Unskilled Work

There are three commonly used words for work in Hindi/Urdu—kaam (work), naukri (job) and mazdoori (labour)—accepting that there is a nuanced and biased recognition of work. Women have had to be persuaded that their endless 'kaam' has a monetary and human value, unrecognized though it is. As mentioned above, the statement by women—*'Mein kayina karoon, bas dhool aur gaarnakoon'* (I do nothing, I just dig and scatter mud)—reflects that what they do is valued neither by society nor themselves; it is just drudgery. So long as many continue to work for a pittance, the value of labour will be denigrated and work will have multiple definitions and interpretations resulting in great inequality. It is somehow most apparent in those born as women, and their plight as workers.

There is some theoretical and abstract understanding about hard physical labour. But just as the tedium of daily housework must be experienced to be understood, physical labour too seems simpler than it really is. Understanding the state of workers and their conditions and the pitiful wage they drew, and still draw, comes as a surprise.

There is also a misunderstanding that women, especially in the rural areas, need skill training for better remuneration. Their impoverishment leads a more endowed urban population to screw up its nose and say, 'They don't work. We should teach them skills.' It began with the sewing machine, which became a symbol of possibilities, as well as a mocking image that disregarded the hundreds of jobs the women actually did. The focus on numbers of women engaged in work in agriculture, construction labour, domestic support, animal husbandry and all supportive work for crafts proves that the economy is, in fact, sustained by women. Their contribution needs to be recognized.

In the late 1970s and early 1980s people worked, but did not know their rights nor how to access them. In innumerable meetings and in every casual, serious or deliberative interaction, the people's articulation was a demand for work. The Famine Relief Code, a relic of the British Raj in India in 1833, continued to operate and a few got work every year. The local conversations were full of 'famine', a euphemism for work. We began with a routine training on rights and laws conducted in Harmara village, 4 kilometres from Tilonia. The seven-day curriculum included a discussion on minimum wages.

Naurti was one of the women participants. The training concluded with some hope and little expectation. Until one morning, about a couple of weeks later, I was summoned to Harmara by Naurti. Some 500 workers had gone on strike and were demanding minimum and equal wages on many work sites. The local officials too came along to rope me in to break the strike.

The gist of it was that workers were paid differential wages for the same quantum of work: the Public Works Department paid more, and the Famine Code, which saw this work as a dole to ward off drought, paid less. The same amount of work was extracted no matter under which scheme you worked. When the workers led by Naurti with her newfound knowledge about wages went on strike and refused to accept the Famine Code wages, all hell broke loose. After a day, the wages were accepted under written protest; women had to feed their families. Inquiries followed and some officials were suspended. A public interest litigation (PIL) was also filed and resulted in a landmark judgment in 1983 when a double bench of the Supreme Court, Justices Bhagwati and Pathak, struck down a section of the Famine Relief Code, which were ultra vires of Articles 14 and 23 of the Indian Constitution.[9]

Naurti's strike for equal wages had won the women an astounding victory. This battle drew us into another paradigm, into examining the definition and scope of minimum wages. In a study conducted for the IDS, Jaipur, with Dr Sharada Jain, we proved that work defined as unskilled was indeed very skilled work. In subsequent years we were able to argue that using implements to dig and shovel and to carry headloads did not constitute unskilled labour. In fact, terms such as 'unskilled labour' have originated from literate policymakers who, from their own point of view, possess the finest skills. Cascading down, the effect of such terms ends with the manual worker, whose predicament is worsened by excessive supply, low wages and increased mechanization. Just as the definition of 'drudgery' by experts had initially included cooking (and which the women had listed under 'relaxation'), another set of experts decided that if there was more supply than demand of a skill learnt on the job without certification, it had perforce to be 'unskilled'.

My continued preoccupation with working women labour and their predicament was sharpened by Naurti's struggle for a minimum wage and the consequent PIL filed in the Supreme Court. I felt that, in all honesty, one had to work like a minimum-wage labourer to understand many things. It was hypocritical to profess support from the protective environment of a shady office, and I decided to enlist for fifteen days (a pakhwada) as a labourer with my women friends to offer shramdaan (free labour) in a charagah (pasture land) where they were working.

I didn't have the skill for 'unskilled' work

In the effort to work as a daily wage labourer for fifteen days—digging, lifting and carrying mud with unscientific posture—I permanently damaged my back. My failure was conversely a triumph of my assertion that this work needed skill—had it been 'unskilled' work that anyone could do, I should not have faced any problems in tackling it. The very first day I discovered that using the genti-pawda (pickaxe with two sharp ends and shovel), which looked so simple, was extremely complicated. My friends banned me from using the genti, for fear that I might harm them or myself. They gave me the task of shovelling stones onto a 'tagari', a receptacle for collecting stones. I was bent double all the time and was so slow that I was the victim of much jeering and friendly sarcasm.

Tiring of the stones, I opted to shovel mud, thinking it would be easier. That too was difficult. They suggested that I carry the stone-filled tagari to its destination. The tagari is carried on the head. I tried lifting the tagari, but it was simply impossible. I strained every muscle, but neither my hands nor my shoulders had the strength to lift the 20-kilogram receptacle to my head. Finally, the women had to lift and place the tagari so I could walk the few hundred metres to where the load had to be dropped. I was a write-off. But research, government orders and rules continue to call this very skilled work 'unskilled'! These definitions are only possible because the rule makers have neither worked on a worksite nor conducted a genuine scientific study on the skills required to do a hard day's physical labour.

This experience was part of the study on wages with the IDS. Apart from many other conclusions that the study came to, it questioned the definitions of 'skilled' and 'unskilled' work and the concept of wage labour as being the most casual form of work that anyone can do.

One has not been able to understand the logic behind this preconception (that hard labour is unskilled work), unless it is planned strategy to use cheap labour on a continuing basis, or to craftily use mechanization to end all claim to work for a majority of people who do not know how to use their numbers in a democracy to claim their rights. Work and wages, apart from their technical detailing, are perhaps the primary concerns of every rural household as a means of livelihood. The set of experiences detailed above make it amply clear that such work must be paid for and its skill recognized. It was with this foundational understanding that the MKSS was established.

The recognition of work and its value is political. It is related to caste, class, gender and region. Documents that detail these processes—as stories, as research papers, as history and folklore—help build a conceptual framework and a political position. The perception of an idea and transforming it into action-learning and institutions has a timeframe that cannot be pre-set. It is much easier said than done. The renewal of the campaign for the MGNREGA began in this context.

Work as Politics: Equality and Justice in Practice

Astonishingly, the desert is beautiful. But for people living there it is hostile and unrelenting. The people who courageously live in the semi-desert areas of Rajasthan struggle daily for survival against nature and the desperate conditions of impoverishment—and hunger. Work and employment are imperative to escape hunger and thirst. Demand for work and wage employment in public works is literally a matter of life and death.

Rajasthan describes its droughts as perhaps the Icelanders describe the variations and nuances of snowfalls. There is the drought that destroys the crops, the staple food for the year; the drought in which there is no grain or fodder, but some drinking water; the drought that impacts food, water and fodder—the chapanyoakaal—this is when villages empty out in search of life and a living.

When we moved to Devdungri, where the MKSS was conceived in 1987, it was in the grip of a chapanyoakaal. There were no vegetables to be had, and our meals consisted of dal (a luxury we could afford, unlike the villagers) and rotis. The entire village was able to eat only half a bellyful. Food was, and is, very basic in the Devdungri home—two simple meals, one in the morning and another in the evening, cooked at once. One day a Dalit girl, Papiya, daughter of a local farmer, came to me with a huge sore and asked for medicines. We had basic first aid and homeopathic medicines at home. It was a stroke of good luck that she responded to the medicines very well. Thereafter she came by often, sometimes when we were eating. With the local diet reduced to just roti with water and ground chilli paste in the chapanyoakaal, the dal at our place seemed special. We would welcome Papiya and invite her to eat with us but she would always say, 'I have just eaten.'

I marvelled at her dignity and felt furious with those who equate the hungry and needy with beggary. Her family, like all others, went daily to the 'mazdoor chowkti' or 'mazdoor mandi', waiting in droves for work. The 'buyer' came to drive a hard bargain, hired the stronger among them and paid them less than the market wage. The weaker folk returned home to face another hungry day. No wonder that they wanted guaranteed employment from the government.

A people's political agenda was set. We had come to Devdungri to look for a construct that would accommodate personal and political ethics within a structural frame. It began to take shape, defined by the living needs of workers, a right to a life with dignity guaranteed by the Constitution. Sovereign constitutional rights to life and work are transferred to the people through the delivery of welfare services and schemes.

In the three years preceding the setting up of the MKSS (1987–90), we had conducted a series of studies while living in Devdungri. One of them was a study on the 'Delivery Systems of Government Poverty Alleviation Programmes' with IDS, Jaipur. The study took care of the MKSS's economic needs and we drew the equivalent of the minimum wage as honoraria, to cover the costs of living in Devdungri. Children in the neighbourhood came for English tuition to us. A look at their textbook stimulated the second study—an inquiry into schooling, looking at access to it, and an examination of English textbooks till class ten. In 1991, a year after the launch of the MKSS, the Times of India group awarded a fellowship of Rs 1 lakh in my name. 'Living with dignity and social justice' records the work, thoughts and analyses of our nascent work at that time. It became source material for many years to come, enabling us to link practice to theory and bring rigour to work. It was an exercise in framing questions that took years to answer, and outlined our trajectory of work and engagement.

Power in the Hands of the People

In India, beginning with its campaign for Independence, people saw the occurrence of two distinct processes with compatible but differing objectives. One process aimed at an end result—taking over state power and forging the contours of the nation, while the other process protected the normative principles underlying the struggle; both finally led to the formation of the Constitution. Gandhi saw the next struggle as a continuing process to keep India within the arc of public morality of a secular state. Ambedkar's Constitution had put these concepts into a legal frame and ensured structurally that the secular was enshrined in a legalistic process and was equally accessible to all citizens uniformly. In current times we speak of this as constitutional morality.

In any process, power has to be monitored and structures must be evolved to do so. In the case of electoral democracies, the citizens monitor through democratic institutions created for them—from the village level to the Parliament. However, power has systematically tried to make itself unaccountable and has legitimized impunity. The vote has got completely entangled in identity, the underbelly of caste, religion, class and gender and has been repeatedly misused, in part by people themselves. The misuse of these two processes has corroded the electoral system and representative democracy, considered the seminal structure of democracy.

Many people's organizations or non-party political structures and institutions, now called 'civil society', derive their mandate from the process of the freedom struggle and the principles enshrined in the Constitution. Non-party organizations work in the area of politics outside of political party formations, an idea born with the independence movement, and whose scope is defined by the DPSP (Directive Principles of State Policy) of the Indian Constitution.

The socio-economic conditions of poverty are rooted in unemployment and in the non-recognition of the immense contribution of the 'unskilled' in building the Indian economy. Work and wages are the primary concerns of every rural household; the MKSS began with these.

Sangharsh: An acceptance of satyagraha and struggle

All people's organizations and struggles aspire for a greater degree of power for the less powerful. Their demand for equality and justice challenges the lack of transparency and protective impunity of the executive and the legislature. Funded NGOs, on the other hand, work with and/or critique development policy. The work of these two sectors may or may not be complementary. However, both have to contest the lack of accountability of governance.

My shift from the IAS to an NGO—Barefoot College SWRC, Tilonia—was dramatic. It changed the socio-economic and political context of my life. From Tilonia to Devdungri, where the MKSS office was initially based, was a greater dramatic shift in ideological perception.

I had learnt about the socio-economic context of poverty in my first nine years in Tilonia. Understanding caste came from a determination to make sense of the rural Indian psychology of identity and its rigid framework of rules. The understanding and shaping of people's politics as struggle came with the MKSS in 1990. The politics of the MKSS itself was defined by two major existing struggles—for land and for wages. It chose non-party politics or people's politics as its political frame. In modes of struggle it chose the Gandhian way: satyagraha; and in its perception of understanding social and economic inequality and accountability, it fell within the frame of Ambedkar's design and the Constitution. Today it remains socialist in its belief that structural inequality has to be contested in all its forms. The attitude to representative politics and aspiration for state power is still debated, though the consensus is for it to remain a non-party, people's political organization. It follows that questioning the misuse of power and the denial of rights in its many manifestations, including corruption and arbitrary power, is at the core of its political agenda.

Living and working from Devdungri

Relocating from Tilonia to Devdungri meant a change from the campus life at Barefoot College SWRC to a village hut that became a home office, as it housed not just our group of four—Shankar and his wife, Anshi, Nikhil and me—but also the newborn MKSS.

Shankar came with his experience as a worker in seventeen jobs, of which the most fruitful were the last seven years in Barefoot College SWRC using communication, theatre, puppets and song. He had begun to walk the path to his legendary status—creating a newer mix of genres to influence all NGO work in Rajasthan. But before that he had been a wage earner, a collector of eggs from poultry farms, a pakora-wallah, a namkeen factory worker, a temporary teacher, an adult literacy teacher. He knew what it was to be hungry and jobless. Shankar, an only son, was born way down the economic ladder but to relative privilege. His father was a Patwari, but drank himself to death and left his widow and son under a mountain of debt to fend for themselves. Shankar's worker mother, an illiterate, feisty, determined woman, saw him through school and then pushed him to work. His saga of seeking employment is an interesting story. He went, like all rural unemployed youth do, to the nearest town, which was Ajmer. He was drawn to the newly emerging egg and poultry industry, where he heard jobs were easy to get. He narrates how he went to the poultry manager and proudly said he had completed his schooling and had a certificate. It cut no ice and he was sent on his way. The man who went in after him was an illiterate worker and immediately got the job. The next poultry farm saw Shankar claiming he was illiterate; he got the job! For three years he kept the job, marking eggs with a piece of charcoal. He also enrolled for a BA degree from an open university, taking leave to give his exams. Having become a graduate he proudly presented his degree and a packet of laddus to his employer, who wanted to know what the sweets were for. Shankar answered, 'I am now a graduate.' The employer was none too pleased at having been tricked. Once Shankar came to Barefoot College SWRC, Tilonia, he set up the Communication Section and demonstrated his genius in being able to speak across the board on different contexts to different communities. His Chaplinesque humour made him a unique phenomenon in the activist world. His primary concern, however, was to look for ways to make his people more powerful.

Nikhil Dey, the youngest and a good seventeen years younger than me, was born to privilege. He attended the Lawrence School,

Lovedale, had a grandparent in the ICS and all the credentials for continuing to live and claim all that privilege could give. He had travelled with his parents to the USA, where his father, an air marshal in the Indian Air Force, was the air attaché in the Indian Embassy. Nikhil was an excellent scholar, studying for his bachelor's degree in the USA, with a debate scholarship, until he dropped out to work with people's politics. He had begun to think of politics and people from the age of twelve, when Indira Gandhi declared the Emergency. That year he first saw the Parliament in session and was disillusioned. But this disillusionment pushed him into the world of alternative politics. His decision to return without completing his degree saddened his parents. Finally, to satisfy them, he got a BA from an open university, and finished his law degree from Delhi University while the MKSS was being conceived.

One's physical location determines one's politics in many ways. As do our choice of colleagues. Living together in Devdungri, in the small hut, we knew how it felt to be deprived of amenities. When Shankar, Nikhil and I decided to work together, we were committed for life, and as long as it took, to pursue our dreams. It also made our friendship deeper and tethered it to shared principles. Participation was a guiding principle and, therefore, choices too had to be made with people. Most importantly, the Devdungri home was a statement of our politics in life and our lifestyle. But other variables of caste and identity-based inequality remained similar.

Living in Devdungri forced us to face issues of social discrimination every day. The rules were trivial and rigid. Nagodaji, a Dalit farmer, had a well that was the source of drinking water for the village. Water was drawn with a rope and bucket; the children and I held the rope and ran down the slope as the leather bucket, called a 'charas', slowly surfaced with the water. Shankar, Anshi and

Nikhil would then fill the pots. From Nagodaji's well we carried the pots, balanced on our heads, to our home office, the hut. Local men did not carry the pots on their heads as Nikhil and Shankar did. It was just not done! I must mention here that Shankar was distantly related to many of the families in the area and Anshi, as his wife, had to bear the brunt of local ire, as we had broken social behavioural norms. But to the four of us, working with one's hands and ignoring differentiation in gender roles was a matter of pride and dignity. Our kitchen became a central space for important political discussions as we cooked and ate together.

There were sceptics. Many friends wondered whether shrinking from what are conventionally seen as power centres—the IAS, Delhi, then an NGO—to live in and work from a mud hut in Devdungri would get me any closer to understanding real change or truth. The future would tell, but minimalist living and understanding the true meaning of 'work' with people in idyllic surroundings certainly helped.

Emergence of the Mazdoor Kisan Shakti Sangathan

Even before we set up the MKSS, the issues of wages and feudal oppression had been the first to demand our attention. The contentious issue of wages set the tone and structure for the long-drawn-out battle for transparency and work. The first wage struggle brought Mohanji and Chunni Bai (both poor Dalits) and Bhanwar from Kushalpura into the discussion and debate of people's struggles for equality. This, and the fight with the people of Sohangarh against feudal oppression, laid the foundation for the awakening of awareness and determination for collective struggle. We battled against concentrations of power, whether feudal or of the political ruling class. These two struggles also led us to understand the nature of collusion, and from these struggles emerged the MKSS.

The issue in Sohangarh was feudal oppression. Hari Singh, a Rajput, had usurped public land and levied tax on anyone found grazing their livestock there. India has a Land Ceiling Act, which disallows ownership of large tracts of agricultural land. The excess land either reverts to the state as commons or is allotted to the landless as small holdings. During their fight for their right over the commons, the people of Sohangarh formed a women's society to the astonishment of the people around. The strong and compassionate women of Sohangarh—Bhuriya and Kakima—made sure that we stood in solidarity and friendship. Participation and uniting against the oppression of the feudal landlord gave hope to the people because they saw that it could lead to victory. They realized that uniting could strengthen the weak to the point where oppression by the powerful could be resisted effectively.

These two struggles also seeded the idea of what was eventually to become the MKSS. Bhuriya and Kakima, the two women opinion makers of Sohangarh, were strong, ethical people and adopted us politically and emotionally. Sohangarh was the first village to understand and shape the ethical struggle in the long battle that followed. We, for our part, shared the anxiety and determination of the villagers.

Government assurance, fudged accounts and underpaid workers

It was 1987. India was on the verge of 'opening up' its market. The contours of the economy, technology and business were changing. Many critics felt it was the wrong time to start talking about the obligations and continuation of the welfare state. But for the people in the semi-desert tehsil of Bhim in Rajasthan's Rajsamand district, their only hope lay in continuing to demand enrolment in public works. At that time, no matter what their nature, public works were called 'famine relief'. The term stemmed from the Famine Relief Code passed by the British colonial rulers to facilitate the opening of works in drought-affected India in 1878. Since Rajasthan is always affected by drought in part, the code was used every year by the Government of Rajasthan to implement works. Historically, the 'feudal system used drought relief to build forts and palaces, rainwater conservation tanks, and lakes'.[10]

The demand for the right to information began during our engagement with workers on public work sites who were denied their wage. It is no easy task to break through to a community, to get them to believe that you are there not to exploit them. If we had any great advantage in Devdungri, it was Shankar's presence, for he was distantly related to many of our neighbours. The mud hut we lived in was his cousin's home. While we did not have to face the usual hostilities, i.e., allegations of being Christian missionaries, mining contractors come to exploit, etc., the villagers were unable to place us workwise in the understood niches of occupations—farmer, middleman, contractor, government servant, mining agent—and this confused them.

One evening in March 1987, Shankar and I walked to the village of Kushalpura in Bhim tehsil to respond to the demand for work. This was the first of many such evening meetings. The demand for work far exceeded the average of five to six days of paid work a year sanctioned per household under the Jawahar Rozgar Yojana (JRY) scheme, till then the most promising of work schemes to come to village India. But for an area peopled by small and marginal farmers, where migration was a set way of life, five to six days of paid work was a pittance. Those who migrated often came back with little or no savings, ill and desolate. Locally available paid work was thus important and not just for economic reasons. Migration disrupted families, denied children healthcare and education; it was imperative that at least a part of the family stop migrating and yet be able to earn enough for subsistence. After an assurance from the government, work was offered at a site called Dadi Rapat with payment as per the norms for the minimum wage.

Chunni Bai and Mohanji, impoverished Dalit agricultural workers, were among the first to recognize the worth of a sangathan. Chunni Bai, who worked at Dadi Rapat, told us that she worked with 100 workers. The work involved not merely digging but also carrying the dug-up soil to the tank bund about 500 metres away. The wages were set at Rs 4–7 a day. We negotiated with the government that they should pay full wages if workers delivered the quota of work assigned to them. We talked to the workers, including those who had come from other places to Kushalpura and now numbered about 100, advising them to work together in groups of twenty. We thought bringing system and rationality would call the government's bluff that workers did not deliver. We went every day to the work site and the workers worked hard to finish their tasks to earn the minimum wage.

Unfortunately, a combination of fudged accounts unavailable for scrutiny and the power of the petty bureaucracy to threaten and misappropriate money made a mockery of the truth and the hard work of the workers. Those who worked more and completed their tasks were paid less and some who did nothing but scratch the surface were paid much more. Two of them—Chunni Bai and Bhanwar from Kushalpura—did not accept their wages, but readied themselves for a long legal battle in 1988 to claim their money.

At a psychological level struggle makes us conscious of our strengths and limitations. It also pushes us to share emotions with a group of people. The matter-of-factness of normal conversations are cemented with shared moments of hope, anxiety and worry. In sharing vulnerabilities, we reinforce the ideas of shared leadership and the importance of a participatory consultative process. My bonds with Mohanji and Chunni Bai were built for life. Even Nikhil, Shankar, Anshi and I entered a different phase in our friendship.

Colonial frameworks and feudal implementation

The colonial structures created for delivering services provided the skeletal frame for building upon after Independence. While policy at a national level introduced the concept of welfare as an obligation of the state as defined in the Constitution, the process of implementation remained feudal. The basic structure of work remained suspicious of people, who were defined as 'mobs' or thieves. This attitude, sustained by a prejudiced bureaucratic and caste hierarchy, retained the double standards within the system. These double standards were most explicit in the way the lazy or procrastinating babus expected work from the mazdoor or worker who toiled mutely and relentlessly in the sun.

The penalty for non-performance was always borne by the worker, while the incompetence and inefficiency of the lower bureaucracy went unchecked and remained opaque and transparent. This situation—of poverty, of an indifferent administration and the inability to access basic services for life and livelihood—was the foundation for the seeding of the RTI movement.

The MKSS realized that in the democratic structure, people were helpless and marginalized in framing policy. Structural injustice and inequality had also to be addressed. The first meeting was held in Bhim, with the workers from Rajasthan. B.D. Sharma, Commissioner

SC/ST and Joint Secretary, Labour, Government of India, attended the meeting to express legal and formal support to the demand for work. A second meeting of experts from Rajasthan was held in Beawar in the form of a public meeting with voices of research, public intellectuals and workers to collectively state that the situation of work and wages needed review. The third meeting, a seminar at IDS, Jaipur, was attended by policymakers and senior civil servants, economists and lawyers, researchers, journalists. Secretary, Rural Development S.R. Sankaran and eminent legal scholar Upendra Baxi attended the meeting, chaired by Director V.S. Vyas, a leading agro-economist. The seminar was critical in redefining work as a part of a democratic right to livelihood and survival. It shifted from the colonial perception of work as a dole to work as a right.

In bringing together those concerned from the smallest to the most eminent in shaping policy, the MKSS made a statement about its political argument for pooling thought and action. There was an assertion that participation of people in shaping policy is vital for its rigour and enables its capacity to implement the programme. It established unequivocally that transparency was a fundamental principle—originating in Article 19 of the Indian Constitution—to sustain integrity and probity in public life, and as a tool to fight corruption and arbitrary governance.

At a personal level, we felt anger and frustration, but collective discussions helped channelize the anger. It was always a challenge, and we met it with creative ways of addressing every argument and working with the details of structural functioning. Shankar's father had been a patwari (a land revenue official). His childhood experiences and memories of his father's work and my days in the IAS came in handy not only to unravel bureaucratic processes but to understand the psychology of its functioning. These were very important days, when we sat in the middle of the situation literally and metaphorically, and tried to find a way out. We knew there was hunger, migration and endless visits to the mazdoor chowki next door. The arguments were endless and alternatives, within the mode of non-violent public action, were explored.

The case that led to the Right to Information Act

The demand for transparency and a law for the people's right to see government records was shaped by simple incidents—wage workers cheated of their wage and unable to see muster rolls, villagers facing dysfunctional development projects, corruption, graft and misuse of power. The Right to Information Act did not come out of an abstract discussion on information. In 1994 a man came to the MKSS office with a complaint of being cheated on wages. It was decided to examine the records of all public works. The acting block development officer (BDO) in Raipur was an IAS trainee who was still straightforward enough to allow Shankar to copy the records with a pencil. The information when shared sent shock waves across the community. The BDO possibly complied because the demand for the right to see records for justice and truth had reached the civil servants training institute as part of the training curricula.

The first Jansunwai (public hearing) was held in December 1994 in Kot Kirana in Rajasthan's Pali district and was attended by over 1,500 people. The information Shankar had so painstakingly copied included records of works and disclosed the names of dead people on muster rolls, wages not paid, suspicious bills for materials used and non-performance. The local mafia had threatened violence and mobilization of its forces if the Jansunwai was held. The local tent house owner had been threatened and forbidden from putting up the shamiana under which the Jansunwai was to be held, so a brave local resident offered to pitch a parachute in lieu of the shamiana.

The Jansunwai duly took place and those present demanded transparency of all records, accountability of the corrupt, repayment of development funds siphoned off and a social (public) audit. The hearing established that transparency was vital for probity in public life and for development.[11]

The public demand for the RTI gained ground and etched its journey, to end with the RTI Act being passed in 2005. For many of us in the MKSS, the impossible had happened. Personal morality and public ethics had come together to make a strong statement about the denial of rights by the nexus of corruption and arbitrary misuse of power. For the first time, I felt a sense of harmony between my public and personal journey for an ethical existence.

The struggle for wages forked out into two demands: for the RTI and for work. The demand for guaranteed work owes its origins in India to the Maharashtra Employment Guarantee Scheme (1977). Workers and workers unions thereafter demanded an all-India law guaranteeing employment. The political energy of the RTI movement merely ignited the existing demand for guaranteed work by organizing a new set of discussions and formulations. The first serious discussion about the need for a national law guaranteeing work was held at IDS, Jaipur. Scholars and activists from Maharashtra came to lead the discussion.

The MGNREGA is born

The demand for guaranteed paid work culminated with the passage of the MGNREGA in August 2005. On 2 February 2006 India saw the implementation of a pro-worker policy, and for the first time rural citizens had a *right* to work. The law guarantees 100 days of employment to all rural households in India, on demand, every year, at minimum wages.

The MGNREGA differs from other poverty alleviation programmes in two significant respects—it demands proof of citizenship and entitlement. The introduction of regular social audits by the gram sabhas, intended to identify and plug pilferage and corruption, are vital if a programme of the dimensions of MGNREGA is to succeed. As the MGNREGA emerged in small part from the RTI campaign, it mandates transparency and accountability in all aspects of implementation. The Act has led to a paradigm shift from arbitrary provision of work by the government to 'a rights-based framework for wage employment'.[12]

When we articulate a popular demand the best vindication comes from people themselves; in the above case the slogans and the songs (with astute crafting of lyrics drawn from popular tunes) for the RTI and the MGNREGA captured their spirit. The demand had come from very large numbers of people. In Rajasthan we saw mobilizations in almost every district, underscoring the need for such an Act. Exhilarating moments were defined by the fusion of law, rights and the human condition, with the joy of a common demand having been met, finally. These two campaigns (demanding the RTI and guaranteed employment at minimum wage) also built a consensus across conventional divides such as caste, gender and religious identities. At their peak, the campaigns contributed to building democratic consciousness, and evoking the Preamble to the Indian Constitution, where equality, liberty and fraternity come together to demand justice for the less privileged.

Workers were included for the first time in developing and in building the economic and social architecture of India in a somewhat more equal manner. The MGNREGA was the first Act to recognize manual work as contributing to the economy.

Rich farmers and market economists were quick to critique it and continued to do so regularly; but the democratic and participatory voice of workers had carried the day. Gram sabhas and panchayats across the country saw a large increase in fund flows for the first time. With the MGNREGA, for once the assertion of the poor for democratic power was seen as a right. Even today, many years later, despite the MGNREGA being condemned and mocked by the Prime Minister in Parliament, it has proven to be the only standby for preventing starvation.

In the huge reverse migration during the Covid-19 pandemic, the much-maligned MGNREGA proved to be a lifeline, absorbing the millions of workers returning home. Prime Minister Modi had stated in Parliament in 2015 that 'MGNREGA will continue; it is [a] living example of Congress failure.'[13] On the contrary, it was a fall back for the lakhs who returned to their villages. It has been a record number in absolute terms as well as being the buffer between unemployment and starvation. In Rajasthan alone in the financial year (FY) 2020–21, 74.3 lakh families and 1.8 crore people got paid work under the MGNREGA. Prime Minister Modi has been quiet on his incorrect assumption. Even during this time of distress and need, in 2021–22 the Government of India cut the MGNREGA budget to Rs 60,000 crore, while Covid still continued and with the lockdown still partially in place.[14]

The migration during the pandemic would have been an even more terrible nightmare than it was had it not been for the MGNREGA, and of course the National Food Security Act, 2013 (also known as the Right to Food Act). The NFSA ensured the distribution of rations through outlets nationwide; people needed to only show their ration card to collect their rations. It is a fact that the MGNREGA prevented food riots in the period of Covid lockdown and the NFSA also helped provide affordable food to families to prevent distress.

Trade Unions in a Participatory Democracy

Any struggle seeks to wrest agency from unequal structures in some part, to redress the power imbalance. The argument was, and is, that the government—the largest of 'people's organizations'—is mandated to deliver economic rights to the people. Such an agency needs to be both transparent and accountable to the people. For laws and policy to be participatory, people must be able to easily engage with the government. Ambedkar's constitutional guarantees, Gandhiji's emphasis on the dignity of working with one's hands and the socialist principles of the rights of the working class combine to place the plight of the workers high on the list of independent India's political priorities. This allows political and welfare spaces to be used constructively by workers movements, trade unions and people's political organizations to attempt to bring parity and equality to the unorganized sector, which happens to be the largest workforce in India.

Worker-related unions and federations, such as the Hamal Panchayat (loaders at warehouses and railway stations union), have been formed over the years to address specific issues. Formal workers unions like the All-India Trade Union Congress, Centre of Indian Trade Unions, Indian National Trade Union Congress, Hind Mazdoor Sabha and even Bharatiya Mazdoor Sangh have been active in protecting workers' interests. Their recourse to laws protecting the rights of workers, mandated by court orders, has enabled them to fight these battles. They have been a force to reckon with and have proved a deterrent to exploitation.

However, most, if not all, trade unions are affiliated to political parties. It is a matter for historical critique that India did not form workers unions independent of political parties, and these have, therefore, been muted by party policy. The right to work under the MGNREGA has broken this pattern to some extent, by bringing sections of the unorganized labour in rural areas in India under one banner. The RTI, MGNREGA, NFSA and Forest Rights Act are all logically connected, and many campaigns have come together to form a strong voice for rights-based legislations to ensure delivery of basic services, such as the Suchna evam Rozgar Adhikar Abhiyan (SR Abhiyan) in Rajasthan. These campaigns have claimed agency in making policy that has worked towards greater distribution of power. Multiple campaigns have engaged with the state to demand compliance to the rights assured in the Constitution's chapter on fundamental rights. However, the craze for privatization and the attack on labour laws have come down very hard on workers.

The new labour codes disempower trade unions considerably. The National Democratic Alliance (NDA) has merged approximately forty-four federal labour laws that outline rights related to wages, industrial relations, social security, health and safety, etc., and removed many basic entitlements in the name of simplification. Most of the trade unions were against codifying the labour laws under four categories, and contested that the government was benefitting the employers at the cost of the worker.[15] This use of the Covid-19 lockdown to pass these immoral and inherently undemocratic orders by many NDA coalition governments pushed India back many decades, reducing the worker to bondage.

'Reforms' usually indicate a change for the better. The more appropriate word would be regression, or the stripping of rights. Equality as a principle has been threatened with dire consequences by these laws, which, therefore, is a threat to democracy. All of which ricochet on the Constitution itself.

6

Voices of Conscience: To Act or Not to Act, That Is the Question

> 'In times of universal deceit telling the truth is a revolutionary act.'
>
> —GEORGE ORWELL (attributed)

The Activist and Activism

ACTIVISTS ARE COMPELLED to respond to injustice and speak with the powerless, vulnerable and those without privilege. An activist works to make power transparent, accountable and just. As we are also the butt of many jokes and derisive remarks, it is important to see ourselves in perspective.

We were in Jhabua district in Madhya Pradesh. A group of social activists were working with the tribals. Khemraj was the initiator. We walked miles every day, visiting villages and talking to countless tribals. All night we talked and analysed, quarrelled and argued. The local teacher who lived next door could hardly close his eyes. Fed up with the noise we created he knocked on the door at 2.30 in the morning and said, 'Can the revolution wait till the morning? I want to sleep.'

As a child, I was led to believe that wickedness would lose to good and the just would set right the world of wrong. In a child's mind, evil was lodged in one bad persona, the giant, the witch or the bad king. Adulthood brought awareness that 'evil' takes many shapes—poverty, hunger, unequal opportunities, mindless violence, torture, sadistic use of religious prejudice and cultural power. The world when seen up close, like a drop of water under the microscope, houses a million social bacteria and viruses. Social activists, social workers are seen as a species that lives on streets, creates noise and confronts the status quo, mistakenly called 'law and order', and 'disturbs the peace', but does little else! This of course is a stereotype promoted by the media that has the public imagination in its grip. I remember travelling from Rajasthan to Delhi to attend a music concert where eminent vocalists T.M. Krishna and Bombay Jayashri and danseuse Leela Samson were to perform. Delhi's south Indian elite was out in force.

I remember the then election commissioner asking me, 'What are YOU doing here?' I replied, 'When I am not in dharnas and protests, I am a music lover just like you.' Attending a music concert is neither connected with being an activist nor with being an election commissioner, so why single out the activist?

Activists see themselves as amplifiers of the voices of people and advocates of civil, democratic and human rights, and, therefore, willing to take adversarial positions against injustice in any form. They speak for some form of equality and for justice in policy and governance. They highlight instances, situations and events that lie outside the perception of popular media and of day-to-day understanding. There is a strong conviction that prompts them to act to try to set things right.

It would disquiet me as a human being if I could not speak out about whatever I think is going wrong. I may not be able to do anything about it, but I would at least need to articulate it. This is what keeps me going. I say this with a sense of humility that change cannot be brought about by one individual or even a set of individuals. But every set of individuals can contribute to make that little difference, which together with other efforts can turn many wheels, so that the larger wheel will be forced to turn.[1]

If you ask me what I am, I will say I am a socio-political activist who, along with a group of people, fights for democratic, civic and human rights for the people, in the context of the Constitution and the principles enshrined in it. Activism and activists have a background of life experiences that guide the actors to choose this method of self-expression. They also have the need to see something through, to perceive the predictability and causality of action.[2]

Their voices are largely raised to magnify the collective assertion of people who are not heard or even seen. Speaking truth to power is never easy. Power reacts to its status quo being threatened, with violence. The latest fashion of labelling activists and activism as disrupters of life has further enabled the status quo to protect itself. It is easy to construct a new vocabulary of fear and tension, to damn critique and criticism. The mention of a word or phrase—urban Naxal, anti-national, conspirator, atankwadi, Khalistani—conjures up an image of violence, ushering in fear.

Not very long ago activists were described as those who 'sacrificed', 'dedicated', words of approval that were often used to describe the sacred. The activist or social worker's conscious choice to do without creature comforts, to walk the ill-trodden path, was appreciated. But there is now a sudden shift towards apprehension and censure. This is further propelled by a morally bankrupt political system that stokes social condemnation to serve its own ends. The attack has lately taken reprehensible forms, disempowering activists who engage in public action, made them targets of persecution, incarceration and potential violence.

The critical core of public activism is to contest the gap between legal, ethical and basic human rights and the failure of the system to deliver.

Working Outside the 'System'

The tradition of non-violent protest goes back a very long way to the Buddha, Christ and even before. But in recent Indian and world history, Gandhiji's ideas of satyagraha and non-violent civil disobedience shaped people's political protest, challenging the misuse of power by the state. These methods have spread globally and, as most of us know, influenced the politics of Martin Luther King Jr and Nelson Mandela. In India this tradition continued with Jayaprakash Narayan (JP) and many others who used these methods to disempower immorality within power formations and state controls; JP's total revolution was a large movement that put ethical resistance and non-violence at the centre of its struggle.[3]

Activism is often juxtaposed against electoral politics, as the politics of conscience vs the politics of power. In the early years after Independence, young people did not see politics as a profession, and bureaucratic power became the focus of all those who saw themselves playing a role in nation-building. In the 1960s and '70s 'electoral politics' was seen as an avocation for those who could not succeed in procuring conventional jobs. This was notwithstanding a range of great political thinkers and politicians, who lent dignity and respect to political action: Gopal Krishna Gokhale, Annie Besant, Mahatma Gandhi, Rabindranath Tagore, M.N. Roy, Jawahar Lal

Nehru, S. Radhakrishnan, Sardar Patel, Maulana Azad, Aruna Asaf Ali, Sarojini Naidu, among others.

In the India of the 1960s, politics and social work were seen as professions for the failures in society. Politics and politicians were seen as 'notional' power centres, largely monitored by the civil service, except for a powerful few. 'Neta' was a word of abuse. Social work was seen as a milder subset of even that classification, mainly doing charity work or continuing with 'safe' ideas like khadi and charkha. The status of a social worker, or that of a politician, was low when I entered the civil service. Social workers were dismissed as 'time wasters', those who could not qualify to get jobs. During my years in university in the 1960s just a handful of youth were willing to consider development politics as an option. The majority felt service to the nation meant being a part of government (specially the civil service) or private employment.

When I was an SDM in Parliament Courts, Bunker was already in Rajasthan, working out a basis for integrated development with people in partnership. He came to pick me up sometimes, when he was in Delhi. The chief metropolitan magistrate, with whom I shared a retiring room, asked me what he did. When he was told Bunker was a social worker, he dismissed him with '*Kahin naukri nahin mili hogi*.' A few days later, Bunker came to pick me up in squash gear. When the same magistrate realized Bunker was the then national champion, his contempt disappeared in an instant and he fawningly asked whether he could be helped with getting membership to the Delhi Gymkhana Club!

The prestigious Tata Institute of Social Sciences was not on the popular horizon of academic alternatives in the early 1960s, and social work was not a discipline in university academia. Yet, within two decades, the social worker had graduated to become a partner in development with the growth of NGOs and non-profits, then called 'voluntary organizations'. It began to dawn on planners, policymakers and the government in general that they needed the support of these community-based organizations in mobilizing people to ensure the delivery of welfare programmes. In the seventh Five-Year Plan, through the efforts of a group of people including Bunker Roy as consultant to the Planning Commission, the government provided financial outlay for funding projects run by NGOs, and the Council for Advancement of People's Action and Rural Technology was set up as a nodal institutional centre. The institutes of social work and the need for governance and private enterprise to hire specialists thereafter promoted the status of social work.

The politician is still to gain ethical credibility and the argument about the need to see politics as an alternative profession is still a discussion in progress. The politics of conscience fills the ethical gap between professed principles of the Constitution and politics in practice. Activists fill some of these important gaps. In common parlance, they are part of a broad classification: NGOs or civil society organizations. 'NGO' is a nomenclature that blurs the basic differences in approach and strategy.

As India has 'progressed', so has the awareness of the citizenry to question and critique policy and legislative measures. The mantra of growth came in for severe criticism as it displaced people, distancing them from access to livelihood and resources. The first promise of freedom is after all the freedom from hunger and want. The larger awareness of this predicament came about due to, among other factors, the struggles of the Narmada Bachao Andolan, which took strong exception to and opposed the building of the Sardar Sarovar Dam on the river Narmada. Critiquing development policy and desiring to shape policy and development, activists began to demand equal share in making decisions.

The idea of development design espoused by Nehru—who said 'dams are the temples of modern India', while laying the foundation stone for the Bhakra Nangal Dam in Punjab—began to be questioned by a maturing understanding of both development and democracy. The role of public action in demanding accountability from the government beyond the vote gained strength. People's voices were raised against policy. It was the beginning of awareness of participatory democracy and the expression of rights by the people. Just receiving welfare was no longer enough. The movement against big dams had an impact on development policy the world over, with the setting up of the World Commission on Dams. It raised basic questions about who had the right to decide on development design and the rights of citizens impacted by displacement, which destroyed livelihood, culture and life itself in one stroke. This alienation became an issue of fundamental concern and led to the recognition of many such battles for equal development rights. From participating in the welfare programme of an existing system to demanding the right to decide development policy was a paradigm shift. It marked a watershed in the history of public action. Those who believed in the grand design of growth, i.e., the government and powerful investors of money, the World Bank, the International Monetary Fund (IMF) and private ventures, were united against allowing people to decide for themselves. The debate further defined the two categories of public action: social work and social activism. Social work filled the gaps in implementation of government welfare and development programmes, whereas social activism questioned the premise and shaping of development policy, demanding direct involvement in decision-making. The social activist also claimed to be political without party affiliations and identified with the politics of conscience, calling the process 'the non-party political process'.

Continuing Dialogue

The process of dialogue or engagement between the state and the individual is a complex one. The role of the state and the activist in India is clearly defined by the Constitution, in specific, by inference in the chapters on fundamental rights, and in the Directive Principles of State Policy. This engagement needs platforms that have been continually formed for dialogue with the state. There are different kinds of engagement today—such as Jan Sarokar, Pension Parishad, National Alliance of People's Movements (NAPM), Suchna evam Rozgar Adhikar Abhiyan, NCPRI, workers campaigns (by building and construction workers, trade unions in the unorganized sector), rights-based campaigns like Right to Food and Right to Education, Jan Swasthya Abhiyan, People's Action for Employment Guarantee, the MGNREGA, Sangharsh Morcha and so many others—all demanding involvement in the making of policy, to reclaim development, economic and political rights.

Activists are attacked because they provide a constant critique of state mismanagement. They are seen as an inconvenience as they often ask questions of ethical propriety and feasibility, disclosing information the government wants to keep under wraps. The voice of activists carries more weight for most often they are not in competition for status and are able to influence public opinion. They are concerned about the violation of the essential contract between the state and the individual. Activism could also be seen as an attempt to speak for constitutional rights against the misuse of political and executive power.

The deceit and violations of democratic rights in intent and action of the government are primary concerns of the activists. If the articulation of truth, simple facts of existential and life-threatening dilemmas of the people constitute a threat to the state, then 'telling the truth becomes a revolutionary act'. It explains the incarceration of activists, the murders of strong voices of rationality, difference and protest, such as Narendra Dabholkar, Govind Pansare, M.M. Kalburgi and Gauri Lankesh, and the annihilation of the powerless in countless numbers. The frame allows the indictment and institutional murder of Stan Swamy and the labelling of many innocent people like Sudha Bharadwaj, Anand Teltumbde, Khalid Saifi, Umar Khalid, Shoma Sen, Arun Ferreira, Vernon Gonsalves, Varavara Rao and G.N. Saibaba, among others, as anti-state terrorists.

An indifferent and uninformed people buy the propaganda of the status quoists, and even the judicial process, once an inviolable space for justice, has been compromised.

Perception of Activism: The Outsider's Point of View

The MKSS has been perceived ideologically in different ways by a variety of people, ranging from dholki-wallahs (drummers), Gandhians, reformists, communists, Friends of Bengal and Congressites (because of expressions of allegiance to constitutional values, especially of secularism and scientific temper) to even popular definitions of public action like sewa bhavi and tyagi, those who sacrifice personal comforts and ambition, etc. Activists are commonly seen as people who 'complain and don't create'. A mischievous argument is that all activism is not only adversarial but also destructive and that any opposition is 'unwholesome' and, therefore, to be viewed with hostility.

When we went to the Hyderabad Literary Festival in 2018 to release *The RTI Story*,[4] a book detailing the MKSS's role in fashioning the right to information, an irate petty businessman from Rajasthan came up and said to me, 'You are always against something. Why don't you do something creative?' In response, I asked whether he had done anything to creatively tackle the issues of constructive work in India. He was silent. I told him that the RTI benefitted 60 lakh to 80 lakh users annually, and the MGNREGA fed 20 crore households a year. What would he define that as? He skulked away.

The activist both articulates and questions. The activist's articulation is a threat to the corrupt, and when amplified, is seen as a crisis by those who are privileged. The reaction is very often an act of violence against these individuals who dare to think differently, honestly state what they think and stay true to the path they have chosen. A combination of Ambedkar's strong positions on equality and caste and Nehru's views on placing scientific temper in the discourse made the socially and economically privileged very uneasy and resentful. When such people are deliberately projected by governments as being anti-state, vested interest jumps in to exploit the situation.

The disquiet and apprehension of those in influential positions comes largely from the *fear of losing power* and being questioned. The privileged cannot, even in principle, accept any change that demands equality with equanimity. The status quo carries with it the comfort of continuation of 'normalcy'. It is impossible to disturb the sense of comfort of those who enjoy benefits of that power without arousing fears of loss of various kinds. It makes politics link this fear with dispossession, to construct myths that effectively destroy the credibility of activists. The ultimate aim is for the affluent and the power elite to enjoy unquestioned power in collusion.

Campaigns and movements have been powerful in achieving their ends, but have not reformed traditional prejudices upheld by the conditioning of caste, rituals and religious taboos that have persisted for centuries. They are very difficult to dismantle but easy to manipulate to instigate a violent agenda. Any opposition to rituals or irrational categories of classification of caste evokes extreme reactions. It is at such moments that we need a strong state to back the Constitution. However, governments in power at the Centre and in the states are reluctant as they are electorally dependent on identity vote banks and calculations. But in provoking violence and hatred, the 'Lakshmanrekha' (crossing the Rubicon) of ethics has been breached.

Those whose self-interest and power is challenged by activism have reacted by trying to build a discourse using pejorative branding and labels. 'Urban Naxal', the latest, claims that socially motivated literate amplifiers of protest are anti-national. 'Naxal' is a word that originated from the tea-garden labour uprising in Naxalbari in 1967 and has become synonymous with violent, left-wing struggle against the state. The propaganda machine of the right-wing has used branding, a marketing technique, to create fear by evoking the loaded apprehension behind the word 'Naxal'. 'Urban Naxal' is a new brand, as until a few years ago Naxal activity was confined largely to the rural/tribal belts. The term 'urban Naxal' was coined to increase fear and gain popular support to justify illegitimate suppression of dissent by non-violent fearless individuals with independent minds. The state now silences its own people, contravening the basic right to freedom of expression.

Privileged India is wary of the other India of poverty and marginalization, wary of a serious argument that may prove them wrong. Activists are at best seen as necessary but unsettling. They are to be kept away from sons and daughters of privileged homes, for fear that their idealism may make them abandon the market fantasy.

I occupied a weird space between welcome and wariness in the 1990s, when the children of my urban middle-class friends were growing up. They were worried my preoccupations and concerns might influence their children's choice of profession. Friends were anxious when their children visited us to get 'the experience' of rural India. There is a famous Hindi saying, '*Bhagat Singh janme, magar padosi ke ghar.*' (May a Bhagat Singh be born, but to a neighbour.) In other words we all admire revolutionaries, but from a safe distance.

Strangely the urban privileged get angrier over being stuck at a roadblock for half an hour than over a budget cut or the passage of laws. Inconvenience and discomfort are greater forces driving positions of moral disagreement and disengagement than the corrosion of justice and democratic politics. The politics of comfort and convenience wins over rights.

People come together only when their personal links with the political. We saw this in the campaign for the RTI, which stitched us together in a common demand. We are divided by sub-cultural identities. Each part is socially held together by common prejudices, faith or identity. Activism works at many points to unify people across sub-cultural identities. Common concerns pushed back parochialism, for example, when 2 million signatures on all kinds of cloth—old saris, dhotis, sacks that when laid end to end stretched across 2 kilometres—were sent to Delhi to flutter on the trees in Parliament Street in 2004 to demand that the MGNREGA be passed.

The RTI dharna at Chang Gate in Beawar in 1996 attracted people from all walks of life. They came from different professions—workers, doctors, lawyers, students, tradespeople, poets, trade unionists and so many others—to participate in a moral battle to cleanse public life. This dharna raised many possibilities of united public action. It was a platform that kindled hope of building a more ethical nation, and gave people the space to 'do good'. It even drew members of political parties who protested political corruption!

When I came to Rajasthan, I used to receive thanks from people who actually gave their time and energy to either me specifically or a collective cause. They used to say, '*Sewa karne ka mauka diya, uske liye dhanyavaad.*' (Thank you for providing us the opportunity to serve.) I was a bit perplexed by the sentiment behind this statement. I discussed it with my mother and she explained that there is an old Indian concept of 'kritagyata', the expression of thanks for providing one the opportunity to be of service. She was not surprised by this sentiment.

The RTI and MGNREGA campaigns created many such platforms for expression of concern about public ethics, to demand justice. The Jansunwai, for instance, is a continual process of disclosure and verification by people, and empowers citizen monitoring. As 'social audit', it is now a mandated part of the MGNREGA and governance systems for accountability, in India and the world. The millennials who are unfamiliar with the history and use of these tools for protecting their rights and ethics in public life need to acquaint themselves with them. These are citizens' democratic tools for ensuring rights.

The Jansunwai was designed during the right-to-information struggle by the MKSS. Faced with lies and prevarications, authenticated information had to be placed before the people for verification and arriving at the truth. Public questioning has power, but it needs a collective platform with rules, and has to be supported by enabling legal tools and structures. The power of the Jansunwai lies in this rigorous process.

In the first Jansunwai organized by the MKSS in December 1994 in Kot Kirana, the entire power nexus united to stall the sunwai. Information was collected from the BDO office and verified, but those who came to testify were threatened. Those who resisted were supplied with liquor to inebriate them. The 1,500 people assembled were witness to the fact that a half-finished building had been falsely certified as completed, and heard the names of dead people being read out from a muster roll. They were furious. The collective fury of being cheated made news, and the information spread quickly. Election campaigners were prevented from entering villages; they had to either promise the right to information or were sent away.

The Government of Rajasthan, adopted the process of the Jansunwai, and it became known as a social audit. The 'social audit' got further public sanction when the then comptroller and auditor general (CAG) of India saw its power to empower citizen monitoring. At a meeting held in the National Academy of Audit and Accounts in Shimla, CAG Kaul commented on social audit and the RTI, saying, 'This is an opportunity for every citizen to become an auditor,' and held that the CAG's role was strengthened by this process. Participation facilitates the process of an individual demanding accountability and making it obligatory for the state to comply to the demand. The success of the RTI lies in it being able to create the space and a method to allow people to be part-time activists, thus ensuring that the process of governance does not claim impunity from the laws of the land and constitutional normative values.

Single-issue-based agitations, even the successful ones, leave a question to be answered, about larger democratic perceptions and participation. A strident trade-unionist talks against the equality of religions, for instance. A woman's rights activist can also be a believer in caste. It is when these contradictions surface that activism has to face challenges about larger democratic political education. After years of discussion, we set about establishing the School for Democracy as a space to 'reflect'. Interestingly, it has drawn social activists, social workers, academics, civil servants, professional groups and a range of people across the board who are interested in ethical governance. There is both structured and informal space to learn, unlearn, share, discuss and debate about the future of constitutional values in practice.

Political education, much like literacy, is a generational issue. It needs to be repeated over and over to every new generation to make democratic institutions and processes work. It is unfortunate that formal schooling leaves huge gaps in curricula, where the basic structure of governance remains a mystery. The decade from 2005, beginning with the passage of the rights-based laws (like the RTI, NFSA, MGNREGA, RTE, etc.), was a period of positive achievement for activism. The government created space for engagement with critique. It seemed as though Indian democracy was maturing to make space for accountability as part of its formal structure.

Participation monitors economic and political equality and gives a foothold in the business of shaping socio-economic policy. However, those who lost the privilege of impunity opposed sharing power and democratic processes. The corrupt found newer ways of scuttling scrutiny and accountability. Participatory rights for engaging in pre-legislative consultancy processes were set aside, for instance, when the farming laws were passed through ordinance.

7

The Complexities of Activism

STRUGGLING TOGETHER FOR a common cause bonds us. Take the independence struggle for instance, which brought people together across political ideology and eventually got them to largely agree on a constitutional frame. Being part of a collective struggle is remembered for the strength it leaves as legacy. The privations of hunger strikes, lack of sleep on a continuing basis, sleeping on the road during dharnas and eating any available food, no access to toilets and the ensuing impact on digestive processes—the memories of all of these miseries fade away.

People wonder how we sustain hope. Cynicism is often an excuse for inaction and comfort. If a poor woman with all the odds stacked against her can hope, on what grounds of logic do I place my middle-class despair? Being hopeless is an indulgence the poor can ill-afford. For those of us who live on the edge of survival, the appeasement of hunger and getting work seem enough to carry on. This does not take away from the fact that we have to continue to struggle for guaranteed livelihood and long-term survival with dignity. The tenacity of the struggle and the dreams for its achievement can lead to success, as it did with the MGNREGA.

The lifestyle issue was an important one for the older activists and a culture of living styles was built around the notion of 'sadgi', or simplicity. In the activist lexicon it was a tool for measuring one's own place in the struggle for inequality. This was no celebration of poverty, but ostentation was perceived as politically and culturally vulgar given the stark contrast in lifestyle and access to basic needs.

This political or, if you like, moral position underwrote our life in Devdungri without special privileges such as a toilet in the initial years, cooking gas, electricity and privacy. Unlike the rural activist, the urban activist separates home and the workplace and some aspects of privilege continue. In rural India, even though things have changed for the better, it is very much more difficult not to match means and ends.

Challenges that Activists Face

Infirmity and old age have been addressed in political battles for old-age pensions and benefits for the ill, widows and orphaned children. However, the middle-class activist is often left without security of benefits or income. Financial support may or may not come from friends and well-wishers. Many work till they can, changing to softer aspects of public intervention—writing, training, conducting studies and so on. There is also a constriction to conform to stereotypical expectations. There are those who idealize the activist and are appalled that they should ever tire! I remember a friendly reporter telling me that politicians never tire and they keep such odd hours, implying that we should not tire either. I remember muttering that politicians do not camp on the road or wait on the whims and fancies of others, but command!

Exhaustion has to be dealt with over years of work. As I went along from day-to-day, the need for more time to think and reflect became urgent. My insistence very often to stop and think led me to evolve a space for sharing the learnings of many activists and to fill in the gaps—the School for Democracy. Since 2013–14, the School for Democracy has created space for the action-oriented to think, debate and plan.

The psychology of continual struggle, the inconvenience and erratic hours of living push many of us into spaces of either illness or withdrawal. We were once in Jantar Mantar for hours on end and the elderly were packed elbow-to-elbow in hundreds. Apart from the langar (a meal served free to all who visit) in the gurudwara and the occasional chai, there was no food. I recall a woman sat patiently, clutching her tattered pouch, her fragile frame wedged into a tiny space. There were kiosks that sold food, but she could not afford even a cup of tea. Long hours of starvation are part of sit-ins and rallies. Crouching and adjusting to small sitting space is a physical manifestation of poverty and marginalization.

It is seldom realized that access to space is privilege. There is anger with a democratic system that provides neither space for public action nor access to utilities where activists are gathered to protest. Activists face a running battle with the municipality for the provision of mobile toilets, tankers of drinking water and the permission to pitch tents wherever they have gathered to protest. When I was an SDM in 1972–73, protests usually took place on the roads and lawns around Delhi's India Gate. This went on till the protestors were pushed into the premises that housed the Jantar Mantar, located beside a small winding road close to Parliament. The Modi government, on the pretext of environmental violations, banned protests at Jantar Mantar. Ultimately, the MKSS filed a writ in the Supreme Court to get the space back, with limitations of time and restrictions.

'Am I right?' is another sword that hangs over the head of a conscientious activist wrapped in endless action. There is the fear that often arises from refining too much on moral choices, of becoming enmeshed in circular arguments, indulging in Hamletian procrastination. Such discussions need to be taken to the collective to contest cynicism and inaction.

While the collective is important, it has to make space for both individual expression, difference and dissent. Discussions of political correctness tend to gloss over basic cultural perceptions and differences. The urban-born activist comes from a background where work and home are clearly defined and boxed. Political commitment does not mix with the personal and the domestic. In rural India, the concerns overlap, and lines are not easy to draw. Most often sensitive issues arise out of different ways of understanding gender, caste and religion. Dissent is sometimes expressed through 'irrelevant' emotions—anger, tears and angst. Exigencies of immediate action push sentiment and feelings away. We engage partially and turn a blind eye to the person. It is no surprise then that a friend with whom we fought a battle for rights suddenly sees release from misery only through identity politics and religious affiliation. For a collective to remain healthy, individual angst must be dealt with. Dealing with reactions may consume time, but they are an investment in solidarity and evolving an ideological constitutional commitment to equality, liberty and fraternity.

Women activists face gender inequality and patriarchy in many forms. This has particular reference to the ingrained social conditioning of masculinity, so fine-tuned and internalized that it needs a sensitive and reflective persistence to unpack. Unpacking masculinity, therefore, becomes a part of many important debates.

Vulnerability is considered a weakness and is not recognized by the average male. For most men introspection and self-assessment are not important and they do not accept weaknesses. Masculinity and vulnerabilities are now being discussed increasingly in activist meetings than elsewhere, but still leaves even a 'powerful' woman like me at the edges, struggling to make colleagues give space for emotional expression.

Friction stemming from internalized masculinity is dismissive of anything that doesn't fit into preconceived boxes. There is also the battle of agenda vs process. Male activists tend to be agenda-driven, whereas women activists are keener on processes and in looking at pluralities. It could even be said that male arguments tend to be linear, whereas female expression tends to be lateral and cyclical.

Sometimes the desire to be politically correct may overwhelmingly tilt an argument in favour of a process that may not reflect the situation on ground. This is particularly true when there is conflict between empowerment as an ideal and the reality on ground. Two areas of social interaction—caste and gender—require careful handling. Faith and belief in traditional values is deeply entrenched, and has its own architecture. It is very complex and the emotional response is also a political statement. The activists and change agents mistakenly believed that uniting the community on concerns of the poor, for example on 'work and wages', could build a strong enough understanding to oppose caste inequality. But it does not. We have not developed a discourse to deal with its presence in the communities we work for. Caste is often 'social security', despite its oppression and discomforts. Religion and social custom are the most difficult to challenge. My greatest friends in rural India agree to disagree when we discuss inter-caste marriages or even the freedom of women to choose a husband. I am happy to see that there is a generational difference now, and young women show acceptance of these changes; however, they do not have the courage to put it into practice.

Reflections

Reflection has not been a priority for activists. However, the quick changes brought in by technology and changes in laws and the attacks on the Constitution have made activists realize that there is more to public action than struggling against specific forms of injustice. The NAPM, which is one of the oldest people's political campaigns, has brought movements together. There are platforms for Dalits and for women, such as the National Federation of Indian Women, the National Campaign on Dalit Human Rights, the All India Democratic Women's Association, the National Commission for Minorities, the All India Dalit Mahila Adhikar Manch and many others. The MKSS, for instance, has formed specific campaigns for specific issues.

In moments of extreme distress, of life and death, sickness and betrayal, people take solace in faith. When a statue of the god Ganesh allegedly started 'drinking' milk, thousands flocked to see the 'miracle'. Activism, on the other hand, takes on unpopular positions, such as critiquing blind faith and absolute irrationality. Activism must be careful not to present a grim future and an unhappy face continuously. A well-known writer once said that it was hardly surprising that massive numbers flocked to hear 'god-men' who promise instant paradise, with flowers and music, while a comparatively smaller number went to a neighbouring pandal, to discuss the grimness of poverty, discrimination and oppression, which demanded long-term commitment without guarantees. One of the reasons for the success of the MKSS has been the genius of Shankar, his gift for theatre, lampooning and song. The lilting lyrics and truth laced with humour and satire never failed to swell the crowd. The use of song, theatre and sometimes the joy of a beat can make all the difference to people's energies in sustaining what is a back-breaking effort with little guarantee of success. Protests call for the best in creativity, to use simple language and metaphor to convey important messages.

For protestors, sometimes the weight of conscience and an increasingly callous system can become unbearable. The voice of someone, a politician or a guru, who says 'leave it to me, just pay me homage and I promise happiness', becomes a moment of release from the constant vigilance that moral public action requires. Perhaps this explains the rise of gurus and the parallel rise of mega politicians who claim the divine right to rule, who claim theirs is the only right vision and opposition is not to be countenanced.

Living a Life without Borders

We often speak in and of absolutes but live in areas of grey. Formal positions are careful to be politically correct or wary of stepping on people's sensitivities. Caste, religion, comfort of belonging, the exhaustion of continual contestation and identity are to be found in the cracks between polarities. In Devdungri these occupied the space between kneading the dough, rolling the rotis, peeling onions (and of course garlic) and lighting the wood fire that was always resistant to kindling quickly. Most of the debates that led to understanding of political complexities took place while cooking in Devdungri. Informal conversations allowed us to face reality. If the walls of the Devdungri kitchen could speak, we would have a great narrative. It would also be an editor's nightmare as profound thoughts would be interspersed with requests to pass the salt!

The first constriction of protest begins with the denial of space. Almost all power structures are worried when people gather anywhere, but particularly in front of their offices. For the protestors, it is the most appropriate space for democratic protest. The government office represents both the promise and its denial. Protestors chanting the slogan '*Yeh* office *kika hai? Hamara hai, hamara hai!*' (Whose office is this? It is ours, ours!) never fails to irritate and even frighten those inside.

The activist is permanently on call for issues that threaten the life and liberty of individuals. The recent spontaneous support to a call for medical help and supplying food during the 2020 riots in north-east Delhi, and the provision of food, shelter and safe passage for migrants during the Covid-19 pandemic, was philanthropy. Political malevolence has deliberately misrepresented humanitarian action (delivering food and medicines) by calling it terrorist or anti-national activity. The rule of law and justice have been derailed. People at large have kept quiet and watched from the sidelines.

Activists nevertheless continue to respond to calls for help. But there are moments of indecision arising from a variety of complexities. The personal tentativeness and anxieties about the consequences have to be quietened for action. Where two rights clash for precedence, the female activist is sometimes caught in a dilemma: Am I a woman first or a worker? There is a need for continual political analysis at all levels. The personal and political come together in dealing with these issues. However, the personal must find the vocabulary to make itself comprehensible, and the political has to allow its boundaries to be smudged. Women have forced public action to examine issues that were shelved. As one sees the best and worst of fellow human beings, questions multiply and remain. The struggle for fundamental changes in politics, society and human behaviour may wound one's reason but the battle continues. The woman activist has a triple burden, children and parents, home management and political confrontation. Often in these dilemmas the activist is compelled to determine what is more critical.

In 2005 when I was to travel to Mumbai to address a press conference on corruption in defence of an honest collector, my mother lay very ill back home. I left Rajasthan with great trepidation and conflict. I had barely arrived at Mumbai Central station when I got a call from home to return quickly as she was sliding and continually asking for me. There was conflict between my love for my mother, her mortality and my political obligations. The arguments continued as I talked this over with friends and colleagues. Would I let down the cause if I went back? Could I forgive myself if I were not at my mother's bedside when she breathed her last? My few quiet moments helped me make my choice. I left to be with my mother and reached in time. What happens in the public domain is constantly monitored by a collective and one can personally afford to be somewhat less vigilant. In the personal sphere, however, quarrels are far more subtle and there is the problem of having to continually prioritize between two disparate and equally important demands.

Adversarial positions and confrontations in the public domain need tact and strategy. The energy of social anger is the basis for public action and pushes us over that last mile to confront and overcome fear and the consequences of speaking out. For some of us who confront inequality instinctively, social anger becomes a part of our DNA. Social anger and ire against institutions have logic on their side, and occasionally activists may carry that anger home and become argumentative and insensitive at home or with friends. The activist has to remember that personal anger and angst can destroy public action, that the battle espouses the value of compassion. In fact, prolonged battles against criminal violence can create a desire for revenge. As an activist, one needs constant vigilance to keep the demand for justice untainted by any need for revenge. Sadly, compassion is often confused with weakness and justice with indifference.

Experience of the MKSS

Leaders, or, in modern jargon, 'change makers', 'icons', are not born with special gifts. They are created in contemporary public space by the clever manipulation of the media. A senior journalist frankly commented in a workshop in Jaipur that it was the celebrity that the media was concerned with. There are, ironically enough, 'poverty' celebrities! The people's leader is one among equals, someone who is open, transparent, collective and accountable. Genuine participatory leadership is collective and transient by nature. It gives a sense of comfort in sharing responsibilities and critical decision-making. It also ensures that every issue is examined from multiple perspectives so that the chances of being incorrect are minimized. The MKSS has internalized these concepts and lives in comparative harmony without the infamous 'leadership struggles' that have brought down greater structures.

The great unsung heroes of history, the person who created the wheel, the concept of cooked food, the discovery of salt, of the first boat that sailed—all these have passed into oblivion. In a world view built on competition and profit, we acclaim the small changes wrought by individuals and groups. The givers of awards look for a single profile, much more marketable than a collective; the end of the arc is to create a celebrity. The Magsaysay Award committee and the middle class singled out Aruna Roy and Nikhil Dey, joined by a host of others from the English-speaking middle class who had worked with the MKSS. The trauma of the first award to the MKSS would be almost comical if it had not been the worst of dilemmas. There was a feeling of guilt and awkwardness in being awarded, with the appalling thought that inequality would come in through the backdoor of public attention. The pressure from the campaign at that time was to set aside these 'minor' scruples and do the interview, give the byte or write the piece. But it accumulated to create the image of a single leader.

The tears and hand-wringing that followed are still remembered by friends as a moment of pathos and irony. Group discussions and collective decisions followed and the MKSS drew its fences by stating that awards should be given to the collective. The immediate counterargument was: Which collective? The MKSS has been the receiver of many awards, but none have traversed a course of comfort. The one exception we really cherish was given by the citizens of Bhim in 2010 at Dussehra. They honoured the collective, the MKSS, for elevating their small part of central Rajasthan to the height of a benefactor to the nation, through the RTI and the MGNREGA. All of us were asked to the ceremony and a 50-foot-long garland was put over the shoulders of all members of the MKSS—Dalits, workers, women and men. It still retains the highest position in my hierarchy of extraordinary moments.

I heard Eduardo Galeano in Barcelona in 2002. He spoke in Spanish, which I do not understand, yet what he said resonated with what we were saying miles away in rural India. Even in translation, he was superb. Expanding on the misconceptions and distortions in our understanding of leadership, he went on to critique the way we first build up two-dimensional leaders, convert them into icons, and when they display clay feet, damn the concept as we bemoan the loss of yet another idol. He said, 'Have you looked at the skies and seen a flock of ducks flying in an arrow formation? If you keep looking, the "super" duck leading the flock, no different from the other "sub" ducks, tires and comes to the end, and a sub duck takes its place, naturally and gracefully.' That fable should serve as a reminder to us that democracy is really a paradigm of changing leadership that is accountable to a collective. The leader is one among equals.

The MKSS is based on equality among its members. The spokesperson keeps shifting, as responsibilities keep changing. The normal struggle for leadership is reversed; we vie with each other to take the back seat. The dialectic between the individual and the collective, between the political necessity and the need for personal and the private, is a constant. There is need too for discipline and freedom. Shankar, Nikhil and I, along with the others, have been friends and colleagues for over thirty years and have shared arguments, disagreements and responsibilities, emerging stronger at the end of each confrontation.

The MKSS effort began with the belief that people can become powerful and control their own destiny. It was based on a recognition that people have potential power in a democracy and the creative use of it can liberate them from oppression and inequality. During the initial years of the RTI struggle, we went to many districts to stage dharnas to popularize the idea and to invite participation. In Bikaner, a man looked contemptuously at our unkempt bunch and demanded, 'Who is the leader?' Laxman from Nilwa, a small person just 5'3" tall, stepped out and said 'I am.' The man replied, 'You are just a bunch of tatpunjas [nincompoops]. Nothing will come of your struggle.'

When we won the first round to get then Rajasthan Chief Minister Bhairon Singh Shekhawat to allow us to see records, we went to a huge crowd gathered in Badi Chaupar in Jaipur and declared that the 'tatpunjas' had won their battle against the might of the state. The RTI campaign provided us with a tool to creatively build this concept—the leader is one among equals—in practice.

8

Mazdoor Kisan Shakti Sangathan: The Early Years

DEVDUNGRI'S LIFESTYLE AND politics brought peace, beauty and harmony for me personally. Actually, Chunni Singh's '*kathni aur karni*' (word and deed; the harmony of thought and action) was life in Devdungri. There was no contradiction between thought as a principle, as a living style and as public action. I have always envied people who are able to live their values, and I will cherish those twenty years in Devdungri when work and life were in harmony and I was at peace with my conscience.

Feminist work had prepared me and given me tools to both understand and deal with the fallout of debates, dissent and emotional reactions. These differences need to be addressed and resolved if possible to keep collectivism alive. Chunni Singh and I have had furious debates but we remain the fondest of friends. We have stood together at the most critical and potentially violent times and derived strength from each other's presence. This is not a singular story; the MKSS history has many examples.

Many of us who are old-fashioned feminists know that we act from the sum of ourselves. This is so important for public action to succeed. There is a consciousness of the relationship that exists between the principles we believe in and the way we act, between thought, feeling and action. The disconnect between means and ends leads to disvaluing the principles and objects of our work. When this happens, struggles are bound to end in failures and disasters.

Perhaps my first conscious teacher in political activism was Naurti. Ours is a forty-year friendship nurtured by shared perception and values. Neither of us could stand by and witness injustice. It has been a political journey for two women from different backgrounds and very different cultural bases, bonded by a search for equality and justice and the compulsion to engage for justice in the public domain. We shared angst and anger and a recklessness for our safety and peace. But Naurti and I have also another trajectory, in which we have quarrelled because of differences in priorities and choices. We have critiqued each other, but are happy that to both of us it's the work that matters. We are friends and comrades. We were both bothered and grew out of a struggle for minimum wages in 1981 for many others. As a Dalit, work for her meant livelihood and life. For me it was the hinge on which the dignity of the economically vulnerable was tethered. We struggled together for the RTI and MGNREGA and against caste- and gender-based atrocities.

My years in Devdungri were the most intensely happy period of my life—where we cooked, ate and worked and lived our principles as a community. This was contrary to the popular perception that it was a period of want, of sacrifice. We learnt the line dividing formal exchange of ideas and informal talk was very thin. The most jealously guarded personal thoughts and attitudes were generously shared. Our political discourse was a normal conversation, peppered with a few difficult concepts and differences that needed explanation and debate.

What began as a loose group of committed individuals coming together to debate, discuss, mix, match and act has grown into the MKSS. The Sangathan also has its share of powerful personalities. We have grown together as a group, forced by collective discussion and decision-making to learn from many at the same time. There are the contrasting characters of Lal Singh and Chunni Singh; the remarkable clear-sightedness of young Narayan; the unquestioned determination and commitment of Mohanji, who lived a life of deprivation and whose simple, powerful lyrics unleashed the power of action. There was Dow Singhji's goodness of heart and his concern for all life. Some who have gone, like Bhuriya, Kakima and Tej Singhji, who encouraged and stood solidly with an ethical struggle, lending dignity and huge community support. Still others who lived lonely lives of struggle who joined us. Sushila and Hans Swaroop, who have questioned norms of caste even in marriage ... The list goes on. We have all inspired, taught, advised, angered, frustrated, cajoled, pushed, comforted, supported each other. Each one has been a guru. But the success in campaigning and work came from a blend of self-worth and dignity in a collective. Over thirty years down the line we can begin to talk in detail about some of our fellow travellers on this remarkable journey.

Our Collective in Sohangarh

There was great scepticism about the history and privilege of two of our little group (of four)—Nikhil and me; air marshals' sons did not look unkempt and IAS officers did not sleep on mud floors. There was a sense of equality in daily intercourse with a number of frontal attacks on what were perceived as upsetting hierarchies of class, caste and gender. Often these furious debates ended with recourse to law and the rule book. Potential violence was stayed, but the rumblings continued.

Shankar's family, especially his wife, Anshi, on the whole, dealt admirably with the huge differences that came with Nikhil's presence and mine. Our families became friendly and intimate. Issues, when they arose, were dealt with one at a time. Schooling for the girls, where and how, and education in general were received well in the traditional family. Inter-community marriages were not acceptable, but untouchability was non-existent and the value of living equality fully accepted.

Activism depends heavily on the ability to work with a community, but also with peers. The proximity of living conditions—activists tend to share homes and the workplace—also places a huge burden on everyone. Very often subtle boundaries are crossed and tensions need to be addressed. As the three of us (Shankar, Nikhil and I) continued to grow in affection and understanding, we also developed the ability to address irritation, friction and conflict. The tensions from work and nuanced differences in strategies and approach also took their toll. Actually, in choosing to work with each other, compatibility was as important as was the freedom to quarrel, the confidence to settle our differences. The fact that I was a woman and that Anshi, Shankar's wife, stayed with us, made a difference to the collective conversations and perception.

In our growing acquaintance with Sohangarh, Tej Singhji and Lal Singh also played important roles. They were our equals in understanding and courage and shared our ethics. As with Chunni Singh and so many others earlier, the friendship was established on shared values and later evolved into working relationships. Tej Singhji could have been a teacher on ethics and action anywhere. He was a fearless man and confronted cheating, thieving and even feudal authority to demand justice for oppressed people. He spoke excellent English with a rural accent and thought like a leader. Lal Singh, who was willing to sacrifice his job as a constable by joining a protest against the misuse and oppression of the lower constabulary, was also an equal. He was accepted as leader by the village, and all knotty problems came to him to be solved. He was laid-back and patient.

Two later entrants, no less in importance, were Bhuriya and Kakima, mother and aunt to Lal Singh. They were remarkable women and strong in their commitment to oust the Thakur's authority.[1] Without them the other women in the area could not have been mobilized. Kakima had her initial grounding in Sabarmati with Gandhiji. Her ethics were learnt in Sabarmati and could not be faulted. She was literate, unusual for a woman in her generation. The nucleus of ethical persons drew many more to join the group.

In a sense, Sohangarh naturalized me as a local Rajasthani. It began with cultural acceptance, much more than I had ever felt before. I became a member of that community in much the same sense as an aunt is, and I was called 'Buaji' by the children. Their final acceptance came through their reference to Bunker as 'Bunker Singh', drawing him into their caste! The community formed a women's self-help group, the Sohangarh Mahila Van Vikas Samiti (Women's Forest Development Committee). This ensured that the Rajput Thakur and his men could not seek membership, and as the Rajput women from the Thakur's family observed purdah, they would not become members.

Redefining Power

My move to Devdungri worried some of my friends. One of them, a senior activist, thought I was diminishing myself by withdrawing into a mud hut. Another gave me a book to read about a king who gives up the kingdom he sees as power, and systematically lives with less, till he lands up as an ostler in his own stable; yet his existential question remains unanswered. Perhaps in the scale of diminishing comforts there was important political education, and answers to some bigger questions.

I was not running away from power, though it must have appeared so. I was only redefining it. The second friend was perhaps philosophically correct. Because the small and the big correlate in every way. There is a universal context—the whole is in the part and the part is in the whole.

For me, Blake's sublime poetry came alive in Devdungri and its minimalist lifestyle.

> To see a World in a Grain of Sand
> And a Heaven in a Wild Flower
> Hold Infinity in the palm of your hand
> And Eternity in an hour[2]

The journey to Devdungri was like studying the microcosm in a laboratory—observing the details of socio-political interaction and understanding why things happened in a certain way. Great political downfalls have occurred not only because ideologies are defective but also because of the misuse of unquestioned power and impunity. The slogan of the MKSS is: '*Nyay samanta bandhutva ho adhaar, aise rachenge hum sansaar.*' (We will create a world based on justice and equality.)

People's organizations in general, and the MKSS in particular, have been labelled in diverse ways. Among them, the non-party people's organizations, the broad left, people's democratic movements describe political presence outside the frame of representative politics. The bulk of the people who vote are not members of any political party. They select a candidate without understanding the role of the representative or the benefits they can get from the formal constitutional obligation. Governance is a mystery. Ordinary people vote for the candidate who offers them and their identity the best bargain. They do not vote on party lines, except in some of the states in the east and southern India. The current transference of religious veneration to the political frameworks is worrying. The usual voter selects a representative on the basis of identity for small immediate benefits. The mood is to surrender to a human being to take care of everything, such as the Indian Prime Minister, who is expected to remove all obstacles. The social contract of the vote is replaced by 'faith'. Like our relationship with God, the occasional ritual of offerings—in this case our vote—is expected to deliver us all from evil.

Political discourse has become very obtuse and very often incomprehensible. There are many chasms in understanding. Though everyone mouths the same jargon and slogan, the expectations are oceans apart. The political aspirant misleads people, and the committed activist often speaks a language that demands continual unpacking. The vulnerable vote for roti, kapda, makaan, swasth and shiksha (food, clothing, housing, health and education). The government they know is encapsulated in the smallest cog of the machinery of governance—a sarpanch, a police constable, the village caste panchayats and so on. While they are aware of corruption and the misuse of power, they are unable to make the system work for them. The state assembly and Parliament are too far away to comprehend or matter. This is the space occupied by the god-men and the prophets of a good life, and a baffled people surrender to those who know better.

Activism is political and public education about the mysteries of power in operation. It acts as an ethical conscience to keep society and politics within a transparent and accountable framework. An activist monitors deviation and is a keeper of the collective conscience. It is, therefore, imperative that activists make sure that they live their principles and ensure that their conscience is clear of moral compromise. In doing so they have to ensure that they do not become vigilantes or self-righteous prigs. Nor must they indulge in the luxury of complacence; continual self-examination is critical. Activists are under the critical lens of public opinion, unprotected by formal procedures and structures. Survival needs strength and determination. The activist has to live with hope, in the continual search for justice. If hope cannot be perceived in the larger paradigm of governance and the criminal justice system, it has to be learnt from the people who continue to live on the margins. They continue to sing, love, dance and even be happy. In the face of such expression, most of us cannot and should not lose hope. Unlike the cynics and the privileged who can afford to do so, the vulnerable cannot—and those of us who feel for them and think with them can ill-afford to do so either.

It is also important to remember that protest alone does not define activism; what we protest for or against defines our ethics as well. There is, however, a disclaimer. In contemporary India (in the last four decades: the 1980s to the 2020s), there has been a growing body of protesters and actors who do not believe in constitutional values but in instigating religious intolerance and transferring that to violence and inequality, and who have no qualms about immorality and lack of ethics. They are better defined as a political wing of extreme religious politics that either has co-opted the methods and idiom of civil disobedience, satyagraha and non-violent ethical protest into its jargon, or uses arbitrary and ruthless violence to achieve its goals. They attempt to kill not only people but also the ability to dream. Ceasing to dream will be the ultimate defeat. Hope must guide the possibilities of a better world. As Martin Luther King Jr said: 'We must accept finite disappointment, but never lose infinite hope.'

9

(In) Spite of It All: Parochialism, Identity, Religion and Politics

Asato ma sat gamaya
Tamaso ma jyotirgamaya
Mrityor ma amritamgamaya

[From ignorance lead me to truth/From darkness lead me to light/From death lead me to immortality]

—*Brihadaranayaka* Upanishad (1.3.28)

I WAS ALMOST a midnight's child, born just a year before Independence, post the Second World War and Hitler. With my consciousness of the external world came the partition of India and Pakistan, the smell of death, inhumanity and the pressure to make sense of the fears and gloom of the adult world. Emotions were transferred to me through the tears of the neighbour and the tension of a loving parent. Once, I heard the heartrending shrieks of a man and my mother bundled me up and took me in. Enfolded in her embrace, I saw a Rampuri cap over her shoulder. I still cannot forget the neighing of the horse hitched to the tonga or the smell of burning. Two years later, at Bombay Central, getting off a train with my mother, I saw another Rampuri cap and cried and called to the man to run away from people who would harm him. I was inconsolable. My mother and her brother took me to the man to reassure me that he would be well. The elderly gentleman held me and said, 'Beta, I will be all right.' That visceral reaction to communal violence, emotion and concern have stayed with me all my life.

Living in Delhi with a politically aware and vocal set of adults, even children picked up the 'mood'. Perhaps I was precocious emotionally, perhaps not, but I still bear the scars of Partition—the brutality of killings, hatred, anguish, my father's fearless forays and his confrontation of the Hindu mobs, my mother's anxieties. These were household stories. When I was three, I saw pictures of the Holocaust. The two horrors were born of genocidal politics and partly destroyed my early years of peace, innocence and trust.

Independent India's leadership gave us the Constitution, a secular republic with an implicit promise to ourselves to never let it happen again. Why have we lost our bearings incrementally in the last decades? Can a country born of strife promote it all over again? Why have we forgotten the wise sayings of our greatest minds? We draw narrower and narrower boundaries, fencing ourselves into enclaves, fragmenting ourselves. Tagore's oft-quoted lines from the *Gitanjali* should have been the guiding text:

> Where the mind is without fear and the head is held high
> Where knowledge is free
> Where the world has not been broken up into fragments
> By narrow domestic walls—

A century ago a great poet understood the challenges of a free India fractured by social divisions and the curse of untouchability.

The conditioning of caste and the scars left by poverty and religious strife remain areas of dispute. I was fortunate to be born to progressive parents. My family had a history of addressing social divisions in simple everyday matters. My maternal grandfather was a district engineer in the early 1900s. Social life with the bureaucratic elite was restricted to English-speaking couples. Sometimes the elite dined together. My grandmother, who did her Senior Cambridge, and was comfortable with English, was modern enough to accompany her husband to these formal dinners. She ate with Christians and Muslims. Whenever she could she took her children along, and they learnt to accept plurality with the simple acceptance of sharing food. They were told that 'refusing food offered is not only bad manners, but ingratitude'. The tradition continued with her children and grandchildren.

My grandmother wore her nine-yard sari and looked like a typical grandma. Yet, she was different. She talked of equality and compassion. My paternal grandfather and his uncle were influenced by the Theosophists, J. Krishnamurti, M.N. Roy and socialism. My grandfather took tradition head-on and, influenced by Periyar (Ramaswami Naicker), did not perform the thread ceremony for his sons. He taught them by precept that all human beings were equal. This was the normal in our household. My father and his older brother were sent to Shanti Niketan from 1920 to 1922. They came back influenced in their most formative years by the mind of Rabindranath Tagore and his colleagues.

My recollections stretch back to very early feelings and some very clear and vivid images. The morality of good and bad, right and wrong transmutes its values into a child's mind in mysterious ways. The fact that differences in religious practices do not justify discrimination and killing was etched forever in my mind as that of many in that generation.

Contemporary India post-2014 is so sharp a reminder that caste and religious conditioning are deep, and can revive the horrors of prejudicial action. Islamophobia, which was the fringe discourse, has been engineered to become the dominant one. The Babri Masjid has been demolished, and the yagya has been performed in the temple in Ayodhya. Courts have caved in, political establishments have become conciliatory and the ruling party is aggressively pushing identities of religion and caste to divide humanity. The temple has become the symbol of a nation set on the course of dividing with religion and ruling with inequality, violating basic tenets of our Constitution.

Gandhiji was an unabashed follower of Sanatan Dharma, ahimsa and non-violence—definitive values of the Hindu religion, according to him. He was assassinated by a member of the Hindu Maha Sabha just after Partition. Today Hindutva, as defined by the ruling elite and aggressive social formations, perpetrates hate and violence. For example, Bharatiya Janata Party Member of Parliament Sadhvi Pragya called Nathuram Godse a 'deshbhakt' (patriot) on camera in Parliament, endorsing him and his views.[1]

Today's India has to fight harder than ever to get its sanity back. This is not a BJP vs Congress debate, or a 1984 vs 2002 argument. All genocidal killings must be condemned. We have to speak for compassion, for humanity and for India. This is the land of the Buddha and of seers and poets, of Kabir, the Sufis, bhakti poetry, of Ramana and Ramakrishna, of Moinuddin Chishti and Guru Nanak. It is also the land where Thomas the Apostle landed, fleeing from persecution in the first century, a place where the Zoroastrians found shelter. A discriminatory culture tried to redeem itself from guilt, gave space to Raja Ram Mohan Roy, Ramaswami Naicker Periyar, Phule, Narayana Guru and B.R. Ambedkar, and the whole stream that questioned caste. Violence was not absent, but was questioned and morally condemned. In a society that inherits the caste system, embedded inequality and the apprehensions of implicit violence will exist. Yet there was also space to question the status quo. Today, however, a majoritarian system has taken over the role of petitioner and judge. What is being attacked now is the right to question at all, especially the majority community and its henchmen.

The counter discourse of Hindutva, stalled by Gandhiji's assassination, has now re-emerged as a popular discourse. There are two significant counters to Gandhiji, as intolerance to other religions and the opposition to non-violence. Non-violence is now being projected as a weakness. Gandhiji has been projected as having 'begged' for Independence, in other words non-violent satyagraha is being interpreted as a weak man's tool. Obviously, the non-violent agenda had to be disvalued to promote the agenda of violence. Persistent attacks based on caste, gender and religion are more than worrying, as they have been woven into the many facets of daily politics. The single-minded argument of pinning all failures on a single victim seems to have worked. Ignorance and vulnerability combine to fashion the deadly weapon of intolerance. The movements and even the organized left have taken too much for granted, and the popular discourse has been taken over by the religious right-wing.

Political education needs to be generationally relevant. Every new generation that is born needs to know its history. Gandhi has been interpreted in negative terms through popular subaltern narratives. He continues to be a target of Hindutva forces, whose main concern is the demolition of the multifaith culture sustained by the symbolism of Gandhi. Godse, therefore, becomes the martyr and temples are being erected to him, such as the one in Gwalior.

Misinterpretations of peaceful protests seek to establish hatred, and the demand for equality is seen as anti-national. Mindful peaceful protests, like that for the Citizenship Amendment Act (CAA), and those who spearhead peace and dialogue, such as Umar Khalid, have been targeted and jailed with accusations of being anti-state/anti-national. Their demands are for constitutional equality. The cunning use of the bogey of international 'Islamic terrorism' has managed to build a discourse of fear and hate. What this could lead to, from constant skirmishes to a state of civil war, is left to one's imagination. The shadow play, where violence is instigated by one group and another blamed, is already evident from the riots in north-east Delhi in February 2020. The constant sense of unease and fear is being used as a tool to silence any kind of dissent and difference. The violence of state terror may appear to bring in a hush, but the human spirit cannot be silenced permanently.

Post-Independence: Peace after an Assassination

Gandhiji was assassinated soon after I was born.

The assassination of the Mahatma was followed by worldwide distress and a deep sense of loss in India. It brought an uneasy peace for four decades. Gandhi was not blindly accepted either during his lifetime or after, but he did leave fundamental principles to follow and methods for stitching together a society with a history of religious strife. His satyagraha and passive resistance were located in deep spirituality, yet reflected a shrewd common sense and an understanding of human nature and its capacities.

Immediately after, and for many generations after the assassination, there was a cultivated position where religion was strictly 'private' and kept for personal approval or disapproval, and for opting to be theist, atheist or agnostic. The liberal elite and the left, having cut themselves off from any public discourse on religion, were gauche in dealing with it. The refusal to engage with any kind of expression of religion in the public domain left the space free for a narrow-minded interpretation of Hinduism to occupy and consolidate. Our deliberate myopia in blocking out religious discourse, as a result of strife and tragedy that followed Gandhi's assassination, was politically ill-judged.

The post-Independence progressive generation made a choice to place religion in the private space, with a cessation of religious discourse in public life. A senior Foreign Service officer said to me in a private conversation in the 1970s that this silence was on all fronts. He bemoaned the lack of familiarity with religions in academic courses in schools, allowing myths and fears to take root. He recalled theological discussions between maulvis and pundits, which would end with a cup of tea. The discourse was rational and within bounds of 'decency', a word not currently popular—an indicator of what we have lost in the ability to converse with mutual respect.

A shocking experience in a training programme of teachers in Rajasthan in the 1990s, post the Babri Masjid demolition, highlighted this in a dramatic manner. The forty-odd teachers with post-graduate degrees claimed that Mahatma Gandhi was killed by a Muslim. Godse became 'Gaud Mussalman'. The education system had failed to provide facts, thus allowing a wrong, perverse narrative to take root. This was a political comment on forty-six wasted years of many innocent and ill-informed generations, where public political education was left untended. Cultural Hinduism was not strong enough to take on the bigotry of an extremist point of view.

In the vacuum of political ignorance and bad education, we have allowed half-truths and distorted narratives to take over. Some fifteen years ago, I was in Bengaluru on work. A middle-class woman came to me and asked whether Naxalites would destroy her home in the city. I told her it was extremely unlikely. Naxals were essentially fighting against injustice in areas where 'development' infringed on basic rights and there was economic neglect. They became violent revolutionaries only when all attempts at dialogue failed. A decade later Gauri Lankesh was killed and the phrase 'urban Naxal' was coined. An addition to the political lexicon of hate, to bring fear into the minds of people. Urban India, ignorant of political history and definitions, would be pushed into looking at all questioning of the status quo with fear. The right to question was again under attack.

The Myopia of a Liberal Elite

The neglect of political education has resulted in a lack of political consciousness. In the absence of real understanding, many bogeys have been created, targeted and incarcerated. Fundamentally denying the right to freedom of thought, expression and free speech. People frustrated by thwarted ambitions to relate to the power structure were offered a very seductive argument by the Hindu right-wing, that this was the failure of progressive, liberal India. The liberal elite were, for their part, entrenched in their aspirations and failed to perceive the raw needs and emotions of a rising middle class. Equality has never been accepted by a caste-ridden, feudal society. The mischief has been to misrepresent all those who speak of equality as 'Naxals' or 'anti-national' conspirators. The hierarchy of a socially discriminatory system has developed double speak. The political system talks of democracy but hollows out its content, celebrates Republic Day but works against the Constitution.

The burgeoning middle class has begun to identify with the communal agenda. Its material aspirations have pushed it towards the glitter of the market. All denial of access to worldly goods has been pinned on the welfare agenda and affirmative action for the traditionally downtrodden. The construct of a communal and unequal society, however popular, has had to deal with formidable guarantees in the Constitution. In order to set aside constitutional guarantees, rational arguments themselves would have to be set aside. The subtext has continued to be spread by the whispering campaigns against Gandhi, Nehru and many others. A steady corrosion of constitutional rights through new legal enactments has written the text of a new India without tolerance.

Fear and Control

With the destruction of Babri Masjid in 1992, India's collective faith and respect for all places of worship was seriously challenged. A devastated and shocked section of the Indian people was unable to comprehend how modern India could destroy a masjid, or indeed any place of worship. The government acted indecisively according to Madhav Godbole, who was home secretary at the time. In his book *The Babri Masjid–Ram Mandir Dilemma*,[2] he mentioned that Narasimha Rao had dismissed the home ministry's comprehensive contingency plan to take over the Babri Masjid structure by invoking Article 356 of the Constitution on the grounds that it was not workable.[3] Godbole adds that India was on the decline. Was this the independence we struggled for?

In 1992 the MKSS set up a people-financed kirana or grocery store to demonstrate that workers could intervene in the market. When L.K. Advani of the BJP was entering Bihar with his post-demolition rath yatra to build opinion in favour of constructing the temple in Ayodhya in place of the Babri Masjid, then Chief Minister of Bihar Lalu Prasad Yadav had stopped them at the U.P.–Bihar border. There was a call for a Bharat Bandh protesting this move. Politics entered the town of Bhim and its market when this bandh was enforced. Since it was a BJP bandh, most of the bazaar pulled down its shutters. The traders attempted to forcibly close the Mazdoor Kisan Kirana Store, but failed, despite threats. The workers in the Kirana Store stepped aside and cautioned the goons: 'The two thousand financiers of this shop will come tomorrow and call you to account.' The insulting and belligerent group backed out. Shopkeepers hate to lose business; and the brisk trade of the Kirana Store was irresistible. Slowly the shutters went up and within an hour all the other shops were open as well. The Kirana Store makes a political statement economically, but it is also the foothold in small-town politics. The MKSS joined the Kirana Store to take a public pledge to the Preamble of the Indian Constitution outside the shop in the middle of Bhim on Republic Day in 1993. They were joined by many people despite hostility.

Hatred born of fear is fostered by carefully constructed, oft-repeated narratives. Rationality is long lost to the winds. What remains is fear of the known and the unknown. The biggest hurdle to rationality is ignorance. Ignorance and the unknown breed apprehension. When fear is calculated as an asset and cultivated as a policy for aggrandizement of political power, violence is bound to follow. George Orwell's *Nineteen Eighty-Four* is the story of fear and its controls.[4] Today, 'Big Brother' watches our expressions of dissent in our articles through smartphones, social media and the internet. The fear of Big Brother trails us through many variations. He does not merely watch but distorts and misinterprets intent and words. It is psychological warfare fine-tuned.

The new variable is the fear of losing our comfort, the loss of material goods. The predominant feeling of comfort traps the middle class into silence. The 'urban Naxal' is a bogey with the right fit, to enhance fears and buy acquiescence. Fear is the reason behind the continuing of inequality, fear of having to share, fear of being questioned. Fear is the root of all irrationality and inaction. As Isherwood says in *A Single Man*:

> Let's just talk about fear. Fear, after all, is our real enemy. Fear is taking over our world. Fear is being used as a tool of manipulation in our society. ... Think about it. Fear that we are going to be attacked, fear that there are communists lurking around every corner ... Fear that we are useless and that no one cares what we have to say.[5]

Today, we face a mountain of lies and double speak and are unable to see the wood for the trees.

The current north Indian discourse has fed a politically illiterate part of our population many misleading myths and narratives. That all Muslims are migrants, historically speaking, and that Hindus alone were part of the land mass called 'Bharat'. We have to recognize that the central Hindu identity is deeply internalized in north India, not merely as religion but also as an angst of refugees uprooted from a home, post-Partition. Inciting Islamophobia falls on very fertile sentiments, especially in the cow-belt psyche, in post-Partition north India. Down south, in Tamil Nadu for instance, the populace has no interest in these myths; for them the Dravidian identity is paramount.

Hindutva, Hinduism, Secularism: Manufacturing Hate

As Bertrand Russel said:

> The first step in a fascist movement is the combination under an energetic leader of a number of men who possess more than the average share of leisure, brutality, and stupidity. The next step is to fascinate fools and muzzle the intelligent, by emotional excitement on the one hand and terrorism on the other.[6]

Any expression that does not fall under the discourse permitted by the diktat of a prejudiced Hindutva is seen as a violation of the sentiments of Hindus, and violence follows. Hinduism has been a philosophy with broad and porous contours and has allowed expansion. Hindutva wants to seal these borders.

It is a statistical fact that 80 per cent of India's population is Hindu. Most of them are practising Hindus and a sizeable but smaller percentage are non-practising or cultural Hindus. Who is a cultural Hindu? Hinduism has no single religious text that all Hindus must subscribe to. It has no concept of 'fatwa' or ex-communication; it also does not condemn people to hell if they belong to other faiths. You might say that it is a passive religion. Hinduism as a philosophy proved a point in lasting out with non-violence as a value, riddled as it undoubtedly was by caste and other structural polarities in which it was enmeshed.

The political aspirations and fears of Hindutva are rooted in questions raised against constitutional equality—caste reservation, the secular state, the reformative zeal of many Hindu movements, women's equality, the LGBTQ movement and others. The anti-Muslim mirage is deliberately created so as to present a concept of 'unified Hinduism' while maintaining all the caste divisions and exploiting them for religion as well as electoral democracy. Why is 80 per cent of the population of India afraid of the minority?

Contemporary India is a victim of totalitarianism in its many forms. Do we recognize its presence when it jails people who want the freedom to think and speak? What is even more evil is that while people motivated to violence by hate roam free, mere expression of dissent and critique of a counter ideology is condemned as anti-national. It is a moment of reckoning. If we comprehend the gravity of these actions we would question, just as Dabholkar, Pansare and Lankesh did, and as the many who are in jail protesting against what to many of us is a series of unjust laws—the National Register of Citizens (NRC), the National Population Register (NPR) and the CAA. In the final computation, the question arises: 'Do I have the right to think?'

Every secular Indian is hemmed in by a plethora of graded perceptions and definitions. Being secular is a political position of defining the state as non-partisan; you can have faith in the religion you are born in, or that of choice (Articles 25–28). No individual is less secular for avowing secular principles while adhering to the cultural and religious norms they are born into or adopt. Using branding for damning personal choice is a threat to thought.

What is the centrifugal force that propels this new discourse of Hindutva—a militant world view to 'regain' territorial authority, political control and gain popularity? Why should peaceful protests and women-dominated CAA sit-ins provoke the reprehensible ire of the police and the government in power? What is it afraid of? The following anecdote illustrates the enfolding of innocent people into a framework of fear and hate.

In 1991, Anshi asked me if there were other gods and goddesses and if Muslims and Sikhs were another caste. What were their temples called? Anshi is a serious woman, fighting against the oppression of the poor. When the Babri Masjid mosque was destroyed, Anshi like many other women, was shocked that any place of worship could be destroyed: to do so was a sin. In the thirty years since, the discourse of women like Anshi has become encased in caste and religious prejudice and the threat of isolation. People argue that there is hatred for Islam in the DNA of the ordinary Hindu. If so, where was it before Hindutva politics infiltrated and captured their minds? How much of this is the desire and conditioning to conform to a community identity? Why and where have there been no other discourses that touched the minds of ordinary people? When Karl Marx said, 'Religion is the opiate of the masses,' did he envision this?

The linking of a religious identity with nationalism is a fig leaf used to deny freedom of expression. It is an irony that there is no question raised about national resources that are squandered by multilateral and multinational deals, signing off tracts of forest land and water. The jingoism of nationalism has long been an issue of intellectual debate. In a famous lecture on nationalism delivered in America in 1917, Rabindranath Tagore said: 'There is only one history ... Not on the basis of nationalism but of humanism.' Tagore was explicit in saying that it was his conviction that '[m]y countrymen will truly gain their India by fighting against the education that teaches them that a country is greater than the ideals of humanity.' [7]

Implicit in Tagore's words is the much-ignored difference between a person who is a patriot and one who is a nationalist. What the Indian citizen needs to know is that there is a difference between nationalism and patriotism: the patriot is proud of his country for what it does, and the nationalist is proud of his country no matter what it does. Throughout his life, Tagore wrote on both, and he remained deeply critical of nationalism. His argument was that when love for one's country gives way to worship or becomes a 'sacred obligation', rationality is sacrificed. 'I am willing to serve my country; but my worship I reserve for Right which is far greater than country. To worship my country as a god is to bring curse upon it.'[8] Many of those who are vociferous about national pride are Indians resident in other nations, wanting to glorify 'the Motherland'. In India, nationalism becomes an excuse for political gain through religious oppression to suffocate any dissent, criticism and critique.

The State: Complicit in Communal Tension

In 1984 when Indira Gandhi was shot dead by her two Sikh bodyguards, northern India broke into communal riots. The killing of innocent Sikhs, the destruction of their property and the subsequent indifference of a state that should have sprung into action to prevent the rampage left scars that are yet to heal.

The devaluation of secularism had resurfaced in sharp profile. After Operation Blue Star, forewarned about the threats to her life by Sikh militants, Mrs Gandhi had vetoed removing her Sikh bodyguards. To quote A.K. Antony, 'She had said that even if it might cost her life she will not change the bodyguards in the name of caste or religion. She had said that she does not want to save her life by creating a divide in the society.'[9] They not only killed her but also severely bruised the rational argument for secularism. What followed was a bloodbath of huge proportions, where the emotions of a bereaved family overcame political and democratic good sense. The 'goonda' elements in the Congress reigned free and the complicity of those in power is unpardonable. The carnage that followed alienated a community that had once been assimilated into the mainstream. Unlike the Muslims, there was no history of 'otherness' nor a popular score to be settled with Sikhs. The politics of hate got another shot of energy. We are still struggling with the aftermath of the violence; the upsurge of religious identity as the base for cessation was an emotional consequence.

One of the calculations behind such riots is economic greed. The community that is attacked is seen as being affluent at the cost of their neighbours. A refugee community had flourished, and this bred envy and jealousy. This factor played a role in the Gujarat carnage in 2002 too, when India witnessed a planned, premeditated stoking of violence in the post-Godhra riots. There is sufficient factual information to prove that the genesis of this set of actions went back many decades and its immediate background was a slow building up of hate and violence against a targeted community.

For someone born in the 1940s, who stood witness to the bloodbath that followed, communal politics and any killing of innocent people are anathema. But when such violence is perpetrated with deliberate planning and strategies of elimination, reason is wounded and the questions that arise on the basis of humanitarian concerns have no answers. When the news hit us that fateful February in 2002, India responded with some compassion and concern. Harsh Mander's article 'Cry, the Beloved Country' moved millions to tears.[10] What affected many about the nature of the carnage was the calculated cruelty with which it was all planned. It brought back memories of Hitlerian Germany. Visits to the United States Holocaust Memorial Museum in Washington, D.C. drew parallels between the happenings in Gujarat and the pogroms against the Jews. The deliberate twisting of due process through the infiltration of extra-legal forces into police stations, the unofficial two-day holiday granted to the bureaucracy in the state, a premeditated laying-off of state support to those facing violent mobs—all these were as obnoxious as they were unbelievable.

I was part of a committee set up to investigate the Gujarat genocide. The Concerned Citizens Tribunal (CCT) was headed by the late Justice V.R. Krishna Iyer, with Justice P.B. Sawant and Justice Hosbet Suresh, K.G. Kannabiran and others as members. It conducted a detailed investigation into the Gujarat genocidal carnage (in May 2002) and released a report on 21–22 November 2002, based on the testimonies of the victims and the shocking evidence from witnesses. We saw acute suffering in Naroda Patiya and in Godhra. The findings of the CCT reflect the truth behind a communal incident. A country with a history of multiple religions cannot condone state-sanctioned inequality and inequity in any form. The collusion of regulatory mechanisms, such as the police, undermines their role as keepers of the rule of law. The riots resulted in impunity for the perpetrators and the miscarriage of justice for the victims. Like in all communal killings, reason was massacred along with humanity.

The CCT met and spent weeks interviewing victims, people from the civil services, politicians and a cross-section of society. The testimonies were harrowing, more so as each victim talked without hatred, wishing only that such things never happen to anyone else. Their anger was against a somnambulant state. The complete inertia of the bureaucratic system without a murmur happened for the first time on such a scale, covering the entire machinery from the chief secretary downwards. Trained to address communal rioting swiftly and efficiently during my IAS training in the Foundation Course at Mussoorie, I could not but wonder at the paralysis of governance in Gujarat.

Each day I spent there was an education in how low the human spirit can fall, as seen in the lack of basic humanity and the violence meted out to the innocent. What further horrified me was the sadistic enjoyment in the killing, like the incident in Naroda Patiya where the stomach of a pregnant eighteen-year-old girl was split open and a tilak applied on the foetus. The girl died.[11]

Genocide is a tragedy no matter what the beliefs of the warring factions may be. The victim is innocent. Human life, violence and the loss of reason are the collaterals. In this case a majority population believing in a particular religion worked on non-religious principles of hate and revenge. Hate and revenge are not part of any religion. They are invoked for political ends, as the committee's report amply demonstrates. The deviation from constitutional morality has allowed the entire governance structure to crumble and fall away from the rule of law. It underscores how important the acceptance, and implementation, of an external moral authority is to control and evaluate aberrations in public behaviour. Communal killings perpetrated by different political parties have made us realize the continuing need to build common sense, comprehend political governance and understand the role of accountability in keeping constitutional morality alive.

Religion cannot, by its own logic, preach violence if it claims to deal with the spiritual liberation of humankind. A substantive part of the basic tenets in ancient Hindu scriptures believes that there are many roads to reach spiritual ends. Illogical co-relations between violent revenge and pious acts should be the antithesis of religion. God as vengeance, created by power politics, has taken over the minds of many, and there is little comprehension between revenge and justice. Religious power wedded to politics is a heady cocktail of irrational control. One must differentiate between philosophies, religions, religious institutions and practice. A continuing public discourse by individuals who believed and practised religion with inclusiveness, like Gandhi, has been devalued.

An important message to all of us, following these communal incidents, is the importance of a continuing discourse on religion in a country where so many people have faith. My generation believed quite myopically that post the partition of India, Hitler and the Second World War, genocide and hate would be viewed with disgust and condemned as not worthy of anyone who wished to call themselves civilized. There was also a simplistic assumption that progress of moral consciousness would be a linearity of knowledge and understanding. The greed for political power at any cost has taught us otherwise. We need to iterate and reiterate the need for moral and political education continually. Every generation has to relearn the importance and significance of the arguments for equality, justice, fraternity, the right to freedom to worship. As much as it must work against blind faith, belief, call it what you will, without fear of reprisal.

Identity Politics

The free-flowing nature of an individual's multilayered choices are fast disappearing. Many people have begun looking over their shoulder to make sure that no one is indeed snooping to report it to the persecutors. Opinions that would have been freely expressed are now pushed into silence. It is a marketing ploy to fix a person in a specific stereotype; whether one is selling fear or cosmetics, the technique is the same. 'Urban Naxal', 'andolan jevi' and so on are labels pinned on the MKSS. We are fixed in the public imagination through branding, a new technique to instil fear. Only if we reject the paradigm can we begin a new discourse. Perhaps as a society we have neglected the socialization that is so very important to correct the lens through which we see difference and promote love for those who are unlike us. Compassion, so much a celebrated part of Buddhist teachings, should still play a role in the understanding of the people in this country. It can be evoked and will be quickly understood.

In my childhood, the greatest challenge for my siblings and me was to assert our right to be different. It was surprising that as children we were not 'caught' in the conflict between the liberal progressiveness of our home and the conservatism of the immediate neighbourhood. We were born to parents who were brought up on a mélange of influences, from their progressive homes in Chennai to the learning environment of Shanti Niketan, from the politics of Mahatma Gandhi, M.N. Roy, Periyar and Ambedkar to the influence of the Adyar Theosophists and the iconoclastic J. Krishnamurti. We were exposed to atheism and arguments about the veracity of religious texts, the grandeur of poems such as *Silapathikaram* and *Shakuntalam*, the greatness of Shakespeare, the fables of Aesop and the Jataka tales, the music of Ustad Karim Khan and the evenings at Veena Dhanam's—the list is endless. Appa was a lawyer by training, a writer, a connoisseur of music and a one-man encyclopaedia; his interests arched from politics to cricket, music, theatre, the intricacies of documentary and other cinema. Amma was a student of mathematics and physics, a veena player and a rationalist. Physics was a discipline that she loved and pursued all her life. Discrimination on the basis of caste, religion or class was a cardinal sin at home. We were interesting oddities. My understanding of identity and parochialism as distasteful lies in the hundreds of impressions and the profound influence of those days. When our differences stood out, reactions were mild and reservations were expressed without violence. In later years, I married Bunker Roy, a Brahmo Samaji, a representative of secular India. The friendship grew on shared world views, sympathy and concern for those without privilege and the acceptance of difference. At many junctures it has been a great solace to sit with a family that included many religions, backgrounds and even nuanced differences in politics. It was a comfort and an assurance to be part of that social entity, and to admit the possibility of living with differences in tolerance and affection. The family may not be an active part of the samaj, but the social impact of the Brahmo Samaj catalysed a great tradition, and my in-laws were proof of it.

The deliberate attempt at indoctrination in contemporary times is amply evident in the changes in school curricula. Post-2014, in BJP-ruled Rajasthan, the state board decided not to include historical or contemporary instances integral to the chapter on casteism and communalism in the political science textbook. References to Nathuram Godse and Mahatma Gandhi's assassination have been removed from textbooks. Nor do they mention the 2002 Gujarat riots, the beef ban, the Dadri lynching or the award-wapsi movement by prominent writers.[12] In Gujarat, a school textbook glorifies Hitler as a great leader and dilutes the impact of the Holocaust.[13]

The constructed conversation uses the fallacious argument of dividing India into a children's comic strip of the 'good Hindu' and the 'bad Muslim'. Will Hindus fall into the trap of demonizing Islam to assert a warped Hindutva, defined not by true Hindu philosophy but by politics? It is a contradiction that those who, by faith, celebrate vegetarianism should be ready to lynch a human being for 'stealing' cattle! Are we going to trade off the sophisticated ability to think and work with rational causality, for flimsy, manufactured falsehoods? Are we going to forego the unity of diverse people and faiths that make India what it is, a rich culture?

> India is defined by its multicultural texture. A choice of any single strain is faulty. One way to look at this culture is as a land of Bhakti or Sufi philosophers of the likes of Thiruvalluvar, Basava, Tukaram, Bibi Fatima or Kabir, who spoke persistently of fostering peace and companionship of diverse communities. An attitude of intolerance and violence contradicts any faith's basic tenets of humanism. In fact, most Hindu shlokas end with 'shanti', an invocation of peace and restraint. Many of us born in the Hindu religion, who either practise or culturally remain within its fold, need to ask ourselves some important questions. Is violence against unarmed human beings going to lead us anywhere near the spiritual goals promised by the best in our tradition? Is difference a justification for subjugation or annihilation of life? Will the celebration of a temple constructed on the ruins of another place of worship give anyone 'punya'? As Hindus, we stand guilty unless we express our dissent.[14]

As activists who chose to work in the public sphere, we have been guilty of fractured perceptions. There was no understanding of the multipolar universe of a poor person. Food in the belly is vital, but the poor need more than food when there is death and continual privation. We were too busy to budget for time to discuss issues of religion, popular narratives, superstitions and beliefs. The popularity of Kabir was glorified, but we failed to perceive that the poor Dalit too set as much store by the 'ratijaga' (the singing of Kabir and other bhajans all night), though caste and religion continue to prejudice them. Once the belly is full, there is misery, death and unhappiness, for which consolation is found in traditional religious discourse.

There is a gap, however, in public discourse between the seer and the peddlers of religion. The liberal middle class, which amplified a popular normative discourse, as a class, has turned aside for careers and modern gadgets, for comfort. The popularity of Kabirpanthis and of bhajan mandalis, of rituals and festivals is ample proof that the fear of the unknown—of death and what happens after—must be addressed. Perhaps then fear and the creation of victims and the doctrine of hate and violence will not take over people's psychology.

Non-violent Protests and an Assertion of Secularism

Freedom as a constitutional guarantee is respected, and expressions are permitted—so long as the impunity of the powerful is not questioned. A new low was reached in the history of civil rights in India during the protest against the CAA when challenging the majoritarian state resulted in the clamping down of all freedoms.

Shaheen Bagh was a synonym for defining peaceful protest for justice and rights across the country at the end of 2019, spilling over into 2020. India has seen hundreds of such protests after the enactment of the CAA, with women and youth leading them. These demonstrations have promoted values of collective leadership and the feminist framework of change with peace. Those who dared to talk truth to power were quelled into silence by a campaign of incarceration, hatred and fear. This remarkable collection of people who dared to speak up simply sat together chanting their pledge to the Preamble of the Constitution and singing the 'Ramdhun', which speaks of Ram and Allah, praying for peace and good sense for all. They sat together day after day to protest a severe assault on the principle of equality and democratic processes that independent India has witnessed. They used methods of civil disobedience popularized by Gandhi, and held aloft the principles of the Indian Constitution and Ambedkar. The protest sites were secular, democratic and wholly within the rule of law. They brought hope to other civil rights activists fatigued with fighting the infringement of all, but particularly civil rights, since 2014. They placed India's ancient and modern conscience at the centre of concern.

Amidst the violence of the riots, one witnessed two expressions of 'Hinduism': one, of Hindutva mobs inciting violence and death while belligerently shouting 'Jai Shree Ram', and the other, of Hindu neighbours risking their lives to protect their Muslim brothers and sisters. Multiple Shaheen Baghs across the country proved India's commitment to peaceful resolution of conflict.

In my early years in Rajasthan I realized that very few people knew the story of the Ramayan. Rama meant Ramdev Pir near Jaisalmer. The large numbers of pilgrims who walked to the temple every year did so with faith and tolerance. The temple priest was a Dalit and Ramdev Pir is a place of faith and worship of the original Baba Ramdev and should not be confused with the Patanjali Ramdev. The Ramayan became familiar after the popular TV serial went to every home in the country. Later, when we visited Pakistan in 1988–89, we found the viewership quite formidable there as well. The language of moving pictures was in its infancy and many did not comprehend the story. But the building of a pan-Indian centralized Rama meant the worship of local gods and goddesses was pushed to the background—and with them the folklore, the rich local traditions of songs and the poetry of subaltern India.

Politics actually deals with power, its distribution and oppression in all structures. Organized religion basically addresses our fears of loss and specifically of death. Philosophy deals with principles and physical phenomena. The organization of communities has depended on interpretations in religion and on a moral code. The moral code associated with religion has always been in conflict with modern ethical systems, in our case, the Constitution. The criminal justice system seemed separate and inviolate, but in contemporary politics, the contradiction and compromise seem stark. It seems as if traditional morality has encroached and taken over parts of constitutional morality with disastrous consequences. The political system has to acknowledge that there is a need for religion in the human psyche, but must prevent its prejudices and narrow confines from taking over the business of life. It is a delicate balance.

India's written Constitution defines the right to worship, as it does a secular state. The resistance to secularism has a long history and mocking the concept and distorting its seriousness in popular perception, with the word 'sickular', was the first step. Unable to directly attack the Constitution and to fundamentally question equality, laws based on inequality have been passed, like the NRC and the CAA. Activists, used to discussing the polarity between theism and atheism, have been stumped by their inability to play any important role in the theological, religious or traditional discourse in inter-religious strife. Knowing that there is huge misinterpretation and miscommunication about the scriptures is not enough. Important changes in normative practice happen only when both the heart and mind are equally involved. All basic shifts in perception come from a feeling, and when we disregard it and fail to understand it with our minds, we are defeated.

In Conclusion

The mass politically motivated incarceration of activists is indicative of a diseased polity.

Let us look at the numbers of innocent lives that have been lost for expressing an opinion and speaking the truth, people who have lost their lives for our cause. Shankar Guha Niyogi, Safdar Hashmi, Ghulam Rasool, Chandrashekhar, Satyendra Dubey, Sarita and Mahesh and many more. Here are good courageous people who were killed only because they pursued the truth and fought injustice. Their sacrifice has been noticed and acknowledged, and even though their killers have not been brought to book, their deeds and their lives serve as an inspiration to the many others who follow their quest.

There are hundreds of poor and courageous people whose acts of courage have gone unnoticed and unsung; poverty and oppression have reduced them to invisibility. Almost all regulatory institutions of justice have been corrupted by the lack of principles and the acceptance of opportunism as the only code of conduct. The rule of law has failed the poor, the minority and the dissenters.

What can we as ordinary citizens do to break this bubble? Can we learn from the struggles of people even less powerful than ourselves, who refused to be subjugated by oppression, corruption and deceit? Can we keep alive the faith that the truth will always prevail?

Hatred and volcanic spleen
    Spills over the brim of reason.
The rage of whipped up and illusory
    divides, makes the mouth froth with venom.
Innocent helpless faces, look at this
—eyes lost

In the bewilderment of cruelty
—unprovoked and senseless.
Eyes looking without focus,
At the tidal wave of hatred;
Twisted the solar plexus
Of the human in us.
Enthroned, astride the middle
Of premeditated mayhem
Sits the throned state reasoning,
Calculating the spiral of stratagems and strategies to
Create hate and mindless rage.
It happened in 1947, in the senseless killing
Of innocent people,
When the state ordained the carnage,
When the borders were defined by an unknown
British hand.
But we have recreated
The horrors for ourselves,
Dividing, isolating, boycotting, massacring
For achieving material ends.
It happens with a native state enthroned
By a people's mandate,
Howling slogans of national jingoism.
Distorted mangled information and bodies
Of beloved ones, words pouring
and spewing spleen, setting fire to humanity
The final ritual of the victim makers.
The managers of money and power
Play into our pettiness and
The narrow definitions of identities, the

Broader divisions of money and fears
To destroy us in ourselves, with our own hands.
A land varied, plentiful, manifold, in song
In words and language, in colour and
Prayer, can ill afford to watch this deliberate narrowing,
Of our contours;
The mowing down of our sculpted history
Of shared love for the smell of food
and the caress of the seasons.
We wait like prisoners,
for the executioner's bullet.
Our faces stare at grimy walls
Hands back, tied
To stop expression.
Only fools would wait to see more blood spill,
To turn the earth black with distress.
The anguished shout and protest, they write and argue.
The relentless power of brass and paper
Continue to beguile and crush,
With the intent of
A bulldozer with open jaws
On the rampage.
A phony democracy waits with
Open arms to
Welcome the land grabbers, the river drinkers and
The mountain chewers who run amok!

10

What Shapes Us: Culture—the Subtext of Life

GOD guard me from those thoughts men think
In the mind alone;
He that sings a lasting song
Thinks in a marrow-bone.

—William Butler Yeats[1]

One day in the early 1980s I listened to the music of the Manganiyars and Langas, famous Sufi folk musicians from western Rajasthan, and was introduced to Komal Kothari (Komalda)[2] and Vijaydan Detha (Bijji).[3] It was an introduction to a Rajasthan I did not know. The music was extraordinary, full-throated pure sound rising and moving wave after wave, enveloping the listeners in its magic. This grand musical tradition, the magnificent voices and the epiphany of that moment have stayed with me. This experience was definitive in making me Rajasthani.

Komalda was an unselfconscious, absorbed talker, and his reminiscences were always in context and abundant in scope. He continued the oral tradition in more ways than one; he talked history, culture and politics. He was fascinating, and even casual conversation with him was intellectually stimulating. It was a delight to listen to the way his mind connected impossible dots to make history come alive—it was magical. Little wonder then that Bijji, the recorder of oral folk stories, was his companion. It is a pity that he was no Boswell to Komalda's Johnson,[4] recording every spoken word to enrich Rajasthani cultural knowledge for posterity.

Culture is often reduced in discussion, and even in thought, to a few of its many varied complexities. It is seen as a simplistic description of one of its many parts—religion, traditional practices, rituals, music, dance, painting, theatre, performing arts in general, politics—and not seen as a definition of life itself. Culture is plural, diverse and embedded in the lives of people. It is the subtext of everything in social and political discourse, and in activism. Culture is in the marrow bone, synonymous with life itself and, therefore, the most difficult to define, articulate or discuss as an entity. Cultural expression comes from a mixture of thoughts, feelings, capacities, skills and a desire to communicate with each other, establish a connection with the world outside. It is immensely rich and varied in its manifestation and expression. Even religious texts change in interpretation with location and context. There are many texts of the Bible, the Koran, etc. The Ramayana has many versions—Valmiki, Tulsi, Kamba (in the south)—contextualized and with regional variations. Classic political texts like those by Plato, Chanakya, Kautilya, Hobbes, Locke, Rousseau, Hegel and Marx are located very much in their cultural, political and historical condition. Even a specific document like the Indian Constitution is interpreted differently, depending upon the group that presents the argument.

To paraphrase Tagore, human intelligence lies in humanity. Culture as human expression is a wide canvas, allowing disparity, contradictions and harmony to survive within its expansive universe. All our actions are located in it. Conflicts arise when culture is repeatedly reduced to its narrowest expression and identity. Those of us who comprehend the enormity of this universe are bound to recognize the multiplicity inherent in its thought and formations, and grow tolerant and accepting of differences in perceptions and preferences.

My realization of my own cultural imitations came from my love for 'high culture', classical music, be it north or south Indian, or Western, or dance, painting, folk art and the traditional crafts. But 'popular culture' was merely tolerated and sometimes endured. This was endorsed by two very important years I spent in Kalakshetra, learning classical Carnatic music and Bharatanatyam. I was taught by some of the best in that tradition, including Gauri Amma, one of the many who taught the great doyenne Balasaraswati abhinaya (expression).[5] The time I spent in Kalakshetra in my formative years would influence me all my life. We were not allowed to watch popular cinema nor perform anything less than pure Bharatanatyam as defined by Kalakshetra. If we perchance saw the popular Bharatanatyam performers of the 1950s—Lalita, Padmini and Ragini—who were part of cinematic Bharatanatyam, we were heavily chastised.

I learnt to come to terms with populistic art. Its popularity was not reason enough to look down on such expression. However, as I write, I am hounded in mind and body by a popular loud sound, called the 'DJ'. Four or more massive speakers are mounted on a motorized vehicle. The volume of the beats and the noise level can be fatal to an ill person. Yet whether an election campaign, a birthday, a wedding or a religious festival, the DJ truck is considered a must.

Some village panchayats have managed to ban these violations of public space, but it continues to be a status symbol for the young and a dreaded nightmare for neighbours. The traditional, beautiful, mellow instruments have become almost obsolete. Gods of all hues and in all religions are invoked loudly. No longer are prayers a silent communion between the believer and the sacred being,

The activist has to be a part of the culture of people they work with—food and expression in diverse forms. The connection between the personal and the political is a continuing dialogue; it is not enough to merely understand the other and engage in conversations for a more equal and just world in a political frame. The cultural mores of people have to be understood. The first time I visited the home of a deceased friend in the village, I had knots in my stomach, as I was gearing up to face the pitch of collective wailing.

'The Poor Have No History'

Camus said that the poor have no history, memory or memorabilia.[6] Perhaps he is right in the context of material histories—photographs, mementos, written memoirs. But in my prolonged interaction with worker and peasant friends, I have learnt that they have a great collective memory. It is as full of details as it is full of myths, local history and politics. Many stories have political insights of great value; they talk of pain and oppression, of love, dignity and honour. I wonder what the world would be without the phenomena of folk memory, of stories and parables. The illiterate have memory and nurture it with the oral tradition.

Galkuma had fifty-three different stories for every day we sat at an RTI dharna in Jaipur in 1997. She was a much-loved narrator, even by the posse of policemen who sat on guard near the dharna. Each of these stories had a political message for the chief minister and his cabinet. There were parables—the birds and animals that visited her stories were the people in power. Not too difficult to understand and assimilate. Who would have thought that an elderly woman would hold the audience, and even those hostile to her cause, in the palm of her hand? Mohanji (the MKSS's bard) had a well-known repertoire of Kabir's couplets and his gift with words is legend in the history of the MKSS. This sharing of gifts signals a wonderful culture in itself that is now lost in individualism and copyright laws.

Subaltern histories recorded and presented through cultures of the marginalized—folk songs, oral histories, stories, paintings, etc.—are a way of hitting back at dominant and often violent domination of vulnerable communities. What the oppressed cannot say openly they couch in parables, theatrical renderings, song and verse. The Adivasis in Rajasthan enact intuitive improvisational dramas called 'Gawri', which depict dozens of different characters, from gods and goddesses to corrupt officials. The theatre troupe travels only when the harvest is good. A procession of forty or fifty set off with a flag and as they pass through, any village can request them to stop and perform. In return the villagers organize their stay, feed them and pay them whatever they can for the performance. All the Gawri plays have standard characters, though the story may vary. The plays are about lagaan (levies), moneylending, police corruption and the nomadic Banjara community as vendors. The perennial oppression of their lives finds expression through these central characters, and updated dialogues and anecdotes bring in contemporary events. Increasingly the subaltern culture has been hard hit by the takeover from TV, social media and film. No real voices of the vulnerable find place there.

Art, Craft and Politics

There are some advantages to being resistant to 'popular' ideas and bestsellers. Those of us who consciously resist propaganda often read with a critical mind. The morality play of the good and the bad has continued with variations and embellishments over the years. In the post-Second World War period the juxtaposition was between the eastern and western blocs. Since many of us were conscious of the prejudice and partiality in the narrative, we read the occasional spy story of the CIA vs the KGB with an alert mind. But one does not understand how insidious the conditioning is till something remarkable happens.

In 1981, I went to visit my mother-in-law, who was then posted as the commercial attaché to the Indian embassy in Moscow. I was met by her at the airport with Anatoli, addressed as Tolya. Ma sat in front with Tolya—we were in a socialist country and there was no question of the 'sahib' sitting at the back. As we drove through Moscow that sunny, cold April morning, I was glued to the window, looking out. I saw young people in jeans and men with longish hair strolling in a park, and I caught myself feeling surprised. Would I have been as surprised if I hadn't been a victim of Western propaganda that claimed Moscow was grim and grey, that everyone walked around furtively, and that young people were not allowed to adopt contemporary fashion and did not meet without fear? Ma, in her broken Hindi and Bengali, whispered caution to me that Tolya was obviously associated with the KGB as he worked in the Indian Embassy. He was chatty and funny. He said to Ma, 'Madam, you are Russian construction. Aruna, she is Indian construction,' referring to the difference in our heights. Ma was 5'9", tall and big, against my diminutive 5'2".

In another instance of religious culture and superstition, what explains a population ready to believe that stone gods can drink milk? In 1995 people across India succumbed to the hype that idols of the god Ganesha could drink milk.[7] Thousands of litres of milk were offered. Miracles have a market, therefore superstitions, such as believing that seeing a widow first thing in the morning will bring bad luck, abound. Most of these superstitions end in collective violence against people and individuals who are different or considered different. Witchcraft (daayan pratha), believed to have been set aside by modernity, has come back, sometimes viciously. Women have been abused, hounded, assaulted and sometimes killed. There are modern legal tools that one can use to protect women, but mass violence and hysteria are often difficult to stop. A criminal justice system hypnotized by these phenomena remains an onlooker despite the provision of legal tools.[8]

Politics relies on predictable strategies (aka prejudiced knee-jerk reactions) to divide people and further their propaganda. The invisibility of cultural conditioning of the mind requires vigilance of a special nature. The most vigilant of us may fall victim.

The connection or division between art and politics is a subject of special concern. Visual art and craft have inspired me since I was able to hold pen and paper and see magic in lines and colour. The images, colours and shapes talk to me. I often find myself gazing at the ceiling, the wall or the earth to find faces, forms and patterns. They fascinate me. My views on poverty and alienation were not formed only by political theories or even by personal vicissitudes. The profound impact of van Gogh's *The Potato Eaters* or of Munch's *The Scream* compels us to respond to moments caught forever, as a reminder of our obligation to do something about it. An Amrita Sher-Gil, Frida Kahlo, Picasso, M.F. Husain or a Ramkinkar Baij have made me think. These works of art reflect on the human condition in different ways. Husain, born to poverty and want, evolved into a brilliant icon for art lovers. He was a founder member of the Bombay Progressive Artists Group. He excited my curiosity when he walked out of a cream Fiat, with horses painted on either side, to walk barefoot in Delhi University in the early 1960s.

Art helped shape my mind as it was tentatively searching to both express and understand the nature of poverty, pain and the illogic of inequality. My life has been the richer for perceiving and appreciating visual art. For me the value of art lies in its ability to connect my personal with my political, like the beautiful Warli drawings and those in Gendra Chhoti in Alirajpur (in Jhabua, Madhya Pradesh), as much as the celebrated painters. These beautiful drawings, white on mud-plastered walls, covering an expanse of 10 feet by 25 feet in a large bare room, were breathtaking. These tribal drawings in homes of extraordinary simplicity and beauty capture the dimensions of space. It is art and architecture at its best.

Vincent van Gogh, the painter of the poor, was not merely a depicter but also a political commentator. But as much as he was a depicter, he became an icon. What the Warli and other tribal painters are to the folk historian, he is to some activists. His *Potato Eaters* has haunted me with its message. The colours are evocative and the people are coloured with tints of earth and green. Their figures are like trees, gnarled and rugged, but imbued with the dignity and perseverance of their kind. People have used this painting to work out a grammar and perception of poverty and a new form of art. *The Potato Eaters* talks to the worker familiar with the grimace of poverty and the struggle to keep alive. The painting has also captured the poverty and hunger of the peasants in an eternal moment. Post-Impressionism is not merely about differences in painting technology, it is about the esoteric concepts of a new definition of the subjects of art. The faces of the poor and their condition could now be the subject of art.

When I went to Budapest in 2017 and stayed there for a few months, teaching at the Central European University, I went to the village where Amrita Sher-Gil had stayed and painted. Her mother was a Hungarian Jew. In my naïveté I had assumed that it would connect immediately with the 'educated elite'. Conversations with my new friends deepened my social understanding of the country. I began to understand that the anti-Semite and anti-Roma sentiments are still formidable. Sher-Gil's work is very much a part of Indian art history but unfortunately she does not occupy a comparative position in Hungary.

The inability to acknowledge varied perceptions cripple our politics, a politics that demands standardization and states implicitly and explicitly that plurality is dangerous. The infamous 'if you are not with me, you are with the enemy' is the most short-sighted of political understandings. It conditions the mind to dismiss different perceptions and understandings, which makes us vulnerable and fearful. It connects directly with the fundamentalist political culture, where dislike and incomprehension of plurality form the base. But since there has never been one standard culture in the past, one has been unprepared for the onslaught.

The Constitution as a Cultural Document

Culture is not mere entertainment. The worst interpretation of culture is its reduction to a 'cultural programme', distinct from the more serious business of the day. The inability to see culture as a kind of politics is to narrow it down to mere entertainment. There are political cultures that are now being understood as part of ideologies and beliefs. The political culture of elections and electioneering has a region-specific profile. The rural elections in India are very much like a mela—a word that has no real English equivalent. It is more than just a fair or a carnival. It combines the social and economic and often includes politics, it brings normal life to a standstill and the occasion is always celebratory. Just as the pre-election period is often more frenetic than when the actual results are declared, the mela is a social gathering and often brings all members of the community together.

Constitutional culture attempts to bring in the concepts of liberty, equality and fraternity, to balance the basic prejudices of traditional morality and divisiveness in India's multicultural people. It guarantees freedom of expression, but provides limits to ensure sentiments are not hurt. In making B.R. Ambedkar the chair of the Constituent Assembly, the new nation chose to give attention to its most socially vulnerable people and to make sure that the legal process genuinely addressed conflicts and hierarchy in society. All work in the public domain must locate itself in this cultural/ political vision. It has to deal with contradictions from time to time, and seek a resolution with justice and equality. The tragedy of contemporary India is its violation of the spirit of the Constitution we gave ourselves, to prevent the dangers of parochial, narrow-minded morality. The vigilantism and moral policing we see today, which reduces everything to fundamentalist scrutiny, predicts a fractured society. There were apprehensions expressed by important members of the Constituent Assembly even as the Constitution was being framed.

India's first Vice President, Sarvepalli Radhakrishnan, warned us at the special midnight session of the Constituent Assembly on the night of 14/15 August 1947, saying: 'Our national faults of character, our domestic despotism, our intolerance, which have assumed different forms of obscurantism, of narrow mindedness, of superstitious bigotry. Our opportunities are great but let me tell you that when power outstrips ability, we will fall on evil days.'[9]

Democracy evokes the greatest of aspirations, of a system in which we control our lives and our political environment. We dream of shaping our collective destiny with a sense of ethics and accountability. In electing to be a democracy and a republic, India chose a political system to accommodate its plurality and faced extraordinary challenges, and through the years has consistently faced its contradictions. On 25 November 1949, Dr Ambedkar spoke of the need to give up the grammar of anarchy, to avoid hero-worship, and to work towards a social—not just a political—democracy.

The cultural reform movements in India (some of which were begun by Narayana Guru, the Brahmo Samaj, Savitribai and Jyotirao Phule, etc.) were the basis of a new perspective on socio-political change. These movements paved the way for a more egalitarian and tolerant society, and built a body of opinion that could shape a constitution and talk of the need to annihilate caste.

The School for Democracy organized a discussion on culture and democracy. The Constitution is a cultural document and it reflects the cultural strengths and shortfalls of Indian society and addresses them. It also reflects the many varied perceptions in Indian culture—of plurality. In one sense the dichotomy is the result of the polarity and tensions between traditional/feudal/conventional society and the Constitution, a very progressive vision that endeavours to safeguard the interests of all people. 'Babasaheb', as Dr B.R. Ambedkar was known, too, with his penetrating vision, saw into our future, and cautioned us of the perils of sectarian divisions. He said, in the same Assembly:

> Will Indians place the country above their creed or will they place creed above country? I do not know. But this much is certain that if the parties place creed above country, our independence will be put in jeopardy a second time and probably be lost for ever. This eventuality we must all resolutely guard against.[10]

The drafting committee of the Constitution sought to address these and other critical issues. The Constitution was a safeguard against the self-recognized cultural fractures within our society. Fractures that are so deep-rooted that they can at any time be used to inflame and perpetuate action that will lead to the dismemberment of the polity. The Constitution is, therefore, a continuing legal and moral framework to make law work for justice. The discussion in the Constituent Assembly addressed all these differences and continued to look at the Constitution as a constant reference. The Constitution has not only offered legal solutions to address social inequality and other flaws in the character of Indian society, but also been a steady refuge in times of the greatest oppression.

Folk, Popular and High Culture: Who Defines and Who Propagates?

Some of us faced a dilemma while opting to work with the 'masses'. It was that mass culture had to be understood. Snobbish values in music or other performing arts can actually alienate us from people. It is essential to sing, eat and dance together. In espousing the serious forms of art, 'fun' is replaced by 'worthiness'. It is only in the rare case that the two disparate strains mix. Anything that is 'pop' is considered lightweight. Serious politics and 'art' have to be dark to convey morality and ideology. It is unlikely that we can invert the form and the message, except through the lampoon and the political spoof. But to connect with people en masse one has to evolve catchy tunes and spicy lyrics that draw attention, not to mention employ the support of drumbeats or rhythm.

The Ghotala Rath Yatra

In 1997 the MKSS undertook a dharna asking for transparency of panchayat records, which continued for fifty-three days.

The location was the Statue Circle in Jaipur. L.K. Advani came to Jaipur to hold a meeting with BJP chief ministers to address 'bhay, bhookh and bhrashtachar', i.e., fear, hunger and corruption. The BJP organized a rath yatra, which was to begin in Kota, with the same intent. The rath was air-conditioned and on a four-wheeler. The MKSS, having failed to get then Chief Minister Bhairon Singh Shekhawat to respond to 'bhay, bhookh and bhrashtachar' and accede to the demand for transparency of records, decided to go to Kota and stage a black flag protest; the anger and angst were palpable.

When the MKSS group came back to Jaipur, the consensus was that we must protest. Already the morning's blockade on the road to the secretariat and the aarti '*Raghupati Raghava Raja Ram/Sarkar ko buddhi de Bhagwan*' had spiked the irritation and anger of the officials and netas who would have had us jailed if we had done a rasta roko. We held a conclave and Shankar, Bhanwar Gopal and other friends said they wanted to stage a rath yatra and follow the BJP rath to show them how hollow their commitment was. Since we could not do that, they decided on a mock rath yatra that would draw attention to the false promises of the state. Shankar became the neta and a pushcart we borrowed became the rath. Ramlal made two stuffed horses in the traditional style, which were tied to the front of the rath. The 'kamdar', the traditional follower, stood in abject subservience with a tattered umbrella adorned with the famous scams of the past ten years. A borrowed chair and a piece of synthetic brocade finished the preparation. Women who had come to the dharna sang a potent lyric based on a popular religious hymn—'*Ghotala raj ki jai jai bolo/Bhrashtachar par Hari Hari bolo*'—accompanied by the dholak. They insisted they were in readiness to accompany the rath. There was an announcement at the pandal that a well-known leader had come to support the demand for information and was resting in the government guest house, and he and the rath would roam the town in full procession beginning at 5 p.m. A police posse, which had seen many important people come and go, decided that they needed back-up for this VIP event. Messages were sent, outback riders arrived on motorcycles and a busload of cops came to prevent any mishaps! At 4.55 p.m. it was announced that the neta had arrived and Shankar, dressed in the recognizable apparel of a BJP or Congress neta, was welcomed with garlands. He ascended the rath and it proceeded with about 200 people. The policemen realized they had been duped but could do nothing. The outback riders had already taken their positions around the 'neta and his rath' and the busload of cops had no option but to follow the 'rath'. People had lined the streets with hands folded, but when they heard the lyrics, laughter followed. Then Shankar, our MKSS 'neta', climbed onto the chair to lampoon all the netas. The 'neta' engaged in conversation with people, even our detractors, with wit and sarcasm, leaving laughter and understanding behind as the Ghotala Rath Yatra made its maiden journey. In the many years that have followed, the Ghotala Rath has travelled to Delhi, Hyderabad, Mumbai and many other cities, and of course has been to Beawar and other mufassil towns in Rajasthan. The RTI used many such interactive communication methods to reach the people. Music has been integral to communication.

Popular art

There is a gradation of art. Pop art, the most heard and appreciated of them all, was low down in the hierarchy, called 'ordinary' by the more considerate and 'vulgar' by the others in 'cultured' circles of art appreciation. The classical form at one time must have been popular music, patronized by religion and the court, and eventually found its way into the popular world. In Rajasthan, because of feudalism, the songs of Mira and the Sufis have been part of popular culture. People know the lyrics and the tunes. The prominent domination is of caste, but class has got intertwined in the emerging socio-economic patronage of the arts. The state has tried to take over patronage with indifferent success.

I grew up listening to All India Radio's broadcasts of Indian and Western classical music. But I also listened to the pop music broadcast. The extraordinary leap in popularity of pop culture has come with films and electronic broadcasts. It is also no longer one genre. It has subcultures, whether in South Asia or in Eastern Europe. I remember disembarking in Bucharest with Nikhil and Kavita Srivastava to attend a conference on methods to address systemic corruption, and being accosted by '*Yadon ki baraat*' sung with perfect enunciation and tune in a baritone voice at the airport. The singer knew no Hindi, but he recognized us as South Asians. Bollywood has taken over the export of Indian culture.

Classical cultural expression in the performing arts has remained with the privileged. It continues to reflect cultural and societal caste hierarchies and religious divides.[11] The state has tried to replace the patronage of the court and religion. Liberation came through the change in patronage from the upper-caste patron to that of civil society and the state. It liberated the musician, as elsewhere in the world, from private patronage. The state has made efforts, but despite all these interventions it has not played as satisfactory a role as it could have, riddled as it is by corruption and arbitrary use of power.[12] However, changing cultural modes of social celebration have seriously affected the lives of performers and musicians who perform on these occasions for livelihood.

Language as culture has perhaps the strongest roots after religion and food. The power of the language of familiarity to break down divides does not require explanation. Speakers of Bengali, a language I love and a people I admire, feel that their idiom is at the centre of the universe. The Hindi speakers—despite Hindi's numerous dialects (Maithili, for instance, is another language)—continue to harangue the rest of the country as speakers of the national language. The Tamils will declare themselves a republic if they are forced to make any concessions on language. Language is the basis for accepting or rejecting a stranger; it is partly communication, but there is more to it—the familiarity of the words, the tone and tune, the intonation. I have learnt to listen and learn. I have also felt the joy of addressing a big meeting in Rajasthani, and of feeling the pulse of acceptance. Appreciation is reward enough for learning to speak a language.

Then there is English. It is the language of power. I remember fighting a battle at a bus stand in Ajmer with a rude and unsympathetic staff. I was in a crushed sari as I was on my way from Devdungri and looked scruffy. I was treated with scant respect and little courtesy. In my moments of social anger I sometimes break into English, as I did that day. That changed their attitude. 'If she speaks like this,' they said, 'she has access to power.'

Urdu was the language of records maintenance in northern India. In fact, it was a language I learnt as part of the IAS-UT cadre in my probation period. Languages become enriched and grow only when their boundaries are porous. English has flourished because it has absorbed words from many languages. Language politics is also discriminatory, as we observe with Urdu, now viewed from a narrow communal context.

There is, however, one fundamental lesson for activists and activism. Political action with a community does not begin and end with a dharna. We have to engage with the community culturally—their songs, their religious beliefs and their ways of life. Have we engaged enough with the socio-religious practices of the people we work with? Why are we not tolerant of religious cultural expression? How much of the political alienation from secularism is the result of lack of comprehension, cultural exclusiveness, superiority or snobbery?

11

Moral Choices: The Continuing Dilemma

'The price good men pay for indifference to public affairs is to be ruled by evil men.'

—Plato

ANY ATTEMPT TO start a discussion on morality, whether public or personal, begins with a sense of apprehension. This has been a difficult chapter to write. The issue is weighty and the interpretations many. Scholars, seers and philosophers, political thinkers and social reformers have dealt with it. But an activist's life is nothing if not a constant series of moral choices, based on and evaluated by a moral scale. This chapter sees print because of collective peer pressure. It may serve, if not for anything else, to reflect the confusions and contradictions, and the irritation we experience. We have witnessed also the incarcerations of many of us because we spoke and continue to speak truth to power. We have acted upon moral perceptions of truth, equality, equity and justice.

Let us say that this is the beginning of an important conversation inviting participation and opinions. As Dr B.R. Ambedkar observed, 'Constitutional morality is not a natural sentiment. It has to be cultivated. We must realize that our people have yet to learn it. Democracy in India is only a top-dressing on an Indian soil which is essentially undemocratic.'[1]

A just, equal society demands probity in public life. Indian ethical systems are caught in two sets of contradictions. The first is the dichotomy that falls between tradition and constitutional morality. The second is the socio-economic hiatus between the privileged and underprivileged—despite relative political equality (i.e., universal adult franchise). The emergence of a third variable is that of neoliberalism emboldened by technological innovations. This has further complicated political processes by reinforcing individualism, ethical myopia, blind consumerism and profit. The two systems that oppose equality—the traditional hierarchical systems reinforced by caste, gender, etc., and the neoliberal market economy—have reinforced one another.

People are unaware that constitutional values determine their demand for rights. They have a splintered perception. The success of many people's campaigns for economic rights and for other development rights, based on constitutional guarantees, did not affect traditional voting patterns, which revert to caste-based choices, often in contradiction of constitutional principles. The perception of the public roles of people is itself trapped in different value systems. Extensive discussions have led us to believe that this is because of being caught in two directly opposite world views: traditional morality with its systems of hierarchy and impunity, and the promises of a modern state, based on equality, liberty and fraternity.

The other structural dichotomy is the persistent dialectic between individual morality and public ethics, which is a part of a set of choices between the predicament of our personal and political search. Often, the resolution for this dichotomy is sought by compromising ethical values. Social and public action needs to be monitored and regulated by the socio-ethical frame and the external justice system of the state. The ethical state should contend with tradition, religious morality, customary rights and a plethora of beliefs that originate from faith and claim a fair degree of public acceptability, heightened by contemporary political positions of religious and caste politics. Embedded in this is a narrative of two intertwined journeys of the personal and the political, of personal morality and public ethics, that shape and contest moral and political choices. It is a continuing dialogue, and often conflicting, to a small or greater degree, every single day.

Morality has a living pulse and has strange dichotomies. The rural woman who is a courageous fighter, braving imminent police brutality in many a dharna, may still believe in 'modern' miracles. Every society needs a moral paradigm and a moral code, as civilizations long gone realized, to regulate human behaviour. The internal sense of well-being reflects or seeks approval from these systems. The struggle for justice is also tethered to a larger vision of systems for guaranteeing justice. The inner conversations and just conclusions define one's personal ethics; you can lie to the world but not to yourself. If you fail to connect with the external system, though, life can become intolerable. For some, however, there is a convenient artificial disengagement between personal and public ethics. Most of us are caught in a dilemma where contradictions are ignored or pushed away. For instance, the same family that has rigid rules against lying and stealing may turn a blind eye to corruption, graft, nepotism by its members outside. The cliché that Indians keep sparklingly clean homes inside and throw all the muck just outside the house is unfortunately true. Strict moral codes at home and opportunism outside. And now the muck is threatening to engulf us. It is time we realize that the public and private are inherently connected.

Unfortunately, most religions are dominated by hierarchy, status and temporal authority derived from them. Sins are pardoned via comfortable compromises, most often with monetary payments. Every religion has formulae and a system of buying pardons, from the simple offering to pledging huge amounts to gods for 'listening to our prayers' for material or other gain. The problem lies in the denial or refusal to accept one's error.

The issue of ethics cannot be dodged by people who congregate to ask for justice. The basis of an effort to decentralize or dismantle power, or just ask for rights, is situated in a moral frame that questions the distorted right to rule unquestioned and without sharing power. The questioning of power has seldom succeeded without the support and bulwarking of a definition of a moral code that holds power accountable. The struggles for the RTI or a demand for an MGNREGA are both moulded and sustained by a moral framework, in this case the Constitution. But truth and appeasement of hunger, the two critical moral factors on which the two laws hang, are also concerns of religious morality.

Questions of equality are seldom raised within traditional structures. Compromise in the outside world and rationalization in one's mind are troubling but constant irritants that demand honest scrutiny and often fail to be fully resolved. Ultimately activism works within a moral frame of public good and personal probity.

Everyone knows discrimination from birth in one of its many manifestations—colour, class, religion, caste, gender—in social interaction. Living in an unequal and discriminating social milieu has been demanding. In the early 1950s when my sister and I went to school in Delhi, we were pinched and taunted for being dark skinned, she more than I. 'Kalikaluti' was the dismissive epithet. It was there that I also experienced my first brush with the injustice of racial discrimination. A south Indian, a Tamilian, living in Delhi did not have to labour to understand that there were many ways in which superiority was established—by where one lived, by colour, by proficiency in English, by dress, etc. The initial contact with morality often arises from a personal sense of injury. But it cannot or should not end there. The attempt to understand why leads us to wrap our heads around the complexities of public morality and mores. There are other ways in which we experience injustice, but most often it is a personal issue that prods us to invoke public ethics.

As an activist, one does not have the comfort of pushing difficult ethical issues aside. Any engagement with daily work raises the issue of right and wrong. The challenges to a solution lie within the complicated frame of caste, poverty, unemployment, discrimination and a host of other issues. There are many hurdles to cross. Prejudice is often paraded as axiomatic truth, and a morality that takes origin from it is very questionable. The Brahmanical control over spirituality had only permitted ritualism to go to the masses. For instance, the 'witch'— 'witchcraft' as a practice is still not extinct—is almost always a poor woman and from a Dalit community.

The almost primitive rituals that cross over from religion to superstition to the forming of a moral code also manifest themselves in dress codes and social mores of inequality. They often confuse form with substantive issues of right and wrong. The intersectionality of problems complicates decisions and actions further. The contemporary Indian discourse is riddled with engineered hatred for or against communities practising a religion other than mainstream Hindutva. In a life of public action, one confronts issues that constantly demand the taking of a moral position. Many of the arguments are based on perceptions of justice, of right and wrong in the world outside. But there is a persistent questioning of the correctness, or fairness, of one's personal, often unarticulated, biases and leanings. In this dialectic, morality as a personal definition and ethics as a frame for public work must work in consonance. If they do not, contradictions continue to harass one's conscience.

Moral choices may not be that simple, given the many intersections of life. How do you bring justice to bear on a person who has stolen to appease hunger? In Victor Hugo's *Les Misérables*, Jean Valjean spends years in prison for stealing a loaf of bread. In the movie *Modern Times* (1936), Chaplin shows how there is benefit in imprisonment for the poor—at least they get to eat at regular intervals. We collect anecdotes as we work, and the amazing range of real-life experiences often overshadow literary and cinematic masterpieces. I cannot resist sharing the story of our bicycle thief, which reflects the human condition—a mix of pathos and humour and the morality that condemns thieving.

The MKSS, in Devdungri, got a call from Bhim Police Station: 'We have a boy here who has stolen a cycle and claims his father works with the MKSS, from Badkochra [in the neighbouring district of Ajmer]. Will you come and meet him?' Shankar and Nikhil went to see what had happened. They were informed that the police were acting upon a complaint from a shopkeeper reporting a stolen cycle. The boy had been trying to sell the cycle for an absurd price. Both he and the cycle were handed over to the police. When the police questioned him he claimed the cycle was his. The constable threatened to slap him. He immediately said he had picked up the cycle in Udaipur. He was ordered to go back and give it to the owner. At that he exclaimed 'No, no, it is not from there.' 'Now what does that mean?' the cops asked. After a few more threats he confessed to having stolen the bike from Deogarh. 'Let's go and give it back,' said the constable and made ready to leave. The boy cringed and said it was not from Deogarh! Infuriated with him, the constable demanded a confession. This was his story: The boy worked in Udaipur, roughly 160 kilometres away from home, and wanted to visit his parents, but his employer refused to give him the fare. Smart and with no great conscience, he decided to take the first cycle he saw and pedal home. He was almost at Gomti Chauraha, about 50 kilometres from Udaipur, when the cycle's chain broke. He was in a fix. As he pushed on, he found another cycle parked on the roadside and a farmer working on his land. He waited for the farmer to turn his back, got onto the farmer's bike and rode on, leaving the one he had been riding as a replacement. As he pedalled on, a tyre got punctured. He looked for a puncture repair shop and found one. While he waited, he persuaded the mechanic to give him another bike 'for ten minutes to shop'. Soon he was on his way again, having abandoned the second bike at the repair shop. It was not as good as this new one anyway, he said. Many hours later he reached Bhim, 25 kilometres from his village. Worried about taking the bike home and answering his father's and the community's questions about how he had acquired it, he had decided to sell it in Bhim.

Eventually he was let off on strict orders of personal supervision and probation, as he was a minor. The cycle was left at the police station. If it weren't for the MKSS, the boy would have been sent to a reform home or his father would have had to bribe the system to release him. There is an interesting coda to the story. Nikhil was made the probationary reporting authority, and the boy chaffed at the fact that he could not outsmart him! One day at a public meeting he got his back, or so he thought, when he whispered to his neighbour, pointing to Nikhil, 'See that man with a beard? He is a rogue,' not realizing that the man he whispered to was the member of the MKSS who had got him out of trouble!

The morality that will punish violence and theft without examining the origins of it is unjust in some ways. While the law comes down heavily on the vulnerable, the powerful get away with impunity for committing real crimes. Vices and illegalities need to be restrained and punished within the law. How humane can the criminal justice system be in this network of human predicament? The issue of daily morality is complex. How do people come to any kind of conclusion of what is right or wrong for themselves?

The first reaction to punishment often is 'he deserves it'. The second could be the damning of a class. But among the many explanations, there would be some which question what condition induces such petty thefts. Village India taught me that the line dividing the private and the public is very thin indeed. One does not have the opaqueness of a compartmentalized home/office life as in a city to facilitate a myopic world view with unquestioned contradictions. I know now that in choosing to live with people in rural Rajasthan, we also chose educators who informed our perception of fundamental precepts that relate to the dilemmas and possible solutions to daily problems. It is this that led us to demand an RTI law and continue to struggle for accountability.

Morality and ethics cannot be associated with religious or spiritual well-being alone. This is a democratic frame and has an obligation to monitor and support public action.

The Discomfort of Our Conscience

As activists we are always on the watch to make sure that we do not allow personal comfort to interfere with our perceptions of right and wrong. The MKSS has evolved a structure and process that allows for moral and ethical issues to be discussed. The artificial division between public and personal morality of many issues, including discrimination and oppression, has been continually challenged.

The average Indian used to be obsessed with morality. In trains and buses questions that raised interest were related to corruption: Where does morality begin, at home or in the public space? How do you talk morality to a child whose father takes bribes in office? Or whose family discriminates on the basis of caste? How can one change and where does one begin?

Morality at home and outside are interdependent and, in influencing each other, form a dialectic. As children we understood equality and tolerance through practice first and then by precept. As my brother often said, at home we did not receive lessons in morality but we were made to understand what was wrong or right. More than that we were expected to live with a sense of justice, compassion and kindness. Equality played a dominant role in our day-to-day routine in a caste-ridden society, where discrimination is a normal state of affairs. It was an overwhelming concern. Everyone who came home used the same plate and cups, sat on the same chairs. It is only later that political understanding and theory came in to unpack these existential conditions.

From as far back as I can recall, even my childhood emotions were affected by poverty and the pain of individuals. The good fairies and the bad giants, popular fairy tales and other stories defined the aspects of good and bad, use and misuse of power. From fairy tales to morality plays, perceptions of ethics evolved into the slightly more complex division of sins and virtue. Theatricals on morality, whether we see the earlier 'morality' plays of sixteenth-century England or the popular folk theatre of India, have stock characters who represent evil and good. But truth always wins in the end. The modern morality play enacted on our nation's contemporary political stage leaves a shattered belief—the truth seldom wins. But we have to battle on.

Adulthood brought a new lexicon in both actual and theoretical understanding to address these issues. In looking for platforms, the civil service was one attempt to use the structure and a legal frame to assist the course of justice. Whether it could facilitate a young woman to do something to address inequality and injustice waited to be seen. This was in the mid-1970s and the big gap between stated principle and practice was often a problem. The system reflects societal norms. The ministries of health and social welfare were seen as 'soft', powerless—in terms of budget allocations and in the matter of weighing in on decisions to be made for the country. There is a sharp patriarchal overtone in its hierarchy. The top three ministries—defence, home, finance—were seen as the ministries eminently suitable for 'powerful' men.

I fled from the discomfort of my conscience and the physical comfort of an urban milieu to a comparatively more honest one in rural India, where relationships were more frank. The journey into the unknown and the fears of a different cultural milieu are not necessarily the result of travel to a different nation or a continent. In rural India villainy did not come with an urbane smile; it came armed with a lathi and illusions were torn apart, leaving one to muster courage to face the truth. Chunni Singh (one of the founders of the MKSS), whose fear of insidious corruption has made him lead a minimalist lifestyle, frequently prefixes conversations with '*Main imandari se kehta hoon.*' (I say in all truthfulness.) That lifestyle has empowered his already powerful voice even more, to articulate that which others hesitate to; he is indeed telling the truth.

The discomfort of our conditions arises from an inability to make two contradictory systems—public and personal ethics—come together. It also arises from a conscience that continually evaluates one's performance. Those who work in the middle of people have to face it every day; they do not have the luxury and comfort of those who are employed in clearly demarcated and exclusive areas of work, away from the human condition. Every evening leaves an unanswered question: 'Did I do justice in resolving this crisis? Was I correct?'

Luckily for me while growing up, my family environment provided the comfort of logic and compassion. Discriminatory behaviour that we experienced outside and the questions we brought back home were challenges to be addressed, and our questions received answers. I grew up in a family where discourse on poverty, inequality, contemporary events were part of everyday life. We understood that physical comfort could not be taken for granted as a norm, that we were privileged to have all we had, that the fact that we went to school and ate well brought us into the orbit of the fortunate. We recognized that the less privileged whom we met needed special attention. However, the larger framework of an ethical universe seemed to totter in public life.

The privileged often do not even know they enjoy special benefits. I have heard affluent people complain of lack of money because it is tied up in investments! There is practically no understanding of hunger and poverty, of constantly worrying about the next meal. In 2009, interns spending a month at the MKSS worked on an

MGNREGA work site and after the four hours of mandated work swore that they would never blame the poor for being poor because they 'did not work'. Many said, 'They work harder than we ever will.' Some even suggested that the workers learn computers, much easier than wielding the genti-pawda.

At some basic level human beings continue to search for values. We use the word 'truth' loosely, stretching its meaning to cover many nuanced perceptions. The good, bad, right and wrong are the daily concerns of all people, especially those who opt to work to reduce inequalities among the marginalized. It inevitably leads to addressing injustice and oppression. These issues take us directly to look at power and constitutional morality every day. Movements and campaigns have a common concern with dismantling concentrations of power as they misuse authority. The issues can range from an inability to access rations to framing national policy and legislation.

For an activist and even for others in more routinized lives, normative values and discourse are imperative as a standard to measure one's correctness. Those seeking truth have to practise what they preach, walk their talk. They are subject to intense detailed scrutiny, as they often live without the defensive and protective layers other structures have. The link between public money, corruption and personal probity used to be a continual public conversation. But why are there grey areas in our moral positions?

In 1982–83, in Aao, an arid, waterless village, Harish Chandra, the pradhan of Silora block, said to me: '*Is desh mein sab ke khoon mein rishwat behti hai. Aap jaise Pavitra mahila hamare beech mein kya kar rahi hain?*' (Corruption runs in everyone's blood in this country. What are you, an honest woman, doing in our midst?) Harish Chandra and I started a debate among the village elite on whether honesty had died and whether, as he was suggesting, we should just accept dishonesty as a way of life—as inevitable—and get on with the business of misgovernance!

We want selective honesty. All of us react so very sharply to being cheated. We quarrel and deride the hawker on the street who cheats just to be able to exist. But we seldom look at the ways in which we cheat as daily routine—officials who do not deliver, teachers who do not teach, policemen who demand bribes for doing their jobs. Why should the hawker not make some extra money through his trade to support his poor family? Graft and bribe are part of a sub-economy, clearly recognized and unquestioned; many in affluent society are aware and willing participants.

I read an article in a US newspaper in the early 2020s that, interestingly enough, traced the logic of moral lethargy and compromise to convenience and comfort. Theoretically some of us (middle/upper classes) may want to lessen wealth inequality but aren't willing to compromise on our branded clothes or hugely expensive luxury food and drinks. We don't want poverty and injustice but wear fancy clothes made in sweatshops. We may have problems with technology and surveillance but are unwilling to question the misuse of technology. We fear that it may impact the convenience of the ATM or Paytm. How do we shape our politics if we want to stay unquestioned in our comfort zones?

Morality is more than chai shop debates. A minimum moral code is essential for public life. But how does one tackle the issue and where does it begin? Immoral behaviour, if tolerated and not protested, becomes consent. Do we speak out? Can we organize to express ourselves on the collective guilt of privilege, the acute sense of responsibility to speak out against inequality and injustice? The freedom to protest needs social life and democracy to be tethered to collective normative values. These normative values—liberty, equality, fraternity—defined in the Preamble of the Constitution are propagated and supported by public ethics, which resonate with the mainstream. People see their individual sense of well-being intertwined with the maintenance of shared public ethics. Loss of life is a tragedy, no matter who dies and what their identity may be. To crow with happiness and a sense of achievement at the death of anyone is a vulgarity that no kind of moral consciousness should accept as normal.

Guilt is often based on being part of privilege. Many of us have a sense of guilt and responsibility, which haunts us all our lives. Mine made me give up formal power, the promise of a comfortable life, and sent me on a journey to face life in its stark realities. I was amazed to realize that I carried power and privilege within me in multiple ways—my confidence, education, the languages I spoke, the development of my mind and skills, my cultural choices, the courage to face want, backed by the unrecognized reassurance that, given a crisis, I would always be supported. The list is long. Even my ability to participate and take decisions, to write appeals, letters and articles came with privilege. I only gave up the privilege of money but the rest remained as part of my baggage. The way of life in the MKSS, a deliberate choice to live without privilege, allowed us to only reduce some contradictions. However, the discourse on simplicity and ascetism allowed self-critical examination.

All privileged Indians wondering whether the second car should be a small one, looking at petrol prices with dismay and ignoring road space, would do well to stop and look at fellow beings just outside their comfortable lifestyles and homes. Have we, in the almost seventy-seven years since the tricolour was unfurled in New Delhi, been able to deliver basic needs to every citizen? Have we wondered why people are helpless? Have we, in our rush to buy more than we can use or consume, lost all touch with logic, compassion and conscience? Morality has its origins in this compassion and search for justice.

Moral contradictions exist everywhere. I remember a woman from the middle class telling us that our (activists') self-righteous positions were hypocritical, even with regard to a simple thing like clothing. The poor could only afford synthetic wear as it was cheap, easily washable with colours that did not run or fade, and dried quickly. The privileged alone used cotton and indigo dyes that faded and needed frequent replacement. The weavers of the handloom we sought to protect were themselves victims of this conundrum; they couldn't afford to wear their own creations on a daily basis.

Answers to these questions and more have come slowly over the years. But the basic question of how best to determine what is right and wrong for ourselves and for society still remains; life and work are always a search for answers. That some of these answers come from constitutional morality brings hope. There is a conviction that as individuals we may falter, but when we are given a chance to be responsible members of a collective, we are our best conscience keepers. This has been further reinforced by the conviction and courage of the hundreds of ordinary people who have inspired me during various struggles. There cannot be a world that lives only on hate and destruction. Evil cannot be a continuing state. The primary desire of almost all of us is to lead honest lives, and we can sacrifice a lot, if required, to be able to do so. Even more important is the general realization that honesty need not necessarily be a narrow concept restricted to financial exchange but can encompass far wider concepts such as honesty of thought.

For those of us who lead our lives fighting inequality and injustice there is a constant, even daily, dialogue between our own moral positions and that of society. It becomes imperative to check the 'correctness' of behaviour and a great deal of collective introspection follows. The preoccupation with the right and wrong of public action bears down on the need to deal with evaluating our decisions, feelings and thoughts. It can be quite exhausting or stimulating, depending upon extraneous circumstances.

Public Morality and Power

Guilt is overwhelmingly more in the realm of the personal, as it is more difficult to ignore. Public ethics can be a minefield with its artificial polarities and divisions; it also has numerous players and complexities, and produces a greater sense of collective helplessness and culpability of inaction. A sense of shared public guilt is necessary for the normative correction of public action, and so long as it exists it acts as a restraint to continuing atrocities and violence. This is further aggravated by political discourses that state unashamedly that this is a 'post-truth', 'post-ideology' universe, neatly withdrawing from any normative accountability that they may have to face. It is a convenient form of myopia. Morality and ideology are too interdependent; justification would become inevitable and uncomfortable. We are left with this easy downturn in ethical standards.

Public space is trapped in a dichotomized ethical world view and personal morality copes by shifting positions continually. The worst fallout of this confusion is the paralysis of action, as it needs moral clarity and determination guided by normative values. Most social reform comes from an attempt to resolve this conflict, with a clarity about the intersections between personal and public morality. Activist action is tethered in this space.

Politics has everything to do with power. Every ideology deals with power, gender, class, caste transparency and its manifestations—codes for apparel, strict social codes, stereotyped definitions of propriety and broken into small details of etiquette. Personal choices are influenced by public morality. Interplay between power and a sense of public morality educates and poses choices. They also influence one another. Organizations have to cut moral corners to keep public face and to maintain power.

The Indian state as represented by its governments has compromised on moral values. The functioning of governance, prodded to be more open from 2005 onwards, has now shifted once again towards concealment. Afraid of the RTI and written records, the governments are looking for paperless governance. It is much easier to destroy a file on the computer than a physical one. Thus making corruption and complicity difficult to prove. Records are critical for transparency and for accountability to be established. The opaqueness of the government always remains just a news item, with a few murmurs from some activists. The demand for accountability, and a strong counter-response, lies in critiquing the decision-making process. There are no consultations, no platforms and no space for dialogue. By narrowing and dismantling such spaces, the very foundation of participatory democracy and accountability is threatened. If justice is the yardstick and injustices like caste discrimination must be countered, we need platforms.

Almost all journeys to seek the truth have to, at some stage, contest power. The battle against poverty and inequality is, therefore, a contestation, non-violent but persistent. Perhaps that is why the play out of corruption, thieving and graft has become an issue of concern both for the individual and the community. Nevertheless, petty thievery always highlights the human predicament and can even come with a dose of black humour. There was a theft in the MKSS's Kirana Store in Todgarh and the police were convinced it was an inside job, as the lock had not been broken and there was no other way of entering except for a small ventilator. We, however, were convinced of the integrity of the people who managed the shop. A few weeks later the MKSS got a letter from an unknown young man, confessing to the crime. He said he had crawled in through the ventilator, stolen the items and handed them to friends outside. Since he was the tiniest in the group, he alone could go through the small opening. The gang of young thieves had fallen apart over the spoils and denied him his share. He wanted justice and had written to us! He had signed off as 'Sincerely, your thief'!

We continually discuss empowerment, abuse and access to power by the lower bureaucracy, the local caste and class power elite. Rural India recognizes power tangibly, as humiliation and oppression in its daily interaction with formal political and feudal structures. There is a need to tweak the definition of power. For instance, we have argued that if democracy is 'by and for the people', the 'people' are the mainstream—the power elite and its periphery, defined by money and power. '*Hamari Sanhkya, Hamari Takat*' (Our Numbers Are Our Strength) is how the people's campaigns describe democracy. The empowerment of marginalized communities lies in making power accountable by dismantling centres of power. Formal power has always been simpler to define, defend and critique. Power derived from self-worth has been an inexplicable part of the consciousness of justice. When one is empowered through this process, it becomes a part of one's life and there are no pangs of deprivation of removal from office.

The state's ability to maintain public probity and ethics is basic to a sense of national well-being. In India's case it drew up a formal constitution to check the misuse and misappropriation of power. The Constitution defined a democratic frame. It also defined the limits that ethical, elected governments could not cross. These deviations from human decency and propriety were subject to scrutiny by a judicial system based on constitutional equality and justice. So long as that remained the basis of governmental action, India would be safe from becoming an unethical and inhuman space. There would be aberrations, but they would be checked by the systems built into the structure—the judiciary and the legislature. The media would be impartial and report unjust and irrational action, or any action motivated by corruption. To some extent personal morality would also be controlled and tempered by the state and its position on justice.

Sadly, there has been steady misuse of power and an erosion of the ethical frame. In the past decade, this rapid deterioration has manifested itself in the passing of unequal laws by a brute majority in Parliament, circumventing the constitutional mandate. The Parliament, in unseemly haste, has bypassed due process of setting up select and standing committees to participatively examine draft legislations. Religious propaganda has shrouded irrational decisions and the abuse of democratic rights.

The already existent mad race to material well-being at the cost of morality has been condoned with hypocritical and plausible marketing techniques and lures. Encouraging inequality has become a justified agenda, based on public action to settle historical scores. An emergent system of violent assertion of superiority claims privilege, has confused revenge and vendetta with justice. The emergent masquerading moral code says, 'Do unto others what you would never do unto yourself.' A technical rule-of-law framework is being built to pass unjust laws to re-establish long forgotten vendettas. The justification—comparisons with foreign governments who chose to restrict their countries to race, religion and language—is a betrayal of oneself. Compromising citizenship for Indians, based on religion, through legal instruments cannot be justified by citing examples from other countries. The government has to be contained within the four corners of constitutional guarantees and contextual morality. The political discourse is equally occupied with the morality of individuals, of society and of the body politic. Nevertheless, it seldom addresses the origins of misuse of power, except superficially, and the real issues get buried. Maybe this is because they are complex and would also threaten formal power.

I recall a story about Mullah Nasruddin: One day, people saw Mullah Nasruddin out in his front yard, searching frantically for something. An inquisitive neighbour asked, 'What are you searching for, Mullah?' 'I've lost my key,' answered Mullah. The neighbour felt sorry and joined the search. Gradually more joined. After some time the neighbour asked, 'But where did you lose the key?' 'I lost the key in the house,' replied Mullah casually. 'Then why are you searching for it in the front yard?' asked the neighbour. 'Because there is more light here,' replied Mullah.

We are all Mullah Nasruddins looking for convenient spaces and, like him, we ditch reason for comfort. When we seek to bring light to darkness, enter inconvenient spaces, listen and talk to people who suffer inequality and poverty, and are unacquainted with policy and law, a genuine participatory legal framework evolves. The demand for the RTI was a silent revolution. Answers do not come easily, especially when one asks questions of our conscience or of the body politic. We must venture into the dark spaces in our mind and in society for answers to come closer to truth. The RTI and MGNREGA campaigns have shown us that it is possible to do so in public action.

The commonsensical reaction to corruption is critical, because defalcation of money is the tip of the iceberg of immorality, the misuse of power and the denial of constitutional morality. Corruption is the veil hiding inequality, injustice, casteism, racism, patriarchy, etc. These arguments have to be logically traced back to the moral frame of constitutional guarantees. Corruption is the disease of a malfunctioning and unaccountable state.

The emerging hate and violence that follow in the absence of a moral frame have vitiated public peace and harmony. The dismissal of non-violence as effete has been challenged. Non-violence as a part of protest and civil disobedience is an established practice for demanding moral and ethical justice, the implementation of laws and rights. Violence has not been limited to public gatherings; women, Dalits, minorities and vulnerable sections have also been victims. Traditional social sanctions and reprisal against violent behaviour have gone underground.

The misrepresentation of Gandhian values has tended to devalue non-violent methods. Non-violence in theory particularly needs reinstatement as a moral and political value. The One Billion Rising campaign, for example, for stopping violence against women, initiated by V (formerly Eve Ensler, author of *The Vagina Monologues*),[2] has drawn huge numbers across the world. Violence ends rationality, discussion, debate and resolving conflict, and prevents morality and ethics from getting space to express their position. The biggest victims are the vulnerable. The feminist philosophy of peace has taken a back seat in public consciousness; public perception has to include much more than the violence against women and expand into equality as a value for peace and well-being. The feminists themselves have to make an extra effort to re-establish the alternative values that define a morally just universe.

Gandhi's resistance to communal violence was connected to a frayed public consciousness and self-critique that had followed the mindless killings of the Second World War. The 1940s saw a public sensibility that responded to concepts of morality. However, Gandhiji's assassination initiated an argument for violence to resolve conflict, the beginning of the annihilation of religious tolerance. The inability of the mainstream leadership to understand the connect between religious practice and morality for four decades thereafter allowed the growth of narrow religious interpretation.

Morality in religion, or is morality religion? When religion is used for identity politics it foregoes its immense capacity for self-examination—and the real moral framework goes for a toss. Identity is all. The real purpose of religion, which is to evolve a moral code, loses all connect with moral tethering. I recall sitting with Naurti, my Dalit worker friend, and finding that we agreed about corruption, transparency, work, wages, but she was still wary of breaking caste norms. Yet she was aghast when her enemies indicted her daughter-in-law as a witch. They had used social fault lines to silence her when she worked against the corrupt. That she was a sarpanch did not deter them from settling political scores with her.

It is possible that at some point of time religion and morality were symbiotically linked but there was a severance—most vividly reflected in the use of religion for electoral politics. The so-called leaders are now mostly 'god-men' with one eye on popularity polls and the other on access to and wielding of political power for material gains. Some of them stand for elections and become office bearers of a secular democracy without accepting the norms of equality, constitutional or otherwise. Once this simplified and self-serving morality steps in, the whole bunch of prejudices arising from religious parochialism seize the discussion. The pre-arranged fundamentalist religious narrative masquerades as moral principles and takes over the debate and debunks any attempt to discuss the simple understanding of 'right' and 'wrong'.

Marx and socialism had to be debunked, Nehruvian scientific temper had to be misinterpreted and Gandhi's non-violence likened to cowardice before the public imagination could be captured and controlled. Intolerance was propelled as defence of one's faith. Ambedkar could not be treated with disrespect for fear of losing Dalit votes, but Dalits continued to be denied entry into temples, and hundreds of manual scavengers die each year in cleaning drains. There is serious damage to Ambedkar's constitutional principles in the many laws that are passed violating equality, like the CAA and NRC.

The lowering of the bar in public and personal conscience allows humanistic normative values to be downplayed. Myths have their unique place but when they replace history in textbooks in contemporary syllabi, then truth and fiction get blurred, stretching the borders of moral permissibility. When irrationality and superstition become the grounds for building an (il)logical argument, it is dangerous. If power so derived gets mass support and the blessings of a manipulative power elite, democracy is threatened. When the state deliberately abandons constitutional morality, then it is only people or civil society that bring in the moral compass—a Kabir or a Mother Teresa.

India's independence was bookended by the Holocaust and the Partition. No new country could have had a more harrowing or desolate beginning. Yet the leadership gave hope and the Constitution provided an ethical architecture for a nascent country to heal and build for the reparation of the living and for freedom for those oppressed by caste prejudices and identity. In the period immediately after the 2002 Gujarat genocide the conversation among its victims was a prayer that the violence they faced should not happen again to anyone. I remember many of them testifying that they wanted compassion to reinstate itself as a core value. When asked who should help them, they asked for support from ordinary Hindus who could re-establish the peaceful coexistence of the past.

India also drew strength from the rebuilding of nations across the world after the ravages of the Second World War. The people chose governance systems based on rationality and compassion. Humanity, after Hitler, was tired of violence, the overweening ambition of nations, nationalism and the propensity to nurture and garner hatred to sustain political power. It seemed as if the world, having learnt its lesson in large measure, had decided to dress its wounds and begin again. In this context, democracy and public ethics came to be defined on the hard rock of rebuilding peace to guarantee the dignity of the people.

To regain 'normalcy' after Partition was critical for everyone. Politics and governance had to take cognizance of poverty; the human condition was still trying to readjust to circumstances, adult franchise, social reform and a new economics of growth. Hunger and economic deprivation had to usher in equality of access to services. The Constitution took care of the larger ethical design but in public life it is the very small things that matter, and if they have a multiplier effect, you manage to either salvage dignity and sanity or lose it. In the period immediately after Partition, in Delhi, a young Sikh boy my age was selling small items from a wooden tray that was belted across his shoulder. I ran to call Amma to see if we could buy something. Soon there was a small group talking to the boy and ready to buy something. Moved by his condition, people wanted to give food and money. He politely declined. As he walked away I admired his extraordinary dignity and grace. This boy became a symbol of reparation and dignity to me and has remained a powerful reminder of a fragile plurality riddled by extremes of poverty, refugees and marginalization.

Public Ethics and the Right to Information

The RTI movement was located in the debate on power and ethics. After all it deals with transparency and accountability as remedies to corruption and arbitrary use of power. The perception of the RTI as central to well-being addressed the issues of ethics as perceived by a cross-section of people—it bridged the external and internal worlds of morality. It was a common understanding that information was vital for access to life, livelihood and justice. A common principle (transparency) and a simple tool (the right to question power) were universally understood. It seemed possible that many ills such as public deceit and injustice could be countered non-violently, democratically and with people. Questions of probity and the demand for ethical standards in public life linked the personal with the political.

The answer to the preoccupation with 'corruption' came with two separate movements. The first was a painstaking participatory eleven-year-long campaign for the RTI, a transparency law, carefully and rigorously constructed, with the preparation of many drafts by people. The first draft prepared by the Press Council proved to be a very useful benchmark. States passed RTI laws and the use of these laws facilitated a realistic evaluation, so that the Central law could use the best practices to modify the fairly toothless Freedom of Information Act passed by the Central government in 2000. The RTI Act (2005) was rigorous and was shaped by both experience and expertise, in which the rural user played a significant role. The critique of governance notwithstanding, it went through the due democratic process of policy and law making as prescribed by the Constitution.

The second campaign began with a bang with the India Against Corruption (IAC) campaign taking a cue from the Arab Spring. It circulated a draft made by a few, did not accept critique and sowed the seeds for a discourse that argued for dismantling the institutions of democracy and representative politics. It negated and went beyond constitutional oversight, and sought to set up a structure to oversee the three wings of the government—legislature, executive, judiciary—giving it unchecked impunity. The leaders of the campaign rode a huge wave of public approval, where the right-wing committed itself on record and liberal India was vociferous in its sanction to what it saw as a mobilization to remedy constant stories of corruption of a sick polity.

But corruption cannot be defined in monetary terms alone; it is textured and layered. You can be monetarily honest, but believe in inequality, genocide and injustice. The RTI campaign, by centralizing the Constitution, its Preamble and the chapter on fundamental rights, made a proactive statement about what was non-negotiable. It also accepted the role of multiple organizations in making public life one of integrity and probity. The IAC, on the other hand, did not differentiate between the role of democratic institutions and their performance.[3] By making the Lokpal omniscient and omnipotent, it granted this structure impunity. Transparency and accountability apply to all structures. The IAC campaign in ridiculing democratic institutions made them a laughingstock, and by implication disvalued the Constitution itself.

Between 2005 and 2013, transparency made the shift from being an idea to a practice. The attempt thereafter, by those whose impunity was threatened, was to bypass transparency, since it could not be killed. The methodologies used have begun with short-changing parliamentary procedures, from the deliberate ignoring of mandatory processes like select and standing committees (which allow public comment to re-examine bills placed in Parliament) to corporate control through electoral bonds to influence policy. Some older Indian parliamentarians were well-informed erudite members, who, regardless of which party they belonged to, kept the sanctity of parliamentary processes intact. Ram Manohar Lohia, Feroze Gandhi, Renu Chakravartty, Minoo Masani, Geeta Mukherjee, Indrajit Gupta, Somnath Chatterjee, Parvathi Krishnan and Rajkumari Amrit Kaur, among others, made considerable contribution in strengthening the democratic process. In 1995, the Indian Parliamentary Group instituted an annual Award for Outstanding Parliamentarian, but there is not much to back it up in terms of performance.

Law has been used to misuse power to twist the rule of law, to pervert constitutional principles and values in keeping up appearances but hollowing out content. The electoral bonds from which parties raise money should be the nerve centre of transparency and the financial probity of the political parties. However, the opaqueness of the process enables big corporate capital to dictate policy. The vote remains, like everything else, a mere procedure without any guarantee about its bargaining power.

We need to look much more at this critical link between democratic reform and our own understanding of ethics. Movements for change, in arguing for involvement with politics and public life, overlooked the eventuality of the majority—already empowered with the vote—running amok. Obscurantism as a weapon to undermine constitutional ethics was used to manipulate and derail political systems. There was a faulty assumption that power in democracy would be naturally controlled through the creation of institutions for checks and balances. Power when absolute corrupts absolutely. Democratic institutions have been co-opted and compromised. Simply knowing there is corruption leads nowhere unless it is supported by factual corroborative evidence. It is merely one opinion against another. Transparency provided the records against which such opinions could be examined. The fear of an open system is the fear of losing privilege and impunity and being forced into accountability. The entrance of the digital world has been double-edged. It promotes transparency, while allowing the state to acquire absolute information to control for surveillance.

The two campaigns (RTI and MGNREGA) coming together had great significance—the former an ethical campaign for dismantling power, and the latter for economic empowerment. It housed transparency and accountability through the social audit to deal with corruption in delivery. However, cheating at the MGNREGA work sites increases hunger and want directly. But WhatsApp messages and propaganda fill the workers' hearts and minds with the divisive politics of hate. The truth is that ignorance of political history gives ample space for prejudice to prevail. The worker falls into a trap, where she/he is accused of either being an advocate of Islam or Naxalism for demanding correct implementation of work on a MGNREGA worksite!

It is strange that questions demanding truth have been feared from the time when Pontius Pilate asked Jesus about the truth and did not wait for an answer.[4] Experiments with truth will always remain a concern of thinking human beings.[5] This is not a treatise on 'truth', relative or absolute; the range of interpretations are a trajectory that cannot be discussed here. The attempt is merely to draw the attention of all of us in public life to the relatively verifiable truth that lies within documents and rights. When we talk of speaking truth to power, we restrict ourselves to our interface with power.

The concept of transparency in governance is not new either in India or elsewhere. But people are now armed with a law for access to information and a growing awareness of their sovereign rights. The gains made in the last ten years have to now contend with the reaction of power structures. Any confrontation with the misuse of power is repulsed by false accusations, violence and additionally with propaganda arising from religious identity. This is overlaid with the constant bogey of being 'anti-state'. The methods used to silence activists incarcerated for amplifying the voice of oppression and the poor demanding a wage fall within a similar pattern. Their call is for, among many things, an open government and system that can be scrutinized for its performance against accepted democratic, constitutional, normative values for food, work, health and education. There has also been a systematic and consistent attack on the transparency mechanisms of the state. In some cases, there have been structural changes for denial and in others brute force has been employed to avoid scrutiny. The concerted attack on those speaking truth to power is too obvious to need explanation. More than 100 information seekers have been killed for raising questions.

Reactions to being questioned come from people when impunity or their individual interests are under threat, or when their personal integrity is questioned. To accuse anyone of theft is a huge insult. The rural Rajasthani knows no greater insult than to be held guilty for theft and misappropriation. Yet the embezzlements and the scams continue. Social audit allows the enforcement of a public discussion, an ongoing debate on the personal morality of those in power and otherwise. This addresses brazen corruption, by providing a public space for expression of a critique on personal morality.

The grey areas arise out of an ingenious method we have devised of dividing and fragmenting our lives into mutually exclusive spheres that suit our convenience, with the professional distinct from the domestic, or the personal. A nuclear physicist may come home to adhere to Rahu Kalam, an astrologically defined period of ill omen! It has been argued that since astrology is also a science, observing such taboos is rational. Proof, so much a part of scientific reasoning, seems dispensable. Equally, many socialists who claim to be atheists participate in the prejudices of caste, not being strong enough to take those battles home. There is no visible cross-referencing to see where logic may prevail. There is rationalization, which allows charitable and religious structures to sell pardons by donations of money from the guilty. These are subtle systems of duplicity, worked out with finesse, with theories and patterns of personal and social interplay. It's a system to buy peace for the guilty. A method to address fears.

The Impunity of Power

Since 2014, the government has taken recourse to passing anti-transparency and anti-people laws. The rule of law has itself been perverted, so that the injustice in policy becomes law and opposition to violations of constitutional principles a matter of law and order. Like the new 'anti-conversion' laws, which are effectively against equality and inter-community marriage, and are contrary to the Constitution. The cunning attitude of the present dispensation in manipulating fundamental rights through legislation has contravened the Constitution again and again.

In contemporary India, the conversation has shifted from its preoccupation with malpractice and corruption to discussing the moral correctness of caste by insidious references to the Manusmriti.[6] The obsessive preoccupation with corruption fell within the larger normative discourse of right and wrong that translated into crime and punishment. The narrative today has expanded from the examination of fact into a presumption that villainy is attributable to birth.

Caste and morality are intertwined in more ways than one. There are communities that were collectively clubbed under the Criminal Tribes Act of 1871.[7] The Sansies and Kanjars, for example, continue to be stigmatized by common prejudices that prevail in the communities. They still live on the edge of poverty, heavily discriminated against and oppressed. The major caste groups considered criminal by birth included Ahir, Banjara, Lodhi, Chamar, Sanyasi, Bowreah, Budduck, Bedya, Dom, Domar, Rabari, Bhar and Pasi, among others. The transgender community was also targeted under the Criminal Tribes Act.

The Sansies live in Nokha tehsil of Bikaner district, in a separate basti (settlement) about 3 kilometres away. They work jobs on the footpath, among others, shining shoes, repairing footwear and doing odd jobs on a daily wage basis. Shankar was on an MKSS yatra with others, promoting the Accountability Bill, when he met a Sansi in Bikaner and witnessed a strange altercation between him and the tempo driver. The fare was Rs 5 per traveller, but the Sansies were charged the full rate of Rs 30 (normally paid for hiring the whole tempo). Outraged, Shankar questioned the driver and was told that if Sansies boarded the tempo, others would not travel with them as Sansies were believed to be pickpockets. They simply had to pay Rs 30 or not board the tempo. This was in the second decade of the present millennia! In other parts of Rajasthan there are other tribal groups, such as the Kanjars and the Girasias, who suffer the same fate. Whether it is the tempo, or the barber who will not cut hair, or the anganwadi where they are not permitted to join, the story is still the same in many places. Those familiar with the Romas—the gypsies of Europe—will recall a similar condition and perception, that of being guilty by birth.

There are many implicit questions. In a society that believes a person is born immoral, what role does a legal system play to change perceptions? What moral role can public opinion play when the population in that area believes that such conditions are determined by birth? When the government in power glorifies the Manusmriti, the message is clear. The poor are always at the receiving end of moral inequality. It is interesting to note that the middle and upper classes believe, in general, that the poor thieve. The stigma attached to the poor has now spread to include religious and other caste groups. It has led to crimes including the taking of lives. The new definitions of criminality have made a huge percentage of Indians vulnerable. The lateral attempts to bring inequality into law, such as the CAA and the NPR, have helped build this unjust paradigm, changing definitions of criminality.

The most cutting accusations and insults in Rajasthan are those of thieving and lies. People take great pains to establish their probity through use of language and anecdote. Even the most corrupt try to don the veneer of integrity. In Hindi, every other sentence would begin with '*Main imaandaari se kehti hoon*' (I tell you truthfully) or '*Main sach bol rahi hoon*' (I am speaking the truth). As a counter to this is suspicion; nothing was taken at face value. Curiosity and suspicion had to be navigated with every new incident or change.

In Conclusion

'The most important human endeavour is the striving for morality in our actions. Our inner balance and even our very existence depend on it. Only morality in our actions can give beauty and dignity to life,' said Einstein.[8]

For those who are conscience-stricken to develop a moral compass, for the personal to look at itself and for the political to locate itself in an ethical frame have become necessities. As problems arise and are resolved, one begins to see the interdependence and convergence—for determining right and wrong, for peace. Peace cannot be a state of being just within oneself; it needs to work in tandem with an external reality that is, at the very least, determined to strive for peace. One looks for comfortable frames and the creation of a counterculture that establishes the immorality of violence, hate, inequality and argues for a culture of tolerance. Different values get affixed to individuals divided by the crassest definitions of difference. The aspiration for affluence and conspicuous consumption as the definition of happiness, in a world divided by huge chasms in income and access to basic living, further corrupts the moral argument.

At no other time in this country's history have we been victims of a situation of sustained duplicity, a contradiction of its own stated intent. Nor one in which the human predicament is challenged at every moment to express its sense of justice against the expression of giddy power. When power loses touch with justice, it is chaos of the worst kind imaginable. One would have thought that the world had learnt its lessons with the wars of the twentieth century and the Hitlerian regime. We look for hope and hunt for the moral compass in individuals and in society. In seeking answers, we look to great minds.

The Constitution continues to make sense and so far has withstood attempts to derail it from being the foci of democratic good conduct. Those of us who are threatened with dejection have rallied around the determined legal structure the makers of modern India left behind for the multicultural and multireligious country India is and should remain. India chose constitutional morality as a frame for defining itself as a just democracy. Ambedkar cannot be quoted enough to emphasize that democratic power and practice must be made accountable to values of equality and justice.

For those of us with a conscience, with a mind that questions and seeks answers, probity, integrity and truthfulness in the public domain, that seeks logical explanations, there is no substitute for the Indian Constitution. It sets these values impartially and uncompromisingly and equally for us all. The personal is alone and unable to connect with the political; the pain, misery and angst today threaten to swamp the public conscience. As decent human beings we are in the battle for a political ethos that will sustain us as reasonable beings.

12

Great Expectations and Hard Times

Democracy: Of, by and for Whom?

DESPITE ALL THE mishaps and distortions of democracy and the plethora of ifs and buts that besiege it, the majority of people all over the world strongly advocate for—and would opt for—it as the best, though imperfect, system of governance. It is perhaps the only system of governance that, at least theoretically, has placed 'liberty, equality and fraternity' at the centre of its political structure.[1]

Even in its very limited and crude form, translated as 'the vote' and elections, it has spoken to the common person universally. Without it, Kamla and Rukmini, all Dalit women sarpanches, confident, competent and remarkable, would not have led their panchayats in Harmara, Tilonia (both in Ajmer district) and Vijaypura (Rajsamand district), with their acquiescent and even occasionally appreciative non-Dalit, macho citizenry to comparative prosperity and 'correct' governance. Democracy has taken root in some significant ways. The panchayats, through the reservation of seats for women[2] and Dalits in a rotating quota, have become far more egalitarian, challenging the obfuscated system that wed democracy to privilege, feudalism and caste in Rajasthan, than what the legislatures and the Indian Parliament have elsewhere in the country. The opposition to reservation of seats for scheduled castes is a contentious issue where there was a majority savarna presence, particularly in universities and colleges.

The principles of democracy may be enumerated, but democracy itself is as difficult to define as beauty.[3] Its specificities derive from a choice of many permutations and combinations, driven by different perspectives of communities and of individuals. Perhaps, because of its intricate nature and its variables, there have been as many manifestations as there are peoples and nations. It remains too elusive to pigeonhole but is as essential as a daily touchstone for our existence. Yet, we must define it in its non-negotiable certainties. That explains why Abraham Lincoln's simple definition, 'of, by, for the people', still retains its relevance and charisma.

Ask a direct question in any rural assembly about whether democracy should stay, and the answer is 'yes'. Yet, the understanding of what democracy is beyond the vote is multiple and selective. Democracy's loose frame and set of principles—liberty, equality, freedom and justice—as stated objectives are universally cited and accepted. But since each country's governance has defined its own architecture of delivering or not delivering these values, it has brought in huge variations. By Lincoln's definition, all autocracies, single-party oligarchies, elected autocracies are legitimate in their claim—*by* and *of*, yes, but maybe not fully *for* the people. Although the question remains, who plans for whom and with what mandate?

India claims its democratic frame, firstly through adult franchise and the vote, and secondly through lip service to the principles enshrined in the Constitution. Cleverly, there have been very few amendments so far of the Preamble, the chapter on fundamental rights and the Directive Principles of State Policy. But in contemporary India, every expression of fundamental rights, particularly of freedom of expression and liberty, unpalatable to the system, has been condemned and perverted by an elected autocracy. Tardy Parliament sessions, ordinances that are passed without discussion, debate or being sent to select and standing committees set up for participation within the parliamentary structure have denied the country and its people the right to differ, dissent and disagree.

Power, Leadership and People's Participation

Most religions and state patriarchy[4] demand supplication and surrender, with the promise of prosperity. A people who have been victims of corruption and arbitrary use of power, of the 'fatigue of democracy' are easy prey. Is it helplessness, laziness, lack of political literacy or immorality that brings in the ethical paralysis? Is it a deliberate plan to mystify, or is it the repression of all protest in the governance architecture that made us silent? Dr B.R. Ambedkar said: 'Bhakti [devotion] in religion may be a road to the salvation of the soul. But in politics, Bhakti or hero-worship is a sure road to degradation and to eventual dictatorship.'[5]

There are two definitive strains: constitutional morality on the one hand and traditional caste and religious ethics on the other. The conflict that leads to continual contestation is a daily struggle. To add to the traditional oppressions are the passage of laws influenced by prejudice, such as the 'love jihad' law, NRC and CAA, demonetization, the labour code and the farmers' laws. The restrictions they impose on transparency and participation make these laws anti-people. So much so that a people fighting for their rights can be declared anti-government and state. The negation of parliamentary processes and introducing laws/ordinances without due process denies citizens the right to democratic participation and bypasses institutionalized checks and balances in the Lok Sabha and the Rajya Sabha. Independent institutions of democratic oversight like the Planning Commission and the CAG have been compromised. The people of India are no longer citizens but consumers targeted by decisions influenced by corporate interests.

The recognition has dawned for some that democracy, as governance and the nature of the state, impacts the smallest detail of life and livelihood for the poor. A negative policy decision taken in Delhi can affect 'roti, kapda aur makaan' (food, clothing and shelter) and change the life of a family, its levels of hunger, health claims, employment or the access to education. A sudden declaration of Covid restrictions becomes, for instance, a call for lockouts and unemployment and dramatically affects daily income and livelihood. The tragedy of migration post-Covid should have more than demonstrated these links.

It is unbelievable that just seventeen years ago people's politics converged with electoral institutional democracy to shape rights-based laws: the Right to Information, Right to Work, Right to Education, Forests Rights Acts and others. It was a period when people also shaped the rule of law and defined its universal parameters. The political climate was enabling. There were platforms to strengthen positions by churning ideas and containing tumult within structural paradigms—all working towards a consensus. People's organizations provided access to an idiom that was intelligible, space to discuss and involve people to make seminal contributions to the legal framework. Leadership, and collective leadership, was a matter of popular discourse. The question of dynastic rule, or the role of power within and outside the electoral process, and internal democracy within political parties and institutions were under debate. There was space within formal politics to express points of view and self-critique. There were also discussions about how leadership should be defined in a democracy: a strong vs an accommodating leader and so on. Embedded in the discussions on leadership and power today is the so-called charismatic leader. A creature is often created skilfully by a combination of sharply timed media reports, aided now by social media hype and images. There has to be process evaluation of the leader's performance, looking at principles of equality and collectivism. Internal democracy has to be continually nurtured. Questioning has to become an important and integral part of the process, measured against norms, rules and legalities. If participatory democracy is not tethered to constitutional mores, norms and morality, it could lead to mayhem.

Lao Tzu centuries ago said:

> What then is the definition of a good leader?
>
> Go to the people. Live with them. Learn from them. Love them. Start with what they know. Build with what they have. But with the best leaders, when the work is done, the task accomplished, the people will say, 'We have done this ourselves.'[6]

A Nascent Nation's Warning

The innocence of a nascent country and its intent was never more evident than in the atmosphere of the late 1940s in New Delhi. Independence was to many a matter of pride or worth as they geared up to face new responsibilities. Despite the Partition and Gandhiji's assassination, which was an act of criminality against normative values that were universally accepted, there was expectancy in the air. The country looked forward with hope, a hope that was more than met by the gift of a Constitution. This Constitution was written in the most participatory of possible alternatives available at that time. The discussions were transparent, and contentious issues were resolved through consensus with a truly representative group that worked hard at resolving India's inherent contradictions and obscurantism. Two stalwarts, B.R. Ambedkar and S. Radhakrishnan, left us with cautions and apprehensions that may today sound like doomsday predictions.

The country had a reprieve to some extent because of the shock of Gandhiji's assassination. Caste, gender and religion seemed to be the dominant discourse in an inclusive and open culture, ready to fight its structural inequalities. The hope of those years was built on the battered collective conscience of a wounded people. In a recent article in *The Guardian*, Salman Rushdie says:

> I have to say that India is no longer the country of this novel. When I wrote *Midnight's Children* I had in mind an arc of history moving from the hope—the bloodied hope, but still the hope—of independence to the betrayal of that hope in the so-called Emergency, followed by the birth of a new hope. India today, to someone of my mind, has entered an even darker phase than the Emergency years. The horrifying escalation of assaults on women, the increasingly authoritarian character of the state, the unjustifiable arrests of people who dare to stand against that authoritarianism, the religious fanaticism, the rewriting of history to fit the narrative of those who want to transform India into a Hindu-nationalist, majoritarian state, and the popularity of the regime in spite of it all, or, worse, perhaps because of it all—these things encourage a kind of despair.[7]

Perhaps, Rushdie talks for so many of us who were born on the cusp of Independence. Two nations, but a common human condition bonded us and pushed the issue of separateness as a necessary practicality to the borders of our consciousness. It now seems that the optimism that rose from the ashes of Partition is steadily being corroded. Despair, however, is the final defeat and has to be countered by looking at both the innate compassion in humankind and the stark necessity of creative action for survival.

Tagore had already cautioned the nation on the dire effects of nationalism. The Indian Constitution was an effort in bringing the cultures of many ethnic groups, of many religions, of the more than twenty-odd languages and a parabola of variations together, with a unity of purpose. The dominant discourse perpetuated by a single identity is injurious to the concept of India as a nation, as imagined by the framers of the Constitution. The contemporary alternate discourse talks of constitutional principles, values and constitutional morality, and holds together the many interpretations and a people. This coming together is a necessity for binding a structure for political cohesiveness and peace. The chapter on fundamental rights guarantees us justiciable rights, to fight a corrupt state if necessary, and the Directive Principles of State Policy gives a direction to our dreams of a more equal India. But the present dispensation has been clipping these rights by curbing the right to freedom of expression. The Constitution defines our functioning as well as the basic federal nature Ambedkar and the assembly imagined to hold our differences together and form a common ideal of governance. The Constitution also draws the frame of representative democracy and much else besides. But the most important contribution of this seminal document has been the normative values it has defined and the culture it has sustained. But there were other fears, of hyper nationalism and the overlay of growth and progress, as Tagore wrote:

> This nation may grow on to an unimaginable corpulence, not of a living body, but of steel and steam and office buildings, till its deformities can contain no longer its ugly voluminousness—till it begins to crack and gape, breathe gas and fire in gasps, its death-rattles sound in cannon roars. In this war [the First World War] the death-throes of the nation have commenced. Suddenly, all its mechanisms going mad, it has begun the dance of the Furies, shattering its own limbs, scattering them into the dust. It is the fifth act of the tragedy of the unreal.[8]

Ordinary citizens were the backbone of the Independence struggle. They emphatically rejected the Emergency. They supported JPs 'total revolution' movement. And it is ordinary citizens who have been the core of every progressive struggle that India can take credit for. It is they who speak with numbers and who have been willing to risk their fragile existence to keep the spirit of the Constitution and the democratic process alive. In contemporary India they are gagged by fear of speaking out and the restrictions on mobility, both legal and, during the pandemic, because of Covid. Democracy in independent India has never been as hollowed out as it is now. The Emergency saw closure of access of citizens to institutional democracy, but once it was lifted most institutions came back to perform within their respective paradigms. In contemporary India, in a matter of ten years, all forms of dialogue between people and the government have been drastically reduced, and attempts at critical dialogue are seen as 'anti-state'.

The attacks on freedom, on singular individuals and entities is now based on popular prejudices and religious prejudices. The individual citizen is caught between the notion of justice, as spelt out in public life according to constitutional morality, and the counter of the centuries-long association with religious morality, which popularly mandates discrimination. What we see today is the popularity of discriminatory practices based on the prejudice of people, rather than on rationality. It raises the question of how dependent constitutional participatory democracy is on the state's following its own directives as laid out in the Constitution, with justice and correctness.

What we are left with is the duality of participatory democracy in economic matters of inequality, where common persons who face an uneven economy loaded against them choose to oppose authority on the issue of income, well-being and a share of socio-economic rights. This also explains why the MGNREGA continues to be relevant and important despite the posturing of a fundamentalist, right-wing government since 2014. The success of the politics of the government is today challenged by the continuing necessity of, if not the continuation of, the demand for rights-based legislations.

Law and Order in Chaos

The state is often seen in the Marxist context as a revolutionary framework where people set themselves the goal of capturing 'state power'. An 'either-or' framework: fighting the state or capturing it. In the Gandhian tradition, the state is viewed with ambivalence. People's political organizations, on the other hand, engaged with the state to ensure the passage of promised laws and policy and later to ensure compliance. The state was also seen as an adversary when it failed to perform justly according to constitutional principles or democratic norms. In a democracy people claim ownership of the government as theirs, voted in to perform according to a social contract.

There were many among the privileged who used the system through nepotism and graft to deliver in their favour. But there was no participation in democratic governance for the less privileged, apart from the act of casting the vote. There was cynicism in the emerging popular discourse, and a desire to wish away the state, using the constricting nature of the 'inspector raj' and state interference in economic affairs as a critique for limiting its role. The increasing privatization as part of democratic economics strikes a death knell for the large numbers who depend on the welfare framework of the state for basic needs. Corruption in a system cannot be used as an argument to destroy it. The IAC campaign disvalued the political system for apparently ethical reasons but, in fact, managed to seed the dismantling of institutions.

Governments daily function at the cutting edge, relying very much in their interpretation of democracy within the scope of 'law and order'. An important lecture we attended at the IAS Academy was on the interpretation of the phrase 'law and order'. The argument was that if these two inseparable concepts went through a divorce, justice suffered. Order at any cost, without deference to law, sacrifices justice. In practice, however, more often than not, law is sacrificed to maintain order. It is also called 'keeping the peace'.

Admiring an authoritarian person, one who controls ruthlessly and reduces governance to discipline, applauding that person as an effective leader is ingrained in the middle class psyche. The details—of nepotism, misuse of power, systemic corruption—are not scrutinized. It was this psyche that brought Indira Gandhi back to office after the Emergency, and what will keep the present government and its cadres in power. Hierarchy, controls and denial—including freedoms enshrined in the Constitution—are justified by pleading the case for order. But this is one side of the case. It also reflects an ambivalent attitude to governance in general and a denial of constitutional guarantees of equality, justice and freedom of expression in particular.

The urge to see order emerge to displace supposed chaos has sanctioned a centralized dictatorship to take over the popular imagination. It has made surrender attractive, unheeding of Dr Ambedkar's visionary statement about the disastrous role of 'bhakti' in politics.[9] Has participation in decision-making tired the people, or did the multiplicity of expression confuse the structures of governance? There was and there is corruption. Corruption and the arbitrary use of power will follow wherever there is concentration of power. A new mode is to legislate to counter constitutional mandates. The electoral bonds, for instance, reinforce the opaqueness of an administration that does not believe in transparency, a Parliament that does not refer its bills to the standing committees and a government that does not disclose information about PM CARES.

It was just twenty years ago, in the early 2000s, when, converse to all these positions, there were campaigns for open governments in India and the world over. It was accepted that it was the democratic right of every citizen to demand transparency and accountability from their government and the state. Every government that assumes office with the people's mandate to govern for the welfare of its citizens has the obligation to answer and deliver. The demand for accountability also imposes on the people the duty to oversee and monitor the functioning of the government. In India we had to change not only the nature of bureaucratic governance that was part of our colonial inheritance, but also the innate conditioning of 'us', the people. The government has been seen by the majority as the 'mai-baap' in a paternalistic system, or largely as a power structure that should be manipulated with sycophancy. Equations are, therefore, established with the civil service and politicians with apparent obsequiousness and inherent contempt.

These representatives define the nature of governance and of 'civil society' both by implication and by specific policies of control. The people's movements and those who formed political formations outside of this 'mainstream' have lost basic democratic space and found themselves on the fringes of both the electoral battles and engineered civil society debates. The discourse is now firmly in the hands of a set of people who, while working within the limited goals of getting electoral power to govern, set the paradigm for national debates and manufacture consent, jeopardizing the basic tenets of the Constitution and the principles of 'democracy'.[10]

Democracy works only when it is located in a normative socio-political structure that depends heavily on the rights to: freedom of expression, form fraternities, work towards equality, guarantee justice and freedom of religious practice. What the RTI managed to do was show how constitutional normative values have to be publicly accepted and made the context of public morality.

Despite all these failures and constraints, we still want democracy for the possibilities it creates for participation. In a theocracy and a fascist state, and in a dictatorship, equality, liberty and freedom of expression are denied structurally. So long as it seems even remotely possible to invoke justice, or work towards justice, one continues to look for improvement, mending or changing the status quo. This is the vestige of hope, the possibilities that egg us on. It is for this very reason that defenders of democratic rights are incarcerated—because they are people who voice reason, invoking hope in the constitutional frame.

We have often been asked whether one can have the right to information without democracy, implying that the right to question fundamentally underscores the freedom of expression, equality and accountability. Our steadfast answer has been that without a democratic frame the right to information cannot be conceived, let alone legislated or implemented.

13

The Power of People's Participation

THE MKSS CAMPAIGN had begun to demonstrate that there could be an opportunity to use elections as a means to 'democratize' ethics and commitment as a basis for political participation.

Social movements by definition are single issue or selective issue-based congregations. The movements base their creativity and work on the politics of constitutional conscience and norms. They call themselves political in the broadest terms. How do they then address the most fundamental structure of democracy, the voting system? They often do not know nor can advise on whom to vote for. Every election the questions come, they bother everyone for a while and then, once elections are over, they seem to dissolve in the humdrum of daily affairs. But the questions remain, to haunt the thoughts of the socio-political activist.

'Children of Our Age'
We are children of our age,
it's a political age.
All day long, all through the night,
all affairs—yours, ours, theirs—
are political affairs.
Whether you like it or not,

your genes have a political past,
your skin, a political cast,
your eyes, a political slant.
Whatever you say reverberates,
whatever you don't say speaks for itself.
So either way you're talking politics.
Even when you take to the woods,
you're taking political steps
on political grounds.
Apolitical poems are also political,
and above us shines a moon
no longer purely lunar.
To be or not to be, that is the question.
And though it troubles the digestion
it's a question, as always, of politics.
To acquire a political meaning
you don't even have to be human.
Raw material will do,
or protein feed, or crude oil,
or a conference table whose shape
was quarreled over for months;
Should we arbitrate life and death
at a round table or a square one?
Meanwhile, people perished,
animals died,
houses burned,
and the fields ran wild
just as in times immemorial
and less political.

—Wislawa Szymborska
(translated by Stanisław Baranczak and Clare Cavanagh)[1]

Socio-political activists live with constant reference to representative politics. I have often been asked, as have many others, 'Why don't you stand for election? You can do much more.' I have been clear that since I did not want to stand and operate in the grey area between exigency and ethics, I could only honestly be an activist, where ethical choices both explicit and implicit are compatible. It is not disputed that electoral politics and state power represent the most powerful structures in a democracy. But the politics of victory brings in a competitiveness where the desire to win may very often cut into the ethics of personal and political decisions. In most electoral campaigns and battles this is visibly so. The role of alternative or non-party politics is based on ethical standards and the power to question authority. Those who question also bear the moral burden of following the ethics they demand.

Power in one area does not get translated easily into the other, as we have seen. Often very credible and successful activists fail the test of the ballot. This is because the voter's psychology sees a pragmatic division between the power to rule and the power to protect and protest. The non-party protagonist draws the battle lines not on winning and gaining but on right and wrong, justice and injustice. Victory does not lie in gaining office but in vindicating the principles of public constitutional morality. The two do not come together often. The failure of public action to impact state decisions involving the lives of millions of Indians on the margin has pushed non-party protagonists into vote politics. In their discussions before elections, the temptation is not so much for personal power and gain, as for the chance of using state power to act ethically and enact and enforce ideals. But almost all efforts by people with credibility in public life to fight elections have ended in severe electoral losses.

The largest organized effort I have been part of was the Lok Rajniti Manch of the NAPM, an attempt to answer the dilemmas of electoral politics. We began with two propositions, both important but with a demand for a different architecture. We could not resolve absolutely whether we were sitting together to discuss alternative politics (movement politics) or political alternatives (to oust the parties in power, replacing them with comparatively more ethical ones).[2] We started detailed discussions within specified time spans, when much of the initial juxtaposition remained to be discussed and cleared. The concept note was not clear, wavering between the two concepts as it was, with varied expectations. The discussions began with trepidation for some and amidst great excitement for the others.

The core issue was to look for alternative politics and not for a political alternative. However, given the complicated demands of alternative politics, which demanded looking at each of the subsets before taking a call *plus* ensuring that the whole structure contained each of the details, led to it becoming a debate on evolving a political alternative. Perhaps, to be fair, the time was too short and the committee too varied in its expectations to come to any conclusion. Looking back, this probably explains the NAPM's divide when the Aam Aadmi Party (AAP) floated candidates, in which some NAPM members stood for election, while others refrained from participation on many grounds.

Ethically rooted political aspirants, who found no comfortable space in formal politics, were drawn into the composition of the Lok Rajniti Manch in 2004. As were the frustrated movement activists, whose failure to impact seminally and on scale on democratic issues remained a continuing sense of concern. It was predictable that the two would not ultimately agree when a document of promises was placed for debate. The promises were idealistic and utopian, and failed to see the inability of a nation to reverse immediately on issues like, say, nuclearization. The document promised immediate cessation of all activities. Within the structure of governance, parties change, but policy can be rescinded only within the space provided by Parliament and institutions built for the purpose. Historical processes also shrink or expand spaces; there is linearity to this process. Issues need to be addressed with great attention to detail and point, counterpoint. Such an exercise was beyond the composition of the large and varied group of people who volunteered to perform this exercise. The only movement not within a known ideological frame that was successful in electoral politics—the AAP—had to renege on many of its promises after the election.

The political argument has to be easily understood. In the case of the Lok Rajniti Manch, given the already existing and embedded political quirks and lack of probity, the intervention, coming midway in the history of electoral politics, began with fundamental handicaps. When people who do not want state power as an end in itself build a political party structure, the architecture has to be set up over time to discuss and arrive at a consensus over a range of issues. We need an alternative form of politics, with constitutional politics as the core, which will perform its role as a conscience keeper. This role that began to develop and mature has been whittled and attacked alternately so that constitutional ethics is no longer at the core of the political culture.

In today's context alternative politics is utopian. It will remain an ideal. But the way to it is warped with every contradiction the political process can fabricate or human ingenuity can invent.

Nevertheless, it is a permanent topic of concern and conversation and has occupied the minds of a huge cross-section of people. Like all utopias, it keeps us walking towards an ideal. The political alternative, a matter of immediate concern, is always a matter of gossip, discussion, worry and often mixed up with campaigning, the exit polls, the stolen electronic voting machines and goonda politics, which almost every party wants not to condemn.

Democratic Institutions

The state is steadily withdrawing from its commitments to the poor. The poor have no access to resources. There is no real hope to access land and there is no land reform. Economic alternatives require capital investment.

The poor are caught in a dilemma between the weakening and disempowering of institutions set up by the state and the argument for privatization as a cure to this malaise. Private institutions in education and healthcare spell exclusion for the poor and all those who cannot pay. While the poor want an accountable state, the state itself is busy trying to offload its primary responsibilities to unaccountable private institutions.[3]

The present regime has fundamentally changed Indian democracy's legal and constitutional framework, diluting the checks and balances that the independent institutions and statutory bodies had on political power. The Election Commission (EC) and Reserve Bank of India (RBI) have all but lost their reputation as being unbiased, 'free and fair' and beyond the influence of party politics. Meanwhile, the electoral bonds scheme—passed via a money bill in a dubious and allegedly constitutional process that violated the parliamentary process—has made political funding completely opaque. Recently, the EC opposed a stay on the bonds. If, along with the EC, the information commissions and other such institutions at the top are compromised, are already hollowed out and lean one way, then the state district and village levels at the bottom have even less power and control over corruption than before. The Supreme Court, EC, RBI, all the statutory and constitutional bodies have the dual role of impartial implementation and safeguarding of political, social and economic rights. Perhaps the most dangerous decline is that the architecture has been insidiously changed from the inside, writing discrimination into law, policy and functioning.[4]

With the disbanding of the Planning Commission into the business-like entrepreneurial 'think tank' NITI Aayog, many state and local planning boards have also become non-functioning. The Planning Commission gave the Indian government a chance to work simultaneously for economic development and social justice. The Five-Year Plans were one of the first ways that the independent Indian government built in accountability to the people. Having these plans gave a chance to review performance, land reform, distributive economic justice, gender, caste and minority equality, and other issues of ongoing and immediate concern.

In rural parts of the country, the effect has been compounded (if not disastrous), as the panchayat, gram sabha, ward sabha, district planning committee, block development/zila parishad, village development council, etc.—already weak bodies—have been written out of planning and participation to an even higher extent. Despite these elaborate branches at the local levels of governance and planning, the task of preparing a reasonably sound District Plan has not made much headway in the states due to many issues, primarily the lack of people's participation. Those who make plans do not want to share the power, make budgets, look at figures and share development spoils, at the district and block levels. The ones who will benefit the most do not comprehend it, and the village looks at the planning gram sabha with disgust and shrugs it off, leaving it to a few officials. If these few people have any interest at all it is shared through spurious resolutions, and they do what they always intended to do: make their pile.

Other reasons include structural lacunae in institutionalized arrangements. The process of seeking consultation with villagers/ stakeholders in the planning process is either not well established or not sufficiently encouraged and developed; there is a lack of appropriate and reduced methodologies for planning, in tandem with the lackadaisical training of planning personnel, planning without addressing realities of resource constraints and the absence of a meaningful way to have collective decision-making.

One could say that in making participation a core principle we reimagine and regain the concept of democracy by looking at the most viable of alternative spaces where we can begin to construct the architecture of decentralized participation. We, the people of India, gave ourselves the Constitution. Where do we, in fact, feature in the making of policy and legislation? People and organizations have pushed for different forms of formal and non-formal engagement with structures of power. Where they have succeeded, power has been shared, demonstrating the potential of participatory frameworks for defining possibilities for a more equitable and socio-economically just democracy.

The People's Campaign for Decentralized Planning (launched in 1996–97) in Kerala was indeed a logical move towards taking democratic structures of participation to people. Kerala's campaign of decentralization had the express purpose of promoting people's participation to increase awareness and maximize the direct involvement of citizens in planning and budgeting. It offered a great example to the central and state governments. The campaign was an exceptional effort at bridging the gap between community engagement and governance. It had been specifically conceived as a vehicle for deepening democracy. As a result, 'all Kerala's 1,214 local governments—municipalities and the three rural tiers of district, block, and grama panchayats—were given new functions and powers of decision-making and were granted discretionary budgeting authority over 35–40 per cent of the state's developmental expenditures'.[4]

Our takeaway from Kerala's participatory initiatives includes the need for the pre-legislative process—by which people see and have access to draft policies and plans, and can suggest changes before these are finally legislated. The pre-legislative process is to be strengthened if policy has to benefit people, and in being transparent allows people to monitor it from time to time.

Idiom plays a critical role in making participation come alive. The overuse of technical jargon and acronyms and incomprehensible use of language leave the average person confused. The efforts to make participatory budgets work is a huge step forward. Even words like 'budgets' and figures in newspapers tend to mystify the common person. The controllers of power then base their arguments for non-inclusion, quoting a lack of interest. The transparency that followed the enactment of the RTI has to a large extent kindled the interest of people in the planning and governance processes.

The promises of electoral politics are supposed to be realized through democratic governance. Democratic governance, in turn, can only be realized through a process of participation. Participatory politics is a constant constructive critique, pointing out the contradictions between promise and action, and the indifference or neglect measured against constitutional provisions, rights and guarantees. Rights-based legislations have been created to overcome the denial of basic promises made in the Constitution. They also aim to hold the administrative machinery accountable for the non-delivery of very basic survival needs—of food, work, education and the rights of tribals to live on the land they have protected and nurtured for generations.

As accountability to superior officers gets more and more diluted, even basic norms of a traditional law-and-order machinery need to be monitored by people; demands have emerged for a Prevention of Communal Violence Act.

The National Advisory Council was set up to look at and advise the government on the implementation of its social policy commitments during UPA I and II. The First National Advisory Council (2004–08) played a significant role in implementing social policy as laid out within the framework of the political promises made by the first United Progressive Alliance (UPA) government in a document called the 'National Common Minimum Programme' (NCMP). This made a broad spectrum of social sector commitments. The overall framework remains the Indian Constitution, but closer examination shows that many of the NCMP commitments relate to the very promising but largely unrealized Directive Principles of State Policy in the Constitution. A few of them were taken up and brought to Parliament in the form of important legislations, including the NREGA, the RTI Act, the Domestic Violence Act and the Forest Rights Act. These legislations sought to address the inequalities in socio-economic policy and access of the marginalized.

The RTI has specifically addressed the issues of involvement of citizens in democracy, drawing upon their sovereign constitutional right to know the what, why and how of governance. It has, therefore, revolutionized and changed the relationship between the citizen and the state, has helped in correcting the power imbalance in governance and decision-making, and has aided people in accessing the basic services due to them.

14

Crafty Inversions of Democracy: Ideas and Ideologies

POST THE DISASTROUS 2020 Covid-19 lockdown in India, when almost all businesses, services and unorganized sectors suffered huge losses and cuts, Oxfam International came out with a report (2020–21) titled *The Inequality Virus*.[1] While poor migrant workers lost their jobs, had no security at all and were treated with callousness and contempt by the arms of government and administration supposed to help them, the extremely wealthy were busy getting richer. Some appalling figures shared by *The Inequality Virus–India Supplement 2021*[2] include:

- India's top 10 per cent of population holds 77 per cent of the country's wealth;
- Wealth of Indian billionaires increased by 35 per cent during the lockdown period;
- The increase in wealth of the top eleven billionaires during the pandemic can easily sustain:
    - the MGNREGA scheme for the next ten years; and
    - India's health ministry for the next ten years.

What does it mean for democracy when the government keeps giving the richest capitalists tax cuts, and either ignores or worsens the conditions of the poor and vulnerable labourers and farmers?

Politics has started working for private capital and big business. The lobbying takes place even before the election, when electoral bonds are bought by companies to finance political parties. Their interest converges with the global surge for privatization, and we need to seriously ask whether the vote has surrendered its power to dictate policy. The nexus between big money and politics has given birth to centralized power and curbs on economic and political freedom of expression. The payoffs ensure that the government will control public protests and keep the people's demands in check by using the might of the state. Slowly, laws to curb freedoms are introduced in the name of controlling terror or protecting national interests. Opposing the government is deemed tantamount to opposing national interest, an argument that needs to be examined in detail to see the serious implications for democratic freedoms and expression.

The assumption that all totalitarian governments are socialist in large measure is proven wrong. There is a misconception among many of us that capitalism promotes freedom and defies totalitarianism. This is a fairy tale, much like comics with happy endings with the good and bad fairies and giants. If both capitalism and socialism work within an ethical frame, with transparency, accountability and integrity, they may shape a more rational and compassionate state. Totalitarianism is not based on ideology but is a form of governance dependent on amassing power and centralizing it, and stifling questioning and critique. It can become a part of any political ideology, as has been amply proved all over the world.

The ideology is separated from the type of governance it chooses to adopt. This is clearer now than ever, particularly if we look at contemporary global trends. We would say in today's idiom that totalitarian governments can and are functioning within frankly espoused capitalist economic structures. The newly emergent capitalist-elected dictatorship has a mix of electoral ignorance with technological controls and free fiscal flow across countries. This sets the scene for a new gulag where questioning, independence and rationality are the first victims of this dispensation. Thrown overboard are free speech, expression, fraternity, equality. Freedom is suspect. Rights expressed by anyone are a threat to the sovereignty of the nation.

Democratic institutions and electoral processes have been taken over by corporations and big businesses. Multinationals and huge corporations have no citizenship. All over the world today, people are protesting against the opaqueness of these corporations. If we do not critique the role of corporate money as part of the governance and corruption debate, we are really only talking about the tip of the iceberg. People's voices drown in statistics of growth rates and the balance sheet of business interests.

Democratic governments run in the name of democracy and electoral politics, but the decisions are arbitrary and corrupt in monetary and other terms. Capitalism, as it is practised today, tends to destroy democracy because it does not want the voices of people's rights and constitutional guarantees to drown out investments in extractive and other industries, aggrandizement and profit. Also, the very idea of 'one person, one value' threatens the core concepts of acquisition, profit and competition that capitalism seeks to nurture. While democratic institutions might toe their line, citizens demand the freedom to choose even their economic agenda and become the strongest defenders of democratic rights. Even as they oppose some policies and demand others, they assert their right to participate.

There are, however, movements that oppose the imposition of the neoliberal development paradigm.

In Odisha the government planned industrial development on the coastline, and acquired land from people who still gainfully lived on their produce. It was their livelihood and took care of building food security. The might of the state did not align itself with the people (whose representative it is) against South Korean steel company POSCO, but with global interest. Nevertheless, the people staged a long protest and finally won their battle, democracy triumphed, POSCO wound up its business in Odisha and went home.

Common sense and the people's will are negated, and basic democratic rights denied to decide what kind of development a community wants. But in Odisha, the local self-government—the panchayat—gave people the freedom to decide, and they decided that they did not want to give up their land to the POSCO project.

Deliberative Democracy

Constitutional guidelines and democratic principles, among other things, ensure a five-year mandate, with the process of election laid out clearly. What has happened quite evidently is the failure of democratic practice. The methods to guarantee that the practice must be democratic lie somewhat outside the strict political frame. The reasons lie in the intersection of feudal social norms and modern political systems, where the latter have been weakened by prevailing obscurantism of social mores. For people to provide the necessary support to guarantee a democratic society, much work needs to be done with political education, even for those who are victims, to understand the real power that democracy provides them to set right the imbalance. This process lies outside legalistic tools available for redress.

When it comes to gross violation of norms, the relationship between communities is regulated by laws and common normative values. The large unchartered domain of 'cultural ideology' has made its impact globally and in India as well. Ordinary people in villages have allowed years of rational build-up of democratic learning to be subsumed by cultural prejudices. The appalling failure of representative democratic structures to stop this has led to a takeover of governance. This demonstrates the flaws leading to majoritarianism, felling democracy itself. It has, therefore, become imperative to sustain the republic and democratic mores.

The polity continues to have its fissures but the question is: How does government contain the occasional communal tension from becoming genocide or carnage? This reflects on the failure of the governance system and the inability of the common voter to sift the notions of democratic governance and apply it in actual practice, until it's too late.

The litmus test in any democracy is the value of the last person—the dignity of the individual and the right to economic and social equality. Laws do not make a democracy, processes do. If the basic framework of the structure of democracy is based on an undemocratic social structure, it casts a long shadow on its principles and practice. It corrodes democracy, as we see now, to distort governance and go back on constitutional obligations. The cultural base has to be sound.

The MKSS for its part has been actively involved with making democracy work. The translation of democracy into modes and methods, which apparently look so mechanical, bureaucratic and of the world of 'babus', is where much of the dismantling of rights and laws takes place. After all, the 'last person' (i.e., the most marginalized) of Gandhiji and the discriminated whose plight is sought to be mitigated by the Constitution created by Ambedkar expectantly await the translation of that promise into reality. This will or will not happen because of a process—one that must change if democracy has to deliver. As Baba Adhav says, '*Satta badalne nahin aaye hain, vyavasta badalne aaye hain.*' (We haven't come to change the government, but change the process.) Much of our collective thought has gone into the fashioning of processes and tools in the last two decades and that is why accountability and methods of interface such as the RTI and the social audit have taken shape.

The act of building consensus begins at home. The family cannot agree very often, there are always diverse opinions. To arrive at a conclusion is always difficult, even in a simple matter of what vegetable to cook that day. Families evolve structures to address what are, in comparative terms, small differences and decisions. It is the practice of taking everyone's opinion into consideration and the tools of communication that help put equality into practice. The fundamental contradiction in social texture is the built-in inequality and the hierarchy contending with the equality we have given ourselves, democratically and constitutionally.

Democracy in action requires a set of principles, a structural frame, and within it platforms for discussion, argument, debate and a set of decentralized authorities for ensuring the normative working of it. This belief in democracy should be reflected in every part of its frame for it to work. The structures of decentralization, like the Panchayati Raj system and the various other supportive functions, are good on paper but have failed to deliver in actual functioning. The reason is the lack of democratic political education of the people.

I went to Denmark once and found that they had set up folk schools at the beginning of their democratic phase. All adults attended the school to familiarize themselves with the process. In India the initial set of leaders, with greater probity and integrity than leaders today, had a paternalistic attitude and guided the citizen. The negative fallout was the reinforcement of the mai-baap syndrome and the walking away of beneficiaries of this process from decision-making—the unattended gram sabhas being a case in point. The citizen who is aware of rights perceives the gram sabha as a people's platform. However, the power elite in villages hijacked the platforms from the people. Conversely the workers who fought for wages did not see the power of their right to govern themselves as valuable. The RTI, MGNREGA, NFSA and other rights-based campaigns did manage to bring in the value of structured participatory platforms to demand justice. All the way up till the Lok Sabha, manipulative processes have replaced real debate and decision-making in a downward spiral. In the Haryana state assembly, for instance, many bills were passed without any deliberation, and research will yield plenty of other examples.

In smaller organizations committed to participatory democracy, like the MKSS, we have had to evolve a structural process that allowed for debate and also showed the way to reaching conclusions through consensus. Every decision had to lead to action. It was imperative that there be equality of expression; time to place the entire case; time for emotional reactions to settle; and to accept that any violation of our self-stated ideals and constitutional norms would be set aside. Once, Chunni Singh and I disagreed with the rest of the group on setting up an independent organization, Kirana Stores, to counter neoliberalization in 1991. We were seen as powerful members and our opinions were generally valued. But both of us lost our argument and the people-managed and people-funded

Kirana Stores came into being. Today a chain of five flourishing shops and their annual turnover of approximately Rs 5 crore every year validates their existence.

The Indian is argumentative. Amartya Sen has captured our national idiosyncrasy in his book *The Argumentative Indian.* The predilection is highlighted in every street corner adda in Kolkata, and every train journey in India, and every evening gathering on the chaupal has proved this over the years. Only two new entrants have come in since, women and Dalits, seldom allowed space to enter into debate. Political party systems have also been examples of how such arguments can be made fruitful, but equally how trivia can destroy the sum of it.

As the boundaries of all our self-defined paradigms have become smudged, we have all been forced to re-evaluate the way we perceive power and use it. We know that inequality in distribution of power arises from a set of preconditions in which the manipulation of conventional democratic processes, primarily now of electoral politics and institutions, has further undermined the development debates and marginalized real issues and the needs of a large section of the Indian population. The people with their separate identities are confused by the overlap of poverty, caste, religion and ideology. The overriding power of religion and caste in vote politics and political decision-making has added to the fear of the basic issues of poverty, tolerance and non-participation in economic processes. This in turn has raised levels of intolerance.

Elections are a process in which the marginalized and the poor feel a short-lived sense of power. There is, however, a growing feeling that there is rarely a real choice at the time of casting the vote. People also realize that they themselves are invariably reduced to their caste, 'bhai ka saval', at the time of the elections, knowing full well that after the election all relationships dissolve into personal aggrandizement and the 'bhai' disappears behind the 'sahib'.

A realization that political power is generated not only through elections, and that there is interconnectedness between asserting the right to food, employment and livelihood issues and the outcome of an election, marks both those affected by it and those others who imagine political power only within narrow confines. Democratic, economic and social rights combine to define political rights.[3]

The recent spate of legislative measures in India has altogether reduced people's engagement, compromised democratic rights and imperilled marginalized communities. This has placed new challenges on social movements and community participation in governance. It has become clear that in the absence of diverse ways of community engagement, development policy can further disempower and dispossess large numbers of people and eventually end up being counterproductive to its own stated objectives. The synergies and intrinsic connections between development and participation are proving to be essential to the functioning of a democracy that espouses justice and inclusive growth.

Bijji retells a Rajasthani folk story in which the lion calls a meeting one day to decide how participatory management of the forest can function. He says that he will not kill at random; instead, the other animals should come together to decide which of them will be sacrificed that day. The story has a wry conclusion, wherein the hare shows up the hypocrisy of the lion. The stark truth that derives from this narrative is that when power is unequal, there can be no true participation. We keep coming back to the conflict that prevents equality in practice: the feudal structure, the caste system and the power definitions within it defined by class and gender. Nothing short of bold assertion will make democracy work.

The dilemma we face today in our political domain is the harsh and brutal putting down of all such assertion.

Democratic Structures and Rights: Falling Apart

We live in a world where real democracies are fast receding into the horizon. The Indian state today has no love or respect for truth, for ethics in governance, nor for an equitable and just social structure. Despite a rigorous Constitution (under constant threat of being amended by the rising right-wing) and the structure of a democracy, almost all regulatory institutions of justice have been corrupted by the lack of principles and the acceptance of opportunism as the only code of conduct. The corrosion of democratic rights began many years ago, even before Indira Gandhi declared the Emergency in 1975. For many years the period of the Emergency was the sharpest and most crippling attack on democracy in India. But what was crude and obvious rule by undemocratic means has now been replaced by the subtle and subversive use of democratic and regulatory institutions, indeed the process of democracy itself, to pervert and deny constitutional rights.[4] We lost all fundamental control over the rule of law when the state in Gujarat connived in the deliberate denial of protection for the life and property of its citizens. What was a perversion of justice became a platform to win elections, thereby giving legitimacy to the state to pervert and misuse the criminal justice system, regulatory mechanisms and institutions of justice. The subtle methods of misuse of information, of deliberate attempts to promote and support fundamentalist elements in society and the use of hate and violence as tools of support of ostensible democratic processes have raised deeper and more profound questions of the polity and the people. The Gujarat 'experiment' was more deadly than anything seen before in independent India, with grave implications for democracy itself.

The contemporary orchestrated attack on the Congress has a complex structure. The attack on dynasty is a legitimate issue of concern that is understandable to a people who still believe in the perpetuation of family above all. But it is a fig leaf for the attack on Nehru. He is really targeted by more calculated moves to destroy scientific liberal thought and intellectualism of all sorts. Scientific thinking stands in direct opposition to the many narratives of obscurantism that are perpetuated, especially with distorting history. The ultimate crudity lies in the destruction of knowledge, followed by the dismantling of institutions and even buildings, historic and sacred, and the propaganda that all wisdom is home-grown. It leads to the question of who is 'home born' in the area of dispute and difference. Even liberal educated India has bought these self-destructive ideas, because of some sense of 'wanting change' from dynasty and the development paradigm of the welfare state. However, political change does not and should not destroy a country's cultural history and one's own carefully engineered knowledge.

The liberal imagination has been captured partly because the 'other' party was posited as 'corrupt'. Corruption was confused with ideology. The promise of change and economic growth was further confused with regulations and the 'inspector raj'. The anti-corruption campaigns were allowed to flourish till such time as they were helpful in bringing down regimes, but always stopped short of progressing anywhere near their logical end. The IAC campaign is a case in point.

A politically illiterate people have bought many narratives. Every argument has been built on a prejudice, an apprehension or fear. These views have been instilled, fanned and literally set afire. The perpetrators have been provided with concepts of heroism and macho ideals that support and condone the violence for which they are all culpable! Bogeys are created, events manufactured and then analysed within the limited political vocabulary of condemnation and fear words like 'communist', 'Maoist', 'left intellectual', 'pseudo secularist' and 'urban Naxal'. The fundamental victims are rationality, scientific thought and all questioning and dissent in its many shades. Finally, the ultimate victim is democracy, which lies in its coffin, waiting to be nailed. The present dispensation is working towards a one-party system, perpetuating the idea of one election for all levels of democratic elections. Popular projection invests political leaders with the overlay of 'divinity'.

A Look into History: Coming Full Circle

It was in the 1960s and 1970s that the Union of Soviet Socialist Republics was indicted for persecuting its intellectuals and thinkers. We heard of Aleksandr Solzhenitsyn and read his *The Gulag Archipelago* (published in 1973), a description of the labour camps that were punishments for the demand for free expression and dissent. Andrei Sakharov was a Russian nuclear physicist, dissident, Nobel laureate and activist for disarmament, peace and human rights, who later became an advocate of civil liberties and civil reforms in the Soviet Union, for which he faced state persecution. The great ballet dancers Rudolf Nureyev and Mikhail Baryshnikov defected. According to a political discourse popular at the time, communist regimes and the KGB promoted the gagging of intellectuals and artists, who thought independently or dared to disagree with the political brass.

In those times the desire for freedom of expression was linked with the capitalist myth of a free market, and the 'free' was confused with freedom. In many bestsellers, pictures of the dark and gloomy streets of Moscow were the background of stories of spying and espionage. When I saw a sunny Moscow in April 1981, I was surprised that such a cheerful, magnificent city should be shrouded in the gloom of propaganda, which it deserved maybe for its Lubyanka and the KGB, but nature shines for all! On the other side, the stories of 'cowboys and injuns' expanded into the CIA and their devastating impact on economies and for real 'freedom' of independent choice.

In the middle of these various discourses emerged the occasional misfit, like the myth of the 'Ugly American', which took on the arrogance and insensitivity of American diplomacy and leadership. This political myth drew clear connections between capitalism and totalitarianism, intolerant systems of governance. There was also *Confessions of an Economic Hitman*, which explained how socialist and low-income economies dependent on aid were destroyed by international financial investment.[5] In Latin and South America, a contrary myth drew different conclusions. The 'Junta' supported by US-based free market exploiters held democracy and democratic action as unredeemable mortgage. Communism went to South America as a liberator from the capitalist–Junta combine. Many interesting ideologies, like the Jesuit Marxists, were born, bringing religion as a force into the debate for principled equal governance. In India the nascent Gandhian–Marxists made their own positions a blend of two apparently contradictory ideologies till lately.

Europe was divided between the West and East, reeling under the impact of its own history that included Hitler's ghost and the carnage of the Holocaust. Colonial history had forced the insularity to question itself to some extent; other cultures were discovered and reluctantly respected. This led to an uneasy truce with pluralism and multicultural expression. The politics was not black and white, like that in the USA and the Soviet Union; it allowed the many shades of grey into its politico-social-cultural understanding. Germany had its own angst as a country divided and yet sharing strong cultural ancestry.

When India initiated the non-aligned movement, Jawaharlal Nehru, Josip Broz Tito and Gamal Abdel Nasser joined together to etch space for a third world. For us this space was critical, because it allowed the multifaith cultural and layered social structural space to exist and struggle for greater equality and rights. Protest was a tool India used to great effect to gain independence, and that it continued as a form afterwards was testimony to the astuteness of its initial leadership.

For the generation that grew up in the non-aligned period in India there was access to the best in literature and culture from the world over. The West and East came to the new republic, and whatever the politics, culture was free to enter and interact. That generation of young people grew up with a cultural internationalism that broke many important walls in the mind. Which in many ways made democratic understanding more plural than it is today. We stood poised between many ideologies, welcoming dissent and arguments as 'argumentative Indians'. We also echoed the sentiments of Europe, whose culture we have contributed to by default. Our heritage has a rainbow of nuanced and differing political interests, including those of Mahatma Gandhi, B.R. Ambedkar, Jyotirao and Savitribai Phule, Narayana Guru, Periyar, Bal Gangadhar Tilak, Gopal Krishna Gokhale, Motilal and Jawaharlal Nehru, Annie

Besant, Aruna Asaf Ali, Sarojini Naidu, C.F. Andrews, Rabindranath Tagore, M.N. Roy, Subramania Bharati, Netaji Subhas Chandra Bose, Swami Vivekananda and a huge collective voice that led to our independence. They managed to set aside the nascent nationalist Hindu militancy.

The paradox of expanding globalization and narrowing minds cannot perhaps be defined or analysed completely. But there are still reasons and we continue to explore them by exposing contradictions at many levels. The chants of nationalism and the waving of flags are sacrosanct but expression of real nationalism is met with incarceration. Ideologies need to have porous boundaries to grow with the rest of the world. We need the perspective of an M.N. Roy who disbanded his own party, or a Gandhi who suggested the dissolution of the Congress after Independence, suggesting new parties be formed. Even a spiritual leader like J. Krishnamurti disbanded his order at eighteen. Institutions have to be seen as instruments for justice, not as citadels of power, which when occupied become fortresses to defend. The essential ingredient of self-critique so vital to the political health of a nation is rubbished.

Individualism developed primarily on two considerations—the market, profit and greed on the one hand, and on the other the desire for comfort. The politics of today is the politics of convenience. That is perhaps why so many are silenced. And though they see the spread of parochialism in every which way, they want to protect self-interest.

Our generation read *Brave New World* and *Nineteen Eighty-Four* as political fiction but we have lived to see it materialize as reality.[6] We are still waiting for a third, to complete the trilogy, to follow. *Brave New World* was about conditioning the victim to accept victimization, *Nineteen Eighty-Four* about the totalitarian state. The new entrant will perhaps talk of global control through the nexus of international finance, national politics and technology. They are a triumvirate guaranteed to suppress genuine democracy. A POSCO of the future, or any local mobilization or protest for that matter, cannot depend on compromised democratic institutions created to protect citizen interest. These institutions are now tools of the power elite, and many feel that the epitaph of democracy needs to be drafted. But the people who remain large in numbers may yet tilt the balance. Human beings continue to see where opportunities lie to awaken collective concerns, whether through environmental concerns or the understanding that the global financial net needs to be broken. Economic well-being of the last person is the last concern of political power. It needs to keep the masses pre-occupied with getting their daily bread, so that they can be used as fodder by the voting machine. That is why genuine democratic empowerment and those who amplify these concerns are framed as anti-national and as terrorists to be put away. In India there are plenty of such examples.

Newton (2017) and the many other films that highlight the condition of the last person show how much harder we have to work to get to vote, even with our limited understanding—the pitiful condition of the voter in a tribal area is a case in point. Many of those who worked to educate people on democracy, as rights, are behind bars. An intelligent people would work out the discourse to make political education the base for improvement, and differentiate between this process and indoctrination. Education provides free choice in an open society, which allows for dialogue and debate. Indoctrination is just the opposite. That is why power sees dialogue and political education with fear, and democracy is hollowed out with jargon. The edifice has to disallow genuine democratic participation and rights to stay in power.

Democracy is about dialogue and the right to question. This space is vital to its structure and the ongoing debates within. Once this is dismantled, democracy as we know it ceases to exist. The contemporary structures of democracy want to keep its shell, while removing space for dialogue through attacks on questioning and space for platforms for questioning unethical action. That is why freedom of expression is attacked and those who speak incarcerated.

Democracy demands time and education. We have not yet evolved an academy of researchers who will do little else but translate public policy into an idiom and language that will reach the people, and enable them to absorb and respond. The time lag between the publication of a policy and the response is so short that the real receiver of the policy, even if interested, stands isolated from participation. Power is happy to shorten the time and short-circuit the process. The demand for a pre-legislative mode, raised by the MKSS and others, did not find support from any political party.

15

No Full Stops: The End Is the Beginning

Where we are now
Pushed, stumbling with chains on our ankles
Eyes glazed bewildered and myopic,
Take me back to the times where there was no killing.
When were those times?
Take me back to my mother's lap
Shield me from fear,
Close my helpless eyes,
watching innocence raped and beaten,
fingers in ears, stop,
stop the cries of pain—
Stop the frenzy of images,
From evil thoughts, that
become huge forms of darkness
Nightmares and fear
To crawl into the skin
Blotches—an itch,
The ugliness of illogic and insanity.
Threatening, drawing lines,

pain playing hopscotch with age.
Take me forward, fast forward
To leapfrog over ugly power.
Heal a torn humanity—
Break into its many parts
A chimera that visited my nightmares.
Reason's wounded, and impaled on
The spikes of mindless proclamations
Force humility on power
Help me search for hope in my mind,
And in my reason,
help me see the beauty of the rising sun,
the bird in flight,
The song that wraps the mind, a journey
a flight through space.
Thoughts joggle,
There are no full stops
Looking, groping persistently, every moment
For reason, to explain and reassure.

IS THERE ANY end to a conversation with oneself? I think not. As I draw the line to end this book, I know many important discussions are yet to be written. Many stories have been discarded by the strict master—the word count.

Writing has given me an opportunity to walk through memories—a gallery of portraits and anecdotes of remarkable people—to think of experiences, events and struggles. They are cameos of unrecognized greatness of many ordinary people. It offers a glimpse into political processes and personal dilemmas. It is a continual struggle for logic in action. Life is and will continue to be confused, complex and illogical. The search for reason, order, meaning and causality will continue lifelong. These are unfinished stories. Only the privileged can think and indulge in the luxury of following an internal emotion or thought towards a 'conclusion'. The less privileged have no time to waste in 'thought'. The daily business of food, hunger, illness, cruelty and violence, the right to question the contradiction between promise and delivery, takes all their energy and time. Their concerns and actions are the substance of 'thought'.

Their actions teach us that in the midst of their lives of relentless trouble there is fun, laughter and joy. Laughter is an antidote to the grimness of poverty, music and poetry its spirit, as they create and sing songs. To laugh at one's idiosyncrasies is a great gift and an important way of dealing rationally with daily threats to life. The poetry of people's articulation gets recorded on the vast canvas of creative human expression. The ceremonies they perform and the religion they believe in offer comfort in a life of unmitigated pain. They also offer a kind of logic that answers, however superficially, the questions that political thought and action cannot—about death, loss and pain. Even now, in places where Hindi is read and spoken, Kabir and his poetry serve to address these issues. Kabir was a believer in rationality and in a world beyond death. Ambedkar, Phule, Periyar, Narayana Guru were interpreters of these thoughts in public life. Of them, Periyar alone was an atheist. His followers have brought in ceremony and interpreted religion. We leave this unfinished, and only set it firmly in the agenda of future conversations.

A very small part of our oral narratives and the written word jostle each other in these chapters, as they do in our separate realities. Heard and recounted, they represent a community's understanding of its lives. It is a political perception born of daily encounters with the denial of simple rights. Their voices build a people's discourse. In this digital age of freezing even oral narratives in frames, videos and podcasts, we need the 'reflective' space of 'writing' as well. The narrative of resistance needs this space.

Technology has helped communication and, as a mode of instant messaging, revolutionized the act of shaping public opinion. Importantly for India, it has helped in working with people speaking twenty-two languages and living in far-flung areas. Contemporary electoral politics has used media to indoctrinate and influence local opinion. Media has reduced the urban–rural divide, but at the same time, the village chaupal has fallen silent. The storytelling elders have few takers. Political propaganda works through a hidden but choreographed control of the media. The centralized planners make sure that messaging and branding will overcome whatever individual views and thoughts people may have. The market has taught us that repeated jingles influence buyers' minds.

Citizens have become consumers and what is on sale is public opinion. The political design builds on the psychology of people wanting identity and a sense of belonging. The political parties that look at details make use of this sentiment to build on identity with the intention of building 'vote banks'.[1]

Political thought and ideology is reduced to democracy's lowest common denominator: the morphing of 'people's democratic rights' with the numbers game of the 'vote'. Centralization and standardization have insidiously fed into the political decision of power brokers to damn basic democratic rights of citizens to differ, disagree and express dissent.

Their real protagonists are the spontaneously emerging centres of subaltern resistance and people's political groups, as they are influential and equally spread out and work intensively with people. The systematic attack on freedom to fraternize arises from a fear of decentralized power, from independent groups that work with details, and is resented by power centres. The deliberate deconstructing of these efforts systematically designs to neutralize the questioning of power. Power unpacked is a real threat. It allows the questioning of impunity of those who aggrandize privilege and authority, not en bloc, but bit by bit. These smaller entities can be deconstructed far more easily and effectively. The discourse of anti-activism derives from this fear. The effort to build a standardized, single and, therefore, dangerous conversation is evident in the attacks on activists and their incarceration. Federalism and difference have to be systematically neutralized and hammered into standardized imaginations. The single dominant identity of religion, the parroting discourse and the hostility to all questioning, is vital for the creation of unbridled power. The strength of this country was, and is, its pluralism. Today, every effort is being made to take over people's minds and dilute the multiplicity, and silence their capacity to differ.

The individuals and the collectives, and their nuanced efforts, need to be recognized for the sustenance of causes they nurtured. The MKSS has been the space where I have learnt the most, as a part of many big and small struggles, campaigns and movements. The people who work at it day after day, who make campaigns succeed, are not even a footnote in history. Their sovereignty ends with the vote. By instinct, even in ways they sit, they find strength in groups. In the world of recognition and acclaim, it is the individual that matters. This book is partly a tribute to those who are unseen, who live their lives naturally and combat ills every day. People too have big dreams and are disturbed by the lack of public ethics. Given a chance, they build the core of successful campaigns, including rights-based legislations. These laws have connected daily life to democratic processes, blending access to welfare with politics, from panchayat to Parliament.

Who are the 'people'?

There is no group that is homogenous and not subject to a criss-cross of socio-economic intersectionality. The difficulty arises when the same individual, motivated simply by pragmatic concerns, aligns with two politically antagonistic ideologies. We have looked at the affinity over single issue formations, broken by serious differences over ideologies, visible when voting, or looking at religious politics. Are we talking about those who fight for rights, brave all seasons to sit on the streets, stand waist-deep in water to demand participation in decision-making on development policy? Or are they the bullies who roam the streets, shouting against minorities and objecting to difference and critique? Or are they part of the silent majority—the ordinary Indian citizen—who engages sometimes with public action but is often silent for comfort?

The reluctance to be a part of a stated political ideology may have different reasons. One of them is the free thinker, who does not want to be hemmed in by lines of intellectual control. The individualist who fiercely protects singular rights may also want to keep away from ideology. Public action and 'single issue' movements offer a compromise, where there is limited ideological commitment. This was the core strength of movements, which is now threatened by the single issue changing rapidly to religious identity and bigotry. It also allows for being part of two contradictory processes.

The book also celebrates the unrecognized protagonist who makes lives better for the community. We search for icons who embody the unattainable, and fail to acknowledge the ones we live with. This book has captured the lives of some of the thousands of remarkable people who populate the universe of activism for justice and equality. Narayan, the MKSS activist who left his battered body before he was fifty for the oblivion of death on 9 January 2022, would have agreed with Plato. He walked with a purpose, casually and with calm assurance, to become a leader of his people. Narayan was just thirty when he was elected the sarpanch of his village. He took no bribes, paid none either. He gave his people all that he could in the five years he was in office. When he died, hundreds of people mourned the passing away of a good, intelligent and shrewd leader of people.

His was a political journey, and he believed that there was a commitment to share his journey with his people. A quiet introvert in part, Narayan's intelligence and his belief that change would come only through shared action compelled him to relate to and educate people, with his slow measured drawl, by precept and example. He withstood tremendous pressure from the Jati Panchayat to suspend the Jansunwai in Kukarkheda Panchayat in 1998, held to question fraud, as the woman sarpanch was from his community. The consequences of his action could have ostracized him and his family socially—and that mattered to him—but compromising public ethics for personal comfort was unthinkable. The Jansunwai was held as planned.

In his end should lie the beginnings of another journey, where fairness and justice above all would judge human action. We hope there are many such beginnings.

Located in this intricate criss-cross of public action is the personal. Normative standards give stability to people. Caught in the corruption-ridden structure of delivery and the blatant corrosion of the electoral process, the ordinary individual seeks resolution. 'People' are generally preoccupied more with the business of living than any preoccupation with public affairs. It is only when they see the connection between their personal lives and public action that they become participants. The success of activist efforts also depends on their ability to make the state's commitment to democratic constitutional morality and its stated ethics (or lack of it) visible.

The objectives and visions of campaigns, which amplify people's response and try and build larger platforms, are situated within the constitutional frame. Majoritarian political processes use the same tools, but they exploit mass prejudice and its psychological fallout in operation. They serve to build exclusion, separateness and hate. Hope lies in the goodness and common sense of humanity of the ordinary person. In spite of mass propaganda and hysteria replacing reasoned argument, individual discussions with many people make us realize that most people can be rational and humane. The challenge is to retrieve the essential human being away from mass conditioning.

How India Was Imagined

Inequality in any form violates basic humanity; when based on birth, colour and location, it is the most diabolical as these factors are beyond personal choice. When agendas of political mobilization depend on these factors, from Hitler to contemporary politics, reason is the biggest victim. Economic inequality touted as progress has come back to laud modern methods of using technology for immoral money-making. The hiatus between classes has taken a quantum leap. To quote Oxfam's 2022 Inequality Report, *Inequality Kills*, validates this assumption.[2] During Covid in India, corporations made money at the cost of the poor, hungry, unemployed: 'When 84 percent of households in the country suffered a decline in their income in a year marked by tremendous loss of life and livelihoods, the number of Indian billionaires grew from 102 to 142.'[3] *Inequality Kills: India Supplement 2022* has also revealed that:

> The collective wealth of India's 100 richest people hit a record high of INR 57.3 lakh crore (USD 775 billion) in 2021 … The pandemic has set gender parity back from 99 years to now 135 years. Women collectively lost INR 59.11 lakh crore (USD 800 billion) in earnings in 2020, with 1.3 crore fewer women in work now than in 2019.[4]

Democracy, which was a promise of equality, fraternity and free speech, has been turned around by shaping modes and structures meant for people into tools to appropriate power for the ruling fraternity. Technology lends itself to manipulation by a power nexus and has played into the hands of the oligarchies and fascist formations that rule in the name of democracy. Electronic voting machines (EVMs) can be manipulated. The passage of the legal right to accept international donations to political parties without transparency or oversight through electoral bonds has legalized corruption and shifted accountability from the people to the corporate funders.

Partisan politics and the use of inequality as a right has been created through the worst form of promoting prejudice and hate. Democracy in name and fascist in practice requires weakening all institutions created for democracy, from the Parliament to the panchayat. The nexus is interfering with the judiciary through appointments, and now with the argument that instead of being an equal in the trio of constitutional governance (judiciary, executive and legislature), the legislature will appropriate to itself supreme powers.

To all of them, inequality is not an issue as the systems they represent believe in unequal access and control. Digital control has been used to deepen the entrenched power imbalances. Extended and greater police control and redefining the role of armed forces has further brought in structural changes. Governments make unequal laws undermining the Constitution; when people react, asking for democratic rights, they are repressed. This resistance to policy and process gets attacked by the state and deemed 'anti-national', and any fundamental opposition, dissent and difference are marked as criminal. All democratic institutional checks and balances have been vitiated by weakening their independence.

Both market and government propaganda use the jingle, an advertising gimmick, to dull the mind and stop it from asking questions or seeking answers. That is why the independent rational question and questioner are at such risk. Political leaders become parochial god-men, and the latter become decision makers and political leaders.

People remain victims, both of economic design and dictatorial undemocratic controls. The 'citizen' is a person without rights, without a voice, and has been changed from a subject to a consumer. The consumerist marketing trick—show the glitter but hide the substance—has numbed public intelligence. The language of commerce has become popular and a more humane idiom has become passé. We are tagged like sheep so that surveillance is easier and values that allowed multiple expressions are replaced by branding and standardization. Artificial intelligence (AI) threatens to take over the human brain and the debate is in an exclusive and unintelligible idiom.

Some of these contradictions have been captured in these chapters from the perspective of communities that needed to benefit the most from the promise of freedom from hunger, want and oppression. Those who have gained voice and vote have lost the connecting dots between their newly found empowerment and the Constitution. The larger vision of an inclusive India, so intelligently and carefully stitched together, has been deliberately ripped, seam by seam. Perhaps the horrors of *Brave New World*,[5] of using technology and science to reinforce caste, destroy history and suppress questioning, were not science fiction after all. Maybe *Nineteen Eighty-Four*[6] was also a prediction, unwished for and feared, but one that has come to pass. In the public normative curve during my lifetime, nightmares have become reality as much as dreams have been realized. Where do we stand?

The chapter 'Great Expectations and Hard Times' has looked at the struggle for a principled and accountable democracy. It discusses how the principles enshrined in the Constitution can become reality. Public campaigns require public space and a willingness by the power elite to listen. Democracy works only if the guarantee of freedom of expression and of dissent work effectively through the executive—the government. The critical importance of transparent and accountable governance is again underscored. Ultimately, there has to be value for common sense and wisdom. Democratic culture is a way of life, and the federal system has to decentralize power.

Economic disparities lie at the base of public discontent. That is why the demand for an accountability law by the Suchna evam Rozgar Adhikar Abhiyan in Rajasthan has drawn such large crowds. Government servants enjoy a third of the year as leave. Despite all the perks, they do not deliver. People support the demand for the law because it will enable the citizen to ensure that the government functions with ethics, enabling delivery and increasing efficiency. A dysfunctional delivery system is the biggest millstone around the public neck. An MKSS yatra travelled many kilometres (fourteen districts in twenty-one days) and drew thousands of people, collected lakhs of rupees in crowd funding, and was welcomed by a cross-section of society. In an amazing incident, a two-minute video of Shankar speaking of the financial hiatus between the government servant and the ordinary worker went viral, with 20 million hits.

All is not lost with public reasoning. The lesson for us is that we must reach out, speak in people's idioms and genuinely look for what really troubles them. The process of evolving a people's policy, and the rights-based laws—the RTI, the MGNREGA, the NFSA, the Forest Rights Bill, the Domestic Violence Act, etc.—stand vindicated as they afford some protection at the time when the government has become anti-welfare and -people, and further restricts the use of public spaces to express dissent. The struggle against the CAA, which discriminated against Muslims and the arbitrary passage of farmers' laws were non-violent protests. The suppression of protests is actually an acknowledgement of their power. It reiterates the importance of participatory democracy, consulting people and establishing platforms for pre-legislative deliberation. Collectively they make a statement about the people's role in a democracy—the right to participate in decision-making and in evolving tools of governance.

In spite of mass propaganda, individual discussions with many people demonstrate that they have not lost touch with rationality and compassion. The campaigns for hate have to be countered with concrete issues of economic concern for the young, particularly jobs and employment. The political opposition has become weak. The farmers' movement, in its determination, its mode of organization, non-violent satyagraha and in the humanity of its concerns, showed India what 'the people' could achieve.

Are we working towards a new ideology or a new language? Is it possible? We are all suspended between the non-negotiables of existence, trying to create bridges between the mind and action as we do between theory and practice. Create, if you like, the 'praxis' of a logical life. If our public lives seek continual order, enacting laws, building conscience politics, our inner lives demand attention to address the cutting of corners, the compromises and critically examining mistakes. The excessive desire for upward mobility is pushing global societies to cut conscience out of politics, to define a political discourse with statements like, 'post truth', 'post ideology'. The first is morally unacceptable; if principles like truth are twisted to justify and rationalize deceit, exploitation of people and natural resources will get legal sanction.

Without truth as a value, life cannot be lived. It is the basis for science, learning and governance. Without truth, the design of the future will be one without justice and fairness. Its denial allows cynicism to grow, and validates the citizen or business pursuing wealth ruthlessly at any cost, promoting corruption and graft. This impacts the life of an ordinary citizen every which way. Every system requires a moral frame. Ideology is a shared vision of a group, a governing elite, of a just state, transparent and accountable. Even pragmatism is an ideology, drawing its limitations and contour. Together, truth and ideology are the ethical mooring of societies across the world. The peace, and the apparent law and order that people desire, cannot last if it annihilates the vulnerable and bans questioning and critique.

We exist with our senses, emotions and minds. We fail to understand that it is a human emotion that has begun many journeys that have led to great thoughts, discoveries and revolutions. It is the touch and feel of earth, both in a literal and symbolic sense, that has shaped our political minds. The political life of the MKSS is tethered to the mud hut so that we never lose sight of reality. It is looking at the condition of poverty that moves us to action in many parts of India, from an Indian slum to an international concern like South Sudan or Ethiopia. The power of that visual and moral stimulus is what actually leads us to connect with political and public concerns.

A new kind of poverty is growing in rural Rajasthan, where former indicators do not deliver. Poverty as un-repayable debt is now the new poverty line indicator.

The comrade-saathi who went with me to Manila to receive the Magsaysay, Chunni Singh, is proud of the home he and his wife have built. We spent a night in Chunni Singh's mud hut in his village, Palona. We had black tea, sat in the kitchen that had a few pans and one spoon, ate thick rotis with some buttermilk (chaach) and walked into the village. He had gone off to deepen his open well. There was the sound of a jeep and we found the SDM of Beawar driving in. The tehsildar came pompously to inform us that the SDM had come to meet us. He commanded some villagers to get Chunni Singh, adding, 'The SDM is a busy man. He [Chunni Singh] should come immediately.' Twenty minutes later the villagers came back to say, 'Chunni Singh is coming. He said that we should tell the SDM that he too is very busy, digging a well. But he will come up.' We walked to the edge of the well with the SDM, and Chunni Singh was pulled out after a while with a pulley, sitting in a basket. He said, 'Zindabad. Now what is it? Better be quick. I have to get the well ready before the monsoons.' Chunni Singh was courteous, but no matter with whom or where he lived, the principle of equality stayed with him. Whether it was Palona or Manila.

People like Chunni Singh place the debate on minimum needs and the politics of simplicity by just living it. Whether from a

Gandhian or Marxian point of view, minimalism and the concept of equality are closely linked in a society that, exists bookended by poverty and hunger on the one end and by convenience and comfort on the other. There may be questions of the acquisitive society; one may challenge it personally in the way many activists live or, in theory, in campaigns against the deliberate, destructive and suicidal attacks on the planet. But big money, corporates and technology have come to stay and perhaps to rule. It could be the new global Frankenstein.

There are many issues we have to struggle against within ourselves and outside. The insidious dependence on transactional conveniences—the ATM card, the plastic that allows entry, pays and relieves one of physical stress—is linked to the same digital system that we quarrel with. Convenience and comfort have corroded the conscience of many of us, who in the final analysis are willing to compromise. These global devices, including neoliberal markets, have to be modified at the least and fought when necessary, both through local and global resistance. Resistance has to redefine itself. The ones who question the contradictions, where the personal and the political meet, mortgage their comfort zones for their conscience.

The market has to be understood as a key player that is changing democracy. But our minds have to work through a new geography and economic design. It is an intricate criss-cross of currents and countercurrents, masterminded and held together by rising aspirations for a consumer-driven society, dealing with greed, the allure of credit and new forms of debt, matched by literacy and access to social media. The examination of the information counter-revolution masterminded by the smart phone and technology needs a book in itself. But every analysis of the human condition has to take cognizance of the new combine of Goebbels,[7] in the many differently programmed misinformation machines, and *Nineteen Eighty-Four*'s Big Brother, who appears through technological surveillance and controls. The swiftness of the takeover has not allowed people the luxury of time, where experience is the best teacher and often the only way these forces can be countered. The nexus of business and politics has forced draconian controls over public action, which is often the quickest and most effective educator of the negative impacts of these changes. Political education remains a work in progress.

It was not forty years ago that rural India was still largely a traditional society. Modernization has come with the smart phone, technology and rising aspirations. Inequalities based on hierarchical caste and discrimination remain, further enabled by the swiftness of information technology to reinforce prejudices and consolidate caste. The business model popularizes an economics based on inequality. The two worlds of business and a caste-ridden society have come together to destroy the ideas, language and policy designed for equality. We look for symbols and ideologies that promote a more humane world. Reducing environmental damage is not merely an issue of looking at the grand design, it is also the promotion of decentralized patterns of development and lifestyles. Perhaps that is why the mud hut in Devdungri has become a symbol of political and economic choices.

The Challenges to India's Diversity

The relationship between the attitude to mud and earth and modern economic dreams of concrete progress are perhaps evident in the critique of the MGNREGA in the media in its formative years. Metaphors used to denounce it were often linked to the absence of 'assets', read visible buildings and construction. Mud/earth became a pejorative word.

The devil lies in the details. Working with issues where the problem lies is pivotal for finding solutions. However, what the campaigns for transparency and work taught us in process and planning was linking the imagination of people to see all the way to Parliament for solutions in the village. They have worked out a way to connect the political dots—the micro to the macro. Those who suffered from a denial of basic needs began to understand the democratic frame of decision-making. In so doing they understood how constitutional rights could be realized. As experience transformed into policy, experience also transformed into new forms of struggle to redefine resistance. The culture of struggle realized the critical role of participatory governance and accountability.

We make a cultural choice, not once but many times over in a lifetime. The current political discourse has imposed polarities of religion and a system of daily choices for survival on the minorities in India. Cultural definitions can both be wide open to allow boundaries to be reworked and reduce themselves to their most narrow definition. The manipulative use of religious difference to divert attention from socio-economic/political-economic campaigns united by a common cause has been the purpose of the communal-market combine. There is an important need to perceive this, and keep our focus intact. We share concerns of economic demands, corruption, the failure of educational systems and other development plans. For those who divide and rule, collectives and especially struggles are targets to dismantle. The tirade against activism, branding and the denial of the right to protest, think differently, or express originates here.

The human mind is ever busy constructing hierarchies. The constant desire to develop and change has to counter these rigidities—caste, religion and gender discrimination, hunger. If we take this metaphor further, there is the creative tension that is life—the personal, and the political, the contradictions, the balance between thought and action. The specific, tangible world of situations in public life is countered by the infinite universe of a mind, chattering, singing, thinking, questioning, acquiescing, protesting. Bothered as often as it is joyous. There is a huge cosmos we carry within us, unarticulated and often unheeded, which influences our choices and action. The politics of concern and activism is situated in a space where public ethics and the troubling question of justice have priority over all other concerns and define action. But the human condition brings in the small doubts and preconceptions, the contradictions that need continual attention. The fears and the prejudices arising from it have been used and manipulated as a tool to suppress, perpetuating divisions and hate, to acquire state power.

Culture as Politics

Culture as politics, the Constitution as culture, and democracy as its practice have found some space in many of the narratives. They have also relived the literal contradictions between different aesthetics—the cacophony of the DJ truck, with eight speakers blaring forth a culturally indefinable sound, where noise with a rhythm passes as music, the false dichotomies between high and low culture, the ultimate failure to understand politics as culture. The music of struggles, on the other hand, has energized millions and crossed boundaries. The lyrics by Charul and Vinay, '*Dharti baanti, sagar baanta, mat baanto insaan ko*' (Divided the land, divided the sea, but don't divide humans), sung in the middle of the Bombay Riots, has become an anthem for communal harmony.[8] The MKSS songs have gone far beyond Rajasthan, carrying workers' issues with humour and political satire. Movement music has broadcast the spirit of political messages across boundaries.

Political groups like the Kabir Kala Manch have used music to draw attention to anti-oppression, anti-caste and anti-communal songs. Even NGOs like the Barefoot College SWRC, Tilonia, have amplified folk songs and poetry far beyond their physical reach. All songs are created to lend voice to feelings and thought, the desire to be heard beyond the immediate, as an assertion or the desire to communicate, give voice to the voiceless. They have been sung, re-sung and sometimes recreated. They have touched emotions and fashioned political thought, bonding beyond words and divides. This book has just touched upon the power of some of these songs, looking at a future of bringing people together through a tune or a beat. Culture and song, notwithstanding limitations of language and accessibility, have touched many. It is the beginning of a dialogue with others and oneself, of political understanding without polemic.

These moments of connectedness are moments of epiphany. Arguably they were not special to a few. Invoking these moments has brought many people together. Personally, I have found connections with cultures far away in space and even time. The catholic love for music led me to listen to Daniel Barenboim playing Beethoven's piano sonatas in the moonlight, one summer night in 1977 in a village, on a battery-operated cassette player, with the stars for company. It deepened my conviction that music reaches profound depths in ourselves and could and did break barriers.[9] Three decades later I heard T.M. Krishna, who too has understood that music is political. Whether it is '*Poromboke*', arguing for an idiom and the environment, or the Muslim Sufi song in Tamil *'Allah-vai naam thozhudhaal'*. They are sung in the Carnatic classical tradition, the latter with lyrics by Nagoor Siddiqui and popularized in Islamic devotional music by Tamil Sufi singer Nagoor Hanifa. He makes a strong point for cultural and religious affinity and plurality. Neither of these great musicians has in any way narrowed the purity of the musical systems they are part of. Religion or development concerns, in the musical context, merely elaborate on how there is an emotional connect with life.

To continue with the musical metaphor, all music is not symphonic. The single voice or instrument retains its individual logic and expression. So also in collectives. The individual activist is both the collective and herself. Chunni Singh's individualism did not permit him to be a part of the structured organization, but he was a part of the political collective.

Justice and Compassion

The MKSS chose non-violence and civil disobedience as its mode. If the end of the road was a life of equality, peace and justice, the means had to match the ends. It was a logic that also found place in the overall constitutional frame in which we located ourselves. All the important non-violent movements have had to deal with many inconclusive debates on how to define non-violence. But the insidious violence of caste, religious fundamentalism and the non-transparent and fascist state have all brought in an illogical discourse, relying on fanning prejudice. What greater contradiction and irony can there be than that we kill a man in the name of vegetarianism for selling meat? The popular approvals reflect moral decadence. We have seen this time and again when Hindutva-leaning political leaders garland rapists and murderers who have attacked minority communities. How can it ever be justified?

Successive governments have devalued constitutional values, but we see now a contemporary threat to dismantle the constitution itself. The movements have been the counterpoint to the deviation from constitutional values by varied governments. The 1980s and 1990s saw an emerging pattern of formations to build counter-campaigns and movements to challenge the arbitrary action of power centres. It was a natural next step to form alliances and campaigns and create platforms for discussing, debating and taking issues further. Many of these platforms are issue-based. They concentrated on ensuring that constitutional guarantees were accessible to the most vulnerable. The NAPM brought together several other campaigns and movements for development, constitutional, human and civil rights, to evolve a platform for collective expression of democratic and political rights.

Electoral Democracy, Deliberative Democracy

These pages also implicitly trace the tensions between electoral and deliberative democracy. There is need for both: a democratic frame for selecting individuals and empowering them to work for people, and a parallel system of deliberative democratic mores to challenge their ethical and constitutional failures to do so. 'Civil society' is attacked because it is the public face of resistance, promoting accountability and equality and questioning impunity. Resistance is defined by the struggles against the controls of technology and big money over independent democracies and the rights of people.

The transition from a normative constitutional democracy to a mere shell of an electoral democracy, with more and more powers of decision-making being centralized and arbitrary, is a cause for dismay. The essence of a democracy is participation, decentralized decision-making, dissent and creating platforms for consultation, discussion and representation, for policy and legislation. We created a federal system with checks and balances, and an independent judiciary, legislature and executive. The dismantling of this structure weakens the citizen. It is imperative that issues like this be raised for attention and to call this centralization to book. The blatant bypassing of structures created within the frame for discussion—like the Parliament, its standing and select committees for allowing testimonies from people—is shocking. The absence of huge public outcry against the abrogation of these processes is indicative of the political illiteracy that the ruling elite exploit. The rights-based laws passed during 2005–14 educated the average citizen on how rights link up with the sharing of democratic power.

Public debates and discussions stimulate thinking that persuades opinions to change and questions the status quo. The School for Democracy's charchas are a mode to share relevant information with the young. These charchas owe their origin to questions raised by a young woman who said she was tired of the shouting matches in the electronic media. Where should one go to be educated? These charchas have persuaded young people to think, using the right moment to stimulate thought. Public action is a great educator. Public protests are also critical; they educate as they chant and sing, and speak. Public hearings not only bring details of financial issues to the fore, but also exemplify the immense difficulty in raising issues of justice. The social audit highlights both public responsibility and government accountability for public action. The public hearing, social audit and similar platforms give space for corrective self-critical inquiry. These processes keep questioning alive and, therefore, the right to dissent and disagree. It is a practical lesson in governance, the need for resolution or consensus, so important a part of democracy. It defines public decorum, language, idiom and responsibility. These may seem superficial but are essential articulation tools for ordinary people to confront power structures.

A thread that runs through the book emphasizes the fact that democratic theory will have to learn from its practice. Participatory democracy and the voices of people have to find space. Political education of the fast-increasing numbers of young people is vital for a healthy democracy.

The end of a process ties the knots or promises hope that is determined to survive the illogic and malevolence of arbitrary power. All of us hope—for achievement, for success, the victory of good over evil. We look for solutions. The solution lies in continuing public action. We look at young people who have come together over the past four years to form a union of MGNREGA workers, with the MKSS. Their energy and determination is palpable. While the manipulation of democracy by the power elite seems relentless and the ignorance of political processes seem daunting, the spirit of inquiry and the desire to know continue in the persistent voices of the many millions in India. They may not have a face, or a Facebook page, but continue to seed the moral values that are so important a part of community life. As long as we fight to keep questioning injustice and public action alive, democratic issues stay in the centre of our discourse.

All dictators and arbitrary rulers know this well. The right to freedom of expression and free speech is the first to be attacked. The stifling of the human voice is not merely gagging protest but killing the human spirit. We witness the fear of those who enjoy impunity in the many killings of seekers of information, those who protest and anyone who questions. The question itself is under attack.[10]

The spontaneous resistance to being silenced has broken the backs of powerful regimes. It is in this process to protect the right to know that our future lies. We have to realize too that it is through these many small struggles for the right to life and livelihood that democratic and ethical principles survive. Even as we ask the polity to be both transparent and accountable, the day-to-day survival of millions of people depends on the immediate translation of these concepts into guarantees of survival. It is in this context that the five-million-plus questions asked through the RTI gain significance. It has kept the right to question and demand answers alive. These millions of RTI applicants push the gargantuan machine to move to stop corruption and arbitrary governance.

Personal battles for equality and justice often transform into public action. We have looked at many narratives—of the role of the feminine consciousness, of emotion, of cultural sensibilities—as much as we did the law and policy, lodged firmly within a political democracy. The tales themselves may seem miniscule and too small for any significance, but they herald real change, a coming together of the individual journey of choices and perception and the politics of poverty, inequality or feminism. They sketch the possibilities of an ethical future at a time when all projections look bleak. These tales, each a small revolution, too many to count, are a force to reckon with.

The shifts are too quick in the technology-driven world to allow for time, to process the nature of change. Successful political ideologies and movements take time to mature and grow.

My life has been like that of an actor looking at one's performance on a stage with two scripts, one for performance and another for its critique. Exploration of the personal and political in contemporary times has been and will be a continuing dialectic. The personal has included constant vigil with personal ethics, the correctness of translating thought into action, the public a continual engagement with struggle against oppression and a failure of justice.

One hopes that these narratives stimulate thought even if they do not provide answers to questions.

> What the caterpillar
> Calls the end
> The rest of the world
> calls a butterfly.
>
> —Lao Tzu (attributed)

The Last Word

FOR THE LAST four decades, we have been part of almost everything in Aruna's life—and she in ours. As the enormous task of writing such a book reaches its conclusion, we felt what in today's language is called 'our FOMO (fear of missing out)' moment. How could we not have our voice in it! This, therefore, is an afterword that has been included on our demand, and an entitlement for us to be in this book—and, quite inadvertently, have the last word!

We have lived forty years together as friends, colleagues, comrades, and have experienced the wonder of building a large family and community—sharing everything we have, including our personal lives, and our political dreams.

Aruna's book is a conversation with herself. But we have been part of those questions and answers too: the dialogues and debates, arguments and deadlocks, songs and jokes, laughter and tears that have marked every single day of these extraordinary years, of an extraordinary life. Aruna's life could define activism; she has spent every day doing something substantial that connects and extends beyond herself.

Yet, as Aruna often strongly asserts, to call her an 'activist' would be to pigeonhole her in ways that are unfair to what she is: a person with such a wide array of interests, skills and knowledge that draws a natural and organic continuum between the personal and the political; the private and the public; the internal and the external; the home and the world; the small and the big. From sharing a house in Devdungri and our families to being a part of an activist collective, it is Aruna's careful attention to the smallest detail that prepares the grounds for the big breakthroughs that we have been privileged to experience together.

We met in the early 1980s and in the course of a couple of years came to realize that among the three of us, we had found a combination that enabled us to pursue our dreams together. The three of us are eight years apart in our ages; Shankar is eight years older than Nikhil, and Aruna eight years older than Shankar. We are different as human beings, but share fundamental principles, and have found it enriching in so many ways to spend time with each other, in the everyday creative challenge of living and working together. And we are extremely fortunate that this family of close fellow travellers continues to draw more and more wonderful individuals into its ever-expanding fold.

But this book is not just a description of an individual and collective journey. This is a serious book, about serious issues, in serious times. Like Aruna, it does not shy away from raising uncomfortable questions, facing them squarely, and understanding that the answers are nuanced with shades of grey. That's what makes this book even more interesting and valuable. It is also not really a story about the 'successes' or big breakthroughs she has helped shape. Her role in shaping the people's movement for seminal legislations for the people's right to information, and the right to work is, for instance, well established. That's a story that will be told and analysed repeatedly, and in many ways. But it is the story of what shaped Aruna, told in her own words, that will help us appreciate the times she has lived in and the positive effect we can have on people and society. We can testify as close witnesses that Aruna has written a book of immense value to those who want to understand complex socio-political processes, the significance of the 'social' in a social movement and a continually challenged, 'social' democracy, and how the 'personal' is inextricably and wondrously woven into those vast tapestries of social change. We are both living testimonies to Aruna's positive influence on those she has lived and worked with. This book too has the potential to be an inspiration for those who have not met Aruna Roy, but who are on a similar search for justice, equality, free expression, dignity and true fraternity amongst large numbers of people. We feel, quite strongly, that this is a book that will spread hope far beyond its own context and times.

Shankar Singh and Nikhil Dey (and the MKSS)

Acknowledgements

THE IDEA OF this book began with Mita Kapur (CEO of Siyahi, a literary consultancy) and Karthika V.K., who was at HarperCollins at the time (now at Westland-Pratilipi). They visited on a sunny day to ask me if I would like to write a book. I was hesitant. They were persuasive, and offered me carte blanche, the freedom to write on anything, any which way I wanted to. The first thing that came to my mind was the famous feminist slogan 'The Personal is Political'. It reflected my dilemma and also my politics. And so it began.

I had to grapple with my tentativeness about writing anything personal. My collective life had conditioned me to see the personal very often as an intrusion. My first acknowledgement and gratitude must, therefore, go to those who helped me overcome my resistance. I owe my family and friends a great deal. They have been supportive at all times and played different roles, shifting between patience, enthusiasm, understanding and exasperation, but always encouraging and pushing me to write. Bunker refused to take my doubts seriously, and his confidence that the book would materialize helped set aside doubts. My thanks to my alternate family, including Nikhil and Shankar, who are an intrinsic part of the book and the many conversations blending the personal and the political.

Ankita Anand was the first to help with the structure of the book, and has continued to advise me from time to time; Laxman Singh and Swati Dhanesh searched the computer and many terabytes of information on hard drives to put together everything from a couple of stray sentences to many pages of spontaneous writing on many issues. Lipi Mehta professionally extracted relevant pieces from archival material the Mazdoor Kisan Shakti Sangathan (MKSS) and I had already published. A big salaam to Nachiket Udupa, Nikhil Dey and Siddhu (Siddhartha), who helped sort out documents and held emergency conclaves to get me going—their advice was invaluable. Thanks to Meera, who applied her critical mind to reassure me that it made sense, and Subham Biswas, who has helped scrutinize the final edits and place the citations in the manuscript.

Thanks also to the MKSS family, whose inquiries about the progress of the book pushed me to write. Vasu (S. Srinivasan) kept at me about the book till he passed away. Dr S. Anandalakshmy built my confidence to write freely about the areas of grey that so preoccupied me. I am sorry she is not alive to see the completed book.

I owe Mita special thanks. She has been an extremely generous and gracious critic and made sure that I did not give up on the book. I owe Ajitha G.S. thanks for reassuring me that I was on the right track after reading one of the first drafts, and also to Praavita Kashyap, who gave positive feedback after reading through the full manuscript. I want to thank HarperCollins India, for putting up with my requests and delays, and for the many rounds of editing.

My special thanks to Saba Kohli Dave, who came during the Covid pandemic to work with me as my research assistant, and volunteered to discuss, collate and help with the first edits for the book, and continued with her invaluable support. Without her sense of cheerful determination and optimism, this book would have never been completed. She helped me see it through with lively persistence. Huge thanks to her, for her patience and commitment.

Thanks to Gopal Gandhi, for the excellent foreword. Immense gratitude to Amartya Sen and Jean Drèze, V (Eve Ensler), Perumal Murugan, Jayati Ghosh, T.M. Krishna, Syeda Hameed, Harsh Mander, Suraj Yengde, Annie Raja, Kavita Srivastava and P. Sainath for reading the manuscript and sending endorsements commending the book. They helped reinforce my hope that the thoughts and narratives may help young Indians understand the republic and the emerging fault lines of change in Indian democracy better.

A special thanks to the Meera and Vikram Gandhi Fellowship at the Watson Institute for International and Public Affairs, Brown University, which provided me the space and time to put the documents together and give it shape in the spring of 2018.

Most importantly I acknowledge all my comrades and colleagues of the collectives I have worked with. Many will never write a book, and some are not able to pick up a pen or put their fingers on a keyboard. But I owe my thoughts and experiences to them. I hope they will see this, in some ways, as their book as well.

Notes

Scan this QR code to access the notes.

About the Author

Aruna Roy was born to progressive educated parents in 1946, and grew up amidst eclectic discussions, arguments and debates. She went to a variety of schools, but her real education came from her family and their friends where constitutional politics were lived values. She married Sanjit (Bunker) Roy, a classmate in Delhi University, who had similar concerns and whose 'Brahmo Samaj' family reflected India's multi-religious progressive politics.

She worked as a civil servant for seven years, between 1968 and 1975, before leaving to work with the rural poor in Barefoot College, Tilonia. In 1983 she moved to Devdungri where she co-founded a participatory peoples' struggle-based organization, the Mazdoor Kisan Shakti Sangathan (MKSS), in 1990, with Nikhil Dey, Shankar Singh and peasants and workers from central Rajasthan. The MKSS's struggle for minimum wages led to a radical demand for the right to know, the right to work, food and social security. These demands led to the developing lexicon of rights, resulting in the passage of rights-based legislations in India, including the RTI, MGNREGA, NFSA among others.